The Lone Flag

Royal Asiatic Society Hong Kong Studies Series

Royal Asiatic Society Hong Kong Studies Series is designed to make widely available important contributions on the local history, culture and society of Hong Kong and the surrounding region. Generous support from the Sir Lindsay and Lady May Ride Memorial Fund makes it possible to publish a series of high-quality works that will be of lasting appeal and value to all, both scholars and informed general readers, who share a deeper interest in and enthusiasm for the area.

Recent titles in the RAS Hong Kong Studies Series:

Hong Kong Internment, 1942–1945: Life in the Japanese Civilian Camp at Stanley
Geoffrey Charles Emerson

East River Column: Hong Kong Guerrillas in the Second World War and After
Chan Sui-jeung

Southern District Officer Reports: Islands and Villages in Rural Hong Kong, 1910–60
Edited by John Strickland

Cantonese Society in Hong Kong and Singapore: Gender, Religion, Medicine and Money
Essays by Marjorie Topley; edited and introduced by Jean DeBernardi

Early China Coast Meteorology: The Role of Hong Kong
P. Kevin MacKeown

Forgotten Souls: A Social History of the Hong Kong Cemetery
Patricia Lim

Ancestral Images: A Hong Kong Collection
Hugh Baker

Escape from Hong Kong: Admiral Chan Chak's Christmas Day Dash, 1941
Tim Luard

Governors, Politics and the Colonial Office: Public Policy in Hong Kong, 1918–58
Gavin Ure

Scottish Mandarin: The Life and Times of Sir Reginald Johnston
Shiona Airlie

Custom, Land and Livelihood in Rural South China: The Traditional Land Law of Hong Kong's New Territories, 1750–1950
Patrick H. Hase

Portugal, China and the Macau Negotiations, 1986–1999
Carmen Amado Mendes

The Lone Flag

Memoir of the British Consul in Macao
during World War II

By John Pownall Reeves

Edited by Colin Day and Richard Garrett
With a biographical essay by David Calthorpe

Hong Kong University Press
The University of Hong Kong
Pok Fu Lam Road
Hong Kong
https://hkupress.hku.hk

The Lone Flag (memoir) and 'About *The Lone Flag* and John Pownall Reeves' (essay)
© David Calthorpe 2014
Other material © Hong Kong University Press

ISBN 978-988-8208-32-6 (*Hardback*)

All rights reserved. No portion of this publication may be reproduced or transmitted in any form or by any means, electronic or mechanical, including photocopy, recording, or any information storage or retrieval system, without prior permission in writing from the publisher.

British Library Cataloguing-in-Publication Data
A catalogue record for this book is available from the British Library.

Digitally printed

Contents

Illustrations	vii
Preface and Introduction by Colin Day	ix
Macao during World War II by Richard Garrett	xix

The Lone Flag by John Pownall Reeves		1
Introduction		3
Poem: The Song of the Second Secretary		9
Chapter I	The Beginning	11
Chapter II	Getting Going	15
Chapter III	'The Situation'	21
Chapter IV	Organization	31
Chapter V	Parochial	41
Chapter VI	Relief	49
Chapter VII	Medical	61
Chapter VIII	Other Countries' Interests	71
Chapter IX	Morale	79
Chapter X	Thrills, More or Less	91
Chapter XI	Odds and Ends	109
Chapter XII	Post-War	121
Appendix 1	'Macao's Greetings: British Consul Sends Congratulations'	139
Appendix 2	'V-J Day Celebrations at Melco Club'	141
Appendix 3	'Mr Reeves Eulogised by Hongkong Portuguese Community'	143
Appendix 4	'British Eurasians Pay Tribute to Consul'	147
Appendix 5	'Festa de homenagem' (Tribute Party)	151
Appendix 6	'Macao Leave Centre Very Popular'	153

Appendix 7	'High Tradition of the Consular Service Maintained by Mr. J. P. Reeves'	155
Appendix 8	Message from Chungking dated 13 August 1945	159
Appendix 9	'Chinese Want British Rule for Hong Kong'	161
Appendix 10	'9000 Cared for in Macao: Untiring Work by British Consul'	163
Appendix 11	'He Kept the Flag Flying for Four Years'	165

About *The Lone Flag* and John Pownall Reeves by David Calthorpe	167
Notes	181
Index	199

Illustrations

Consulate organization chart   *34*
Location of the British consulate in Macao   *xii*
Map of Macao, 1950   (*following p. xxiv*)

Plates   (*following p. 40*)

1. John Reeves
2. John Reeves and his wife Rhoda with their newly born daughter, Letitia
3. John Reeves gazing over the South China Sea
4. A group of friends in Macao on Christmas Day 1941, the day Hong Kong surrendered, but probably before the news reached them
5. Japanese consulate
6. The Macao hockey team, with John Reeves in his Cambridge blazer
7. The badge worn by British consulate employees in Macao
8. Handmade consulate Christmas card during the war years
9. Karl Pope Fletcher
10. Marjorie Pope Fletcher
11. Thanksgiving service, 19 August 1945
12. Medals awarded to John Reeves
13. The Lone Flag, the new Union Jack raised for the first time after Japan surrendered
14. John Reeves in South Africa
15. Sample (Chapter VI, page 59) of the handwritten sections of the manuscript

Preface and Introduction

By Colin Day

John Pownall Reeves was British consul in the beleaguered Portuguese colony of Macao from 1941 to 1946. Immediately after leaving Macao for home leave and during his next posting (in Rome), he wrote an account of his extraordinary years in that neutral enclave, which was surrounded by Japanese-held territory and flooded with refugees who were mainly from Hong Kong and for whom he was responsible. The core of this book is that memoir.

Many people have been involved with this project. The first, both chronologically and in significance, is David Calthorpe, who, as a child, knew John Reeves and heard many of his reminiscences. Both by inheritance and diligent efforts of recovery, David also holds much of the memorabilia of John Reeves. In particular, he has the original of Reeves' memoir and has granted permission for its publication here.

David's biographical essay, which concludes the book, paints a rich sense of the man as David knew him in his later life in South Africa. Embedded in this account are many of the memories of life in China with which Reeves fascinated the young David, thereby inculcating in him a lifelong engagement with Chinese culture and its artefacts.

Victor Millard, David's partner, converted the text to a word-processed file. It was brought to Macao by Wilhelm Snyman, who was introduced by Glenn Timmermans to a number of people who might help with publishing it. Wilhelm gave copies to a few of us, thus triggering the enthusiasm for the memoir that has finally led to its publication. In an essay in Macao's *Review of Culture*, Wilhelm also provided an account of Reeves' activities in Macao and, through his archival research, supplemented the facts in the memoir.[1] He has been of great help to me as I have worked to get this manuscript ready for publication.

Richard Garrett, author of *The Defences of Macau*, has provided a valuable essay that details the historical context for Reeves' exceptional experiences, for readers who may not know of Macao's unique position during World War II. This opens the main text of the book.

Writing just a few years after the war, Reeves could assume that his readers shared much knowledge of recent events. So he makes brief allusions that now need spelling out. It is also apparent that Reeves thought primarily of a readership that had shared his experience of living in Macao during the war, and that would thus recognize names, places and events and so sometimes he simply omitted helpful details.

To provide answers to some of the questions that might occur to readers, a number of notes have been inserted. Richard Garrett provided a basic set of notes; I added further notes, drawing on the expertise and generous help of many people listed in the acknowledgements below. These notes are a very preliminary step towards a full history of Macao in those years, work on which, I believe, is beginning.

There are other good reasons for Reeves' occasional vagueness. He was writing while civil war raged in China and when the fate of such enclaves as Macao and Hong Kong, whichever side prevailed, was by no means clear. Some facts and identities were best left in the shadows. On a more bureaucratic plane, Reeves knew that he would have to get clearance from the Foreign Office in London to publish what he had written — a factor which would have inhibited full frankness. It is quite apparent that he hoped for publication. In fact, permission was refused. Without such constraints, would he have been more open, even indiscreet? I think the answer has to be 'yes'. Indeed if there is one negative about his wartime record, it was frequently said that he was something of a security risk and in his own writing he alludes to such problems. Reading David Calthorpe's biographical essay, one is presented with a man of ebullience and love of life — quite the antithesis of the silent, close-mouthed security operative. But, of course, not all omissions were deliberate: as he states, he was writing without notes and had to elide missing facts and dates. Yet, his errors seem few and far between, insofar as facts can be checked.

To return to the question of security and Reeves' perceived occasional lapses, perhaps the fairest assessment of the security aspect of his work came from Colonel Lindsay Ride, head of the British Army Aid Group (BAAG), an organization established to gather intelligence in China and to aid escaping Allied personnel.[2] Ride said: 'I think he is in an impossible position, absolutely surrounded by enemy agents and no one to fall back on — enough to make any man crack, and if he has made mistakes, I think they should not be held against him.'[3]

Appendices and Map

Thirteen appendices were added to the memoir by Reeves and two have been lost. These were an illustrated scroll from prisoners of war at Sham Shui Po in Hong Kong and a guidebook to Macao. They were Appendices 3 and 13 in the original numbering scheme.

In the light of Dr. Vincent Ho's investigations into guidebooks to Macao, it seems most likely that the guidebook of Appendix 13 was *Macau, Oldest Foreign Colony in the Far East* (Macau: Agência do Turismo, 1936).

An even sadder loss is of the map that Reeves had included and to which he refers in the text. A substitute has been provided following page xvi. Although it is a 1950 map and thus later than Reeves' would have been, there had been few changes of note from wartime Macao by that time. While many locations apparently marked on the original map can be identified, a few remain unknown, and some ephemeral items such as the mooring places of ships cannot be precisely recovered. The substitute map is thanks to Stuart Braga and the National Library of Australia.

Photographs

While David Calthorpe has a substantial cache of John Reeves' photos, very few relate to the Macao years. A small collection is included in this book. Perhaps the most evocative is the photograph of the torn Union Jack, which Reeves tells us he raised for the first time on the day the BBC reported Japan's surrender. Its tattered state is explained by the fact that a typhoon hit just as Reeves was preparing to leave for what proved to be his permanent parting from Macao.

Location of the Consulate

Strangely, at the time of writing, the location of the consulate has not been completely resolved. Perhaps this is because, as the refugee work expanded, additional offices were added. A further complicating factor is that the consulate building itself was not always Reeves' residence and his comments do not always make clear whether he is referring to his home or the consulate.

The location to which Reeves refers (on the first page of Chapter III) was believed to be the triangle of land at the top of Calçada do Gaio where it intersects with Calçada da Vitória, just below Guia Hill. The British consulate was on the southern side (on Calçada do Gaio) and the Japanese consulate on the northwestern side (on Calçada da Vitória). (See map below.) Leo D'Almada e Castro, his wife and Dr. Eddie Gosano, all of whom resided in Macao during the war, recalled this piece of land as the location of the British consulate.[4] This is also where David Calthorpe was later directed by Father Lancelot Rodriguez, who was in Macao in those years.

However, a letter from Consul Fukui gives the address of the Japanese consulate as No. 1, Calçada do Gaio, which is at the bottom, not the top, of Calçada

Location of the British consulate in Macao

do Gaio, and on that street rather than Calçada da Vitória.[5] In addition, a 12 September 1945 report in the *South China Morning Post* describes the British consulate as being in the Rua de Henrique de Macedo. As this intersects the Calçada do Gaio, the report is not inconsistent with the two consulates being side by side; indeed, the reporter states: 'The two diplomatic institutions were separated only by a low wall.'

Although Reeves never mentions it in the memoir, in a letter dated 19 November 1942, he says, 'I have incidentally now moved to 7 Praia Grande, José Conde Fernandez house.' While it is not made totally clear in this letter, it leans — 'I have moved' and 'it is more suitable' — to being a reference to relocating his residence rather than the consulate.[6] This fits with at least one person's memory.[7] However, another person reports: 'It [the consulate] was in a small street running from the Praia Grande to the Rua do Padre António alongside the old Governor's Palace (West side).[8] The street is called Travessa do Padre Narciso. It runs straight up to the San Lourenço church. I found it on an old wartime map of Macao. I think it moved there during the war from another location which I think was near the Japanese consulate.'[9] This description is not inconsistent with the consulate being at 7 Praia Grande, as it could have been on the corner, with entrances on both streets. A location on the Praia Grande would make sense for the story of the Mocidade Portuguesa parade, as well as for the story of the junk sitting in the harbour with its gun 'practically poking in at my window' (Chapter X).

However, also in Chapter X, Reeves refers to the building next to the Japanese consulate as his 'residence'. But as, by the end of the war, his wife and daughter were living in Skyline (Frederick Gellion's large house on Penha Hill), it could be that the house on the Praia Grande had been relinquished by this time (he spoke of having 'to pay an enormous rent' for it) and that, when his family left Macao after the war, he went back to living in the original consulate. To complicate matters, it seems likely that the refugee administration required more office space than the consulate building alone could provide and that there were other offices being used.[10] In fact, even prior to the war, there was a separate immigration office on the Praia Grande.

For once, perhaps, faith should be placed primarily in the oral evidence, and the consulate at the top of Calçada do Gaio.

Mrs. Reeves

The memoir makes little reference to Reeves' wife, Rhoda née Murray-Kidd. They were married in 1936 in Hankow (Hankou), where their daughter, Letitia, was born in 1937.

As the memoir reports, Mrs. Reeves was trapped in Hong Kong when the Japanese attacked. She was finally allowed to rejoin her husband and daughter in Macao on 10 March 1942. She had spent much of the intervening period with other refugees in St. Stephen's College on Lyttleton Road. She seems not to have taken these experiences well. Mrs. Martin, wife of the consul general in Chungking (Chongqing), recalled: 'Mrs Reeves had been running herself into a nervous decline by refusing to eat and crying all the time.'[11] The Argentinian consul's report includes the detail, 'She was in an extremely bad state of nerves and general health, suffering from neurosis on account of a fracture of the base of her skull some time before.' He indicates that the Japanese authorities would not do anything: 'I could not obtain from the Japanese any alleviation of her situation.'[12] But she was finally allowed to leave and a later BAAG document reports that Rudy Choa 'was instrumental in getting Reeves' wife out of Hong Kong back to Macau.'[13] In addition, 'Sergeant Major Honda Isamu asserted in his war crimes trial that he had defied orders to facilitate Mrs. Reeves' return to Macao in March or April 1942.'[14] More information on Mrs. Reeves is given in the biographical essay.

Sources for the History of Macao in World War II

There is no good source for the full story of Macao in World War II; indeed, Reeves' memoir, albeit from one particular point of view, is probably the fullest account. There are, however, several books worth consulting. Geoffrey Gunn's *Encountering Macau* provides the best discussion of the war and is a very good history of Macao. Richard Garrett's *The Defences of Macau* adds further information on the military side. Entangled as Macao and Hong Kong's stories are, especially at this period, Philip Snow's *The Fall of Hong Kong* is the definitive history of its topic and provides at numerous points insights into the situation faced by Macao. It also provides full references to other sources. Finally, I cannot resist recommending Jonathan Porter's *Macau: The Imaginary City*, which captures the unique flavour of Macao more successfully than perhaps any other book.

Acknowledgements

Aside from his absolutely fundamental contribution of preserving and making the manuscript available for publication, David Calthorpe has been most helpful in giving insights from his direct knowledge of John Reeves, and in providing photos and other items. Elizabeth Ride's extraordinary knowledge of and access to documents relating to BAAG and other Allied activities in the region during the war, her patience with my questions and generosity in providing information, filled so many of the gaps in Reeves' narrative. Wilhelm Snyman's researches in the National Archives in London provided crucial documents and with his enthusiasm also helped speed the project along. Victor Millard sought out, scanned and sent over appendices, photographs and other material. Richard Garrett brought his deep knowledge of military history to the task of providing the historical and geopolitical context for the memoir and explanatory notes. Tony Banham has generously offered his encyclopaedic knowledge of the Battle for Hong Kong, its participants and their fates. Solomon Bard has helped with his personal knowledge of Sham Shui Po Prisoner of War Camp and of the medical profession in Hong Kong and Macao. Stuart Braga has been most helpful as a guide to the Braga Collection in the National Library of Australia and in tapping the memories of older Macao residents. Stephen Davies has answered every question with a maritime dimension in wonderful detail and shown just how much can be done by really skilful web-searching. Geoffrey Gunn has provided his deep knowledge of the broader context for Macao's wartime experiences and his access to Japanese materials. Sarah and Peter Cunich have contributed in several ways, especially in generously devoting vacation time to research in the National Archives. Others who made valuable contributions for which I am most grateful are Geoffrey Emerson, Paul French, Jorge Graça, Vincent Ho, Marie Imelda MacLeod, Christopher Munn, César Guillen Nuñez, Rufino Ramos, Frances Wong and Jason Wordie. Finally, special thanks to Jessica Wang of Hong Kong University Press whose careful editing and exceptional eye for detail have made an important contribution to the overall project.

A number of people helped David Calthorpe, especially at the beginning of the process of bringing John Reeves' story to a wider readership. He writes:

> I should like to thank Glenn Timmermans of the University of Macau, who put all the role players together and provided much valued support throughout in his official capacity. Equally, I would like to thank Marie Imelda MacLeod of the Macao Cultural Institute as well, for her support and for giving due recognition to the historical significance of John Reeves' memoir inasmuch as it provides a first-hand account of Macao during the Second World War.
>
> I should like to thank Sharon Warr of Cape Town for her dedication, thoroughness and resourcefulness as a skilled researcher, all of which she placed at the disposal of this project in verifying pertinent historical details. Thanks are also due to Wilhelm Snyman of the University of Cape Town for assistance in co-ordinating the relevant persons and moving this project forward by travelling to Macao and by his moral support even when the prospects for publication seemed distant.
>
> To Victor Millard, also of Cape Town, for the enormous efforts and dedication in terms of researching facts, compiling the photographic record of Reeves' life in the Far East and for giving invaluable moral and practical support throughout the genesis of this endeavour.
>
> Finally, thanks are due to my late mother, Marjorie Calthorpe, for her untiring support throughout the years, and to Tessa Schukking, both of whom kept the manuscript intact and the memory of Reeves alive. Personally, I am sure that Reeves would have dedicated this memoir to all the colourful and selfless personalities mentioned therein, especially to his hard-pressed staff of HM Consulate in Macao.

Conclusion

While some weight has been put on Reeves' discretion and lack of specifics, at the end of the day his memoir provides an enthralling story of one man's unique and challenging experiences. It records his extraordinary efforts on behalf of all the refugees that came under his care and were looked after, despite shortages of food, space and medicine. He achieved all this while living with armed guards and operating in an environment that required him to navigate among the Japanese, Chinese of various political groups, Allied intelligence workers and, not least, the Portuguese authorities.

Editorial Notes

The memoir was, as described in the preface, converted to a Word file from the original document. It is believed that the main body of the memoir was handwritten and then typed by a secretary, probably in Rome. Later, Reeves added a number of neatly handwritten addenda, with indications of where they should be inserted in the main text (see Plate 15 for an example). These have been inserted as he suggested; no effort has been made to differentiate those passages from the original typed text. In one instance, in Chapter XI, the additional text badly disrupted the flow of the narrative, so it was placed at the end of the relevant paragraph rather than where the author had indicated it should be. A note has been provided to this effect.

As well as the additions for which he provided complete drafts, there are a number of places where he wrote a word or phrase on the original, presumably to prompt him to add another passage to the text. Wherever these annotations are legible (by contrast with the handwritten passages, they are very carelessly written, and I owe much to David Calthorpe for help in reading these), a note has been inserted at the approximate location of the annotation. In all these instances, disappointingly, Reeves never got around to adding the extra text.

The transcription of the memoir into Word format has followed Reeves' original. In a few places in Chapter IX, where a sentence or a paragraph was inordinately long, the original transcriber added periods and paragraph breaks. As these aid readability, they have been retained. Stylistically, his conventions have been followed, including his exceptional reliance on the semi-colon.

One oddity of the manuscript is his consistent writing of Hong Kong as one word. Although it started off as two words, in 1843 it was decreed that it should be just one — Hongkong. It stayed like that until 3 September 1926, when Gazette Notice No. 479 stated that instructions received from the secretary of state for the colonies required that henceforth it be changed to two words: Hong Kong. It is surprising that Reeves was not familiar with this convention, but here perhaps we see a small indication of his contrarian nature.

The last three chapters were merely given titles and not chapter numbers. For ease of reference, these have been made numbered chapters, X to XII.

The spelling of *Macau/Macao* is a continual matter of argument. Reeves is consistent in spelling it *Macao* throughout. Most English books have used the

Portuguese spelling *Macau*. However, in recent years, there has been a shift back to *Macao*, which works better phonetically in English.[15] For this reason and to be consistent with Reeves' practice, *Macao* is therefore the spelling used in this book.

Reeves is rather cavalier with Portuguese names. It is customary to use both surnames, for example, Dr. Elsa Senna Fernandes, but Reeves customarily drops the first surname and writes, for example, Dr. Elsa Fernandes. He also muddles Spanish and Portuguese, thus referring to San Domingos whereas in Portuguese it should be São Domingos. While Reeves' spellings have been retained in the text of the memoir, in the notes the convention is to give the Portuguese place name followed by the English equivalent in brackets. Subsequent references use the English version.

Macao during World War II

By Richard Garrett

In early 1942, the British consulate in Macao stood alone as the only British mission between India and Australia. The Japanese were in control of the Far East and despite claims to be freeing Asia from European oppression, they had become the oppressors. John Reeves was the sole British official left in the area, operating from his consulate in Macao. He was on his own and far away from any colleagues, but unlike his counterparts in the occupied territories, he was free to operate. And what a task he had. His memoir only hints at the pressure he was under, with the Japanese all around him threatening his very existence. Nevertheless, he must have had the true British 'stiff upper lip', for he soldiered on, doing what he could to succour those with connections to Britain.

How had Macao come to be left as the only territory not occupied by the Japanese? As explained below, Japan had been trying to take over China for about ten years before they attacked Pearl Harbor. After that they quickly moved against British and French territories in the Far East. The forces in those areas were not properly prepared for the onslaught and were quickly overrun. Macao had been an observer of all this aggression and had all along distanced itself from the conflict, hoping that it could ride out the storm. Amazingly, it did.

The Japanese aggression in China started in 1931, with what is now known as the Mukden Incident. On 5 March 1932, Portugal's foreign minister, Fernando Augusto Branco, according to stipulation No. 13 of the Hague Convention, issued a statement of neutrality in the Sino-Japanese conflicts at the League of Nations headquarters in Geneva. Despite this neutrality, many Chinese in Macao took steps to support their comrades against the Japanese. They raised money for disaster relief and some young men went to join the fighting. Obviously, this was done without official support.

These efforts escalated after July 1937, when Japan began its all-out war against China. On 12 August 1937, activists in journalism, teaching, sports, music and drama set up the Salvation Society of Macao (SSM) to raise money for the war effort and assist refugees. After the fall of Guangzhou, the SSM organized teams of young people to go into Guangdong Province to help the war effort. Many were less than 20 years old, and some lost their lives. Between October 1938 and June 1940, the SSM organized eleven work teams with a total of 160 people, including students, teachers, workers, employees and those out of work.

Macao remained neutral and hoped to gain some advantages from the war by annexing extra territory. In 1938, it stationed troops on the neighbouring Lapa, Dom João and Montanha islands, hoping to make them part of Macao. They were optimistic that, at the end of the war, the major powers would help negotiate their borders as part of the overall settlement. The European powers at this time still envisaged that they would have a role in settling the Sino-Japanese conflict.

In October 1938, the Japanese army captured Guangzhou. Refugees began to stream into Macao, a territory of just 14.47 square kilometres. The population swelled from 157,175 in 1927 to 245,194 in 1939. The refugees included women and children who owned only what they could carry, as well as wealthy foreigners and Chinese, all seeking a safe haven away from the horrors of war. The latter brought their money, skills and connections. This meant good business for the city's hotels, restaurants, inns and casinos. The Bela Vista Hotel accepted overseas Portuguese who came from Shanghai, and the government set up refugee camps for the less fortunate on Taipa Island.

In 1939, Germany's ambitions in Europe led to war against Britain and France. During the First World War, a mainly European affair, the Portuguese had sided with the Allies. That conflict did not greatly affect Macao, although some residents volunteered and there is a monument in São Miguel Cemetery to those who died. This time, despite being one of Britain's oldest allies, Portugal decided to remain neutral. Again it looked as though the war in Europe would have little impact on Macao. That proved to be wrong and Asia was not to remain isolated from the war in Europe.

In autumn 1941, the situation in South China deteriorated to the point that the SSM teams had to withdraw to Macao. Then, on 7 December 1941, Japan bombed Pearl Harbor and the region became a major war zone. The Japanese allied themselves with the Axis powers and proceeded to invade British and French territories in Asia. The fighting in China spread and Macao became a haven for refugees; the situation intensified after the fall of Hong Kong on Christmas Day 1941. Further south, the Japanese quickly took Malaya and Singapore and then Burma. That left Macao a tiny isolated enclave surrounded by Japanese-held territory. Would it be allowed to remain? The Macao authorities held their breath and as a sign of goodwill, they sent their naval ships back to Lisbon. The garrison consisted of only about 500 men. If the Japanese had decided to take Macao, there was nothing the Portuguese could do to stop them. Fortunately, although the Japanese had more influence than before, they generally respected Macao's neutrality.

Refugees from Hong Kong and neighbouring areas increased Macao's population to nearly 500,000. The Japanese encouraged the outflow, to reduce the number of people it had to feed in Hong Kong. Throughout its history, Macao had never had to support so many people. The Japanese imposed a sea blockade. The colony had to survive on its own food and supplies brought in from Guangdong Province, which was itself suffering from the ravages of war and occupation. The Macao government issued coupons to residents to buy grain as a means of fairly sharing the available resources. In February 1942, as the price of daily necessities began to soar, it allowed land in the urban area to be cultivated for food. The governor, Gabriel Teixeira, and members of the Catholic Church were prominent in providing aid. Space in the urban area soon became crowded and refugee camps were set up on Green Island and Coloane. Reeves explains what he did to support those refugees that had some claim to British nationality as well as helping Americans, as there was no American consul in Macao. He gives a good insight into the problems that so many had to face.

The refugees who were fortunate stayed with friends and families or found places in homes, hospitals, schools, clubs and churches. When these became full, those who followed had to live on the streets and depend on charity for their survival. The people of Macao extended their traditional welcome: welfare institutions, lay and religious, Chinese and foreign, did their best to feed and clothe the homeless with soup kitchens and distributions of bread, rice, clothing and blankets. Although Macao became overcrowded, many of its citizens, being mainly Chinese, continued to help their fellow countrymen. However, with the

Japanese being present they had to be careful about what they did, and so they concentrated on providing relief for the refugees.

As noted above, Japan could easily have taken over Macao. But, while it repeatedly interfered in Macao's internal administration,[1] it chose not to annex it, perhaps because its German ally had decided to respect the neutrality of Portugal and its empire, or because it feared reprisals against the hundreds of thousands of ethnic Japanese residents of Brazil. Nevertheless, in February 1942, the Japanese military took over Portugal's other Asian colony, East Timor, as it prepared to attack Australia. Japanese troops were able to enter Macao with little protest from the government, but the British consul was still able to fly the Union Jack. As Reeves notes, he was very isolated, his nearest counterparts being in India to the west and Australia to the southeast.

Governor Gabriel Teixeira strove to avoid incidents with the Japanese and to maintain what was left of his authority. He banned anti-Japanese activities, allowed Japanese ships to dock, and Japanese troops to transit to neighbouring Zhongshan County. As Reeves describes, he did what he could to restrain the Japanese and assist refugees of all nationalities.

The influx of refugees presented the Macao authorities with many difficulties. The government's revenue had already fallen and its economy had declined. The year 1942 was a particularly bad year. The shortages, combined with the strains on the sanitation system, resulted in a much increased death rate. (The death rate in 1930 had been between 3,000 and 4,000 per annum. It rose to over 16,000 in 1942.) In particular, during a cold spell in 1942, as many as 10,000 people died. A mass grave was dug for them on northern Taipa. Jorge Graça relates[2] the story of how the soldiers of the burial detail amused themselves by playing *fantan*,[3] using the bodies as counters. On one occasion, the winner, who was left to complete the job, was shocked when one of the bodies came to life. He was most upset, thinking that this would negate the game and he would lose his winnings, so he wanted to bury the man regardless. Luckily, a sergeant passed by and the man was saved from burial. He recovered fully, going on to establish a pharmacy and to live a long life in Macao.

Money was allocated to help the refugees, including all gambling taxes. Macao was isolated and suffered from shortages of food. To raise some funds for the purchase of food, the government sold the small gunboat, *Macau*, to the Japanese. Things did get better in subsequent years as the Japanese started to use Macao as a transshipment centre. At the same time, since it was the only place in southern China not at war, its restaurants, casinos, opium dens and brothels boomed, attracting those who were profiting from the war, such as gangsters, Japanese soldiers and officials and businessmen who worked with them. A large amount of gold, silver, platinum and foreign currency flowed into the colony.

In August 1943, the Japanese commandeered the British ferry, the *Sai On*,[4] lying in the Inner Harbour. It had been there since the start when it had been stopped from sailing to Hong Kong. This act of aggression showed Japanese contempt for the Portuguese authorities; thereafter, the Macao government was forced to accept Japanese 'advisers' as an alternative to complete military occupation. Later, the Japanese ordered the governor to recognize their authority in South China, forcing Portuguese troops to evacuate their barracks on Lapa, Dom João and Montanha islands. The Japanese were also given the authority to conduct house-to-house searches in Macao. Obviously, Macao was in no position to challenge Japan but it managed to survive through its well-honed diplomatic skills. While the Japanese presence improved the economy, money was still short and food was scarce. At one point, the government was reduced to exchanging some of its guns for food. Somehow, the population was fed and the death rate started to decline.

The head of the Japanese secret police in Macao set up his headquarters in a villa in the Avenida de Horta e Costa, from where he organized the assassinations of citizens prominent in the anti-Japanese struggle. He also set up two newspapers as propaganda organs for his government. Reeves also had a newspaper under his control to provide a balance. Obviously, the Japanese were not friendly towards the British and armed bodyguards were the order of the day. Living under constant threat of assassination must have been a great strain, but Reeves appears to have borne it well.

As part of its strategy, Japan aimed to attack the Chinese government by economic means and force it to surrender. To this end, Japanese firms set up nearly fifty joint ventures with Hong Kong and Macao businessmen, flooding the Chinese market with Japanese goods, draining the country of foreign currency and buying raw materials needed for the war effort. In February 1944, the governor banned the use of Chinese money and ordered residents to use only currency issued by the local Banco Nacional Ultramarino. As Reeves notes, some were able to exploit the currency regulations for personal profit.

Throughout the war, Macao was a vital communications source for the outside world. Short-wave radios continued to function there, as did the only accessible international cable, linking the colony to Lisbon and London. As Reeves notes, he was able to keep in touch with London and receive funds to support himself, his staff and refugees. Reeves' office was also able to assist those escaping from Hong Kong and, in cooperation with the British Army Aid Group, to enable them to be repatriated. However, some were not confident that his activities were totally secure and chose instead to use the help of Chinese Nationalist agents to escape.

In January, February and June 1945, US bombers carried out three air raids on a naval warehouse in the outer harbour: five people were killed and a naval museum destroyed. Reeves suggests that the pilots did not really know that Macao was neutral. However, other commentators have claimed the main reason for the raid was that the Americans had heard the Macao government was about to sell some aircraft fuel to the Japanese. They bombed the hangar of the Macao Naval Aviation Centre, destroying the fuel. Reeves says he was unaware of this, which is surprising as he had a number of informers providing intelligence. The US planes also bombed the Dona Maria II Fort, which was probably targeted as it housed a radio station, and there was some damage to residential areas. The Portuguese government lodged a protest with the United States. Compensation of US$20,255,952 was eventually paid in 1950, for 'damage caused when American planes bombed Macau's harbour during World War II on 16th January, 25th February and 11th June 1945, mistaking it for Japanese occupied territory'. Reeves notes that the compensation appeared to be adequate.[5]

After the Japanese surrender, Macao gradually returned to normal. Most refugees returned whence they came. Hong Kong once more became the principal European-controlled city on the China coast, with Macao in its shadow. Like Hong Kong, Macao encouraged light industry; and like Hong Kong, it later lost this industry, as manufacturing migrated across the border into China. Today, its gambling industry is its mainstay, outdoing Las Vegas. It has managed to retain many of its old buildings and these historic monuments now have World Heritage status. Although they provide a record of much of Macao's past, there is little to remind us of the wartime trauma. John Reeves' memoir is an important document, as it provides at least one person's view of life during that time. The value of this record is enhanced by Reeves' awareness of many factors in the politics of the time and tensions with the Japanese.

Rotiero Da Cidade De Macau
Macao Guide

1 – Cais de vapores de Hongkong.
   Wharves of the Hong Kong Steamers.
2 – Polícia Marítima e Fiscal.
   Revenue Officers Station.
3 – Hong Kong Miu (Templo Chinês).
   Hong Kong Miu (Chinese Temple).
4 – Leal Senado e Biblioteca Pública.
   Municipal Council and Public Library.
5 – Correios, Telégrafos e Telefones.
   General Post Office, Telegraph and Telephones.
6 – Central da Polícia (Comissariado).
   Central Police Station.
7 – Hotel Riviera.
   Riviera Hotel.
8 – Banco Nacional Ultramarino.
   Portuguese National Overseas Bank.
9 – Sé Catedral.
   Cathedral.
10 – Monumento a Ferreira do Amaral.
   Ferreira do Amara[1] Monument.
11 – Colégio de St.ª Rosa de Lima.
   St. Rosa de Lima College.
12 – Liga dos Combatentes da Grande Guerra.
   Club of the Veterans of World War I.
13 – Grémio Militar.
   Military Club.
14 – Quartel de S. Francisco.
   St. Francisco Barracks.
15 – Hospital Conde de S. Januário.
   Government Hospital.
16 – Observatório Meteorológico.
   Observatory.
17 – Cemitério dos Parses.
   Parsee Cemetery.
18 – Farol da Guia.
   Guia Lighthouse.
19 – Centro Náutico da Mocidade Portuguesa.
   Portuguese Youth Nautical Center.
20 – Porto Exterior.
   Outer Harbour.
21 – Reservatório de água potável.
   Reservoir for water supply.
22 – Estação Radiotelegráfica.
   Wireless Station.
23 – Templo chinês de Macau-Seac.
   Chinese Temple of Macao-Seac.
24 – Monumento a Vasco da Gama.
   Vasco da Gama Monument.
25 – Igreja de S. Lázaro.
   St. Lazarus Church.
26 – Cemitério de S. Miguel.
   Cemetery of St. Michael.
27 – Liceu Nacional Infante D. Henrique.
   Macao Lyceum.
28 – Campo Desportivo da Caixa Escolar.
   Schools Playground.
29 – Escola Primária Oficial.
   Government Primary School.
30 – Monumento da Vitória sobre os Holandeses.
   Monument Commemorating our Victory over the Dutch.
31 – Hospital Militar.
   Military Hospital.
32 – Residência da familia do Dr. Sun Yat Sen.
   Residence of Dr. Sun Yat-Sen.
33 – Jardim de Lu Lim Ioc. (Hoje Escola Pui Cheng).
   Loo Yim-Yok's Garden. (Now Pui Cheng School).
34 – Escola lnfantil.
   Kindergarten School.
35 – Jardim da Flora.
   Public Garden (Flora).
36 – Kun Iam Tong (Templo Chinês).
   Kun Iam Tong (Chinese Temple).
37 – Central Eléctrica.
   Electric Light and Power Station.
38 – Jardim da Montanha Russa.
   ‹Montanha Russa› Garden.
39 – Novo Cemitério Protestante.
   Protestant Cemetery.
40 – Fortaleza de Mong-Há.
   Old Fortress of Mong-Ha.
41 – Lin Kai Miu (Templo Chinês).
   Lin Kai Miu (Chinese Temple).
42 – Portas do Cerco.
   Barrier Gate.
43 – Fábricas de panchões.
   Firecracker Factories.
44 – Casas económicas (Bairro Tamagnini Barbosa).
   Houses for the poor.

45 – Lin Fong Miu (Templo Chinês).
Lin Fong Miu (Chinese Temple).

46 – Esquadra Policial
Police Station.

47 – Central purificadora de água.
Water Supply Purification Plant.

48 – Estação Central das bombas de água.
Water Supply Pumps.

49 – Campo Desportivo e Canídromo.
Public Sports Ground and Canidrome.

50 – Casas económicas (Bairro 28 de Maio).
Houses for the poor.

51 – Fábrica de pivetes insecticidas. (Casa Garden)
Factory of Insecticides sticks.

52 – Colégio do Sagrado Coração.
Sacred Heart College.

53 – Estaleiros chineses.
Chinese Ship Yards for junks.

54 – Mercado Municipal Almirante Lacerda.
Municipal Market.

55 – Fábricas de fósforos.
Match Factories.

56 – Fábricas de artefactos de malha.
Knitted Goods Factories.

57 – Bombeiros Municipais (Quartel).
Fire Brigade Station.

58 – Hospital Chinês (Kiang Vu).
Chinese Hospital.

59 – Instituto Canossiano.
Canossian Institute.

60 – Cemitério Protestante.
Old Protestant Cemetery.

61 – Museu.
Museum.

62 – Gruta e Jardim de Camões.
Camoens Grotto and Garden.

63 – Tou Tei Miu (Templo Chinês).
Tou Tei Miu (Chinese Temple).

64 – Igreja de St.º António.
St. Anthony Church.

65 – Ruínas de S. Paulo.
Ruins of St. Paul.

66 – Fortaleza do Monte.
Old Monte Fortress.

67 – Hospital de S. Rafael.
St. Raphael Hospital.

68 – Igreja de S. Domingos.
St. Dominic Church.

69 – Santa Casa da Misericórdia.
The Holy Houses of Mercy.

70 – Serviços de Economia.
Economic Services Department.

71 – Igreja de St. Agostinho.
St. Augustine Church.

72 – Clube de Macau e Teatro Dom Pedro V.
Macao Club and Dom Pedro V Theatre.

73 – Seminário de S. José.
St. Joseph Seminary.

74 – Palácio do Governo.
Government House.

75 – Igreja de S. Lourenço.
St. Lawrence Church.

76 – Instituto Salesiano.
Salesian Industrial School.

77 – Parque Infantil.
Children's Park.

78 – Hotel Bela Vista.
Bela Vista Hotel.

79 – Ermida da Penha e Residência Episcopal.
Penha Church and Bishop's Residence.

80 – Ténis Militar.
Military Tennis Courts.

81 – Residência do Governador (Santa Sancha).
Governor's Residence.

82 – Ténis Civil.
Civil Tennis Courts.

83 – Colina da Barra.
Barra Hill.

84 – Ponta da Barra.
Barra Point.

85 – Fortaleza da Barra.
Old Fortress of Barra.

86 – Oficinas Navais.
Naval Dockyard.

87 – Ma Kok Miu (Templo Chinês).
Ma Kok Miu (Chinese Temple).

88 – Capitania dos Portos.
Harbour Office.

89 – Edifício das Repartições Públicas: Serviços de Fazenda; Tribunais Judicial e Administrativo; Serviços de Administração Civil.
Public Departments Building: Treasury Department; Supreme Court; Civil Administration.

90 – Colégio D. Bosco.
   D. Bosco College.
91 – Monumento a Jorge Álvares.
   Jorge Alvares Monument.
92 – Mercado de S. Lourenço.
   St. Lawrence Market.
93 – Mercado de S. Domingos
   St. Dominic Market.
94 – Monumento a Vicente Nicolau de Mesquita.
   Nicolau Mesquita Monument.
95 – Piscina Municipal.
   Municipal Swimming Pool.
96 – Imprensa Nacional.
   National Printing Press.
97 – Clube Náutico.
   Nautical Club.
98 – Cemitério de Nossa Senhora da Piedade.
   Our Lady of Piety Cemetery.
99 – Doca de Macau Seac.
   Macao Seac Dock (Netherlands Harbour Works Ltd.)
100 – Armacao Refugee Centre
101 – Villa Leitão
102 – Melco Club and Hipódromo
103 – Fat Siu Lao
104 – Skyline

The Lone Flag

By John Pownall Reeves

Introduction

After I had written some chapters of this book of very personal reminiscence I showed them to a friend in the Embassy where I was serving, sufficiently a friend to be really candid. He said he found it interesting but made this criticism. "You take", he said, "the Consular Service for granted". I may say in parenthesis that I am not the only person who does so. He went on to explain that the public knew very little of the work of the Service and thereby gave me my biggest headache of authorship. After fifteen years of Service I think I would find it easier to say what it is not than what it is.

Though the Diplomatic and Consular Services have been amalgamated their functions remain largely separate. A rough distinction is that the Diplomatic (Embassies and Legations) deals with policy as between nations and the Consular Service deals with the manifold problems of the British Subject abroad as a commercial entity or an individual. I am aware that I appear to be ignoring the Commercial Diplomatic Service; but here again the same distinction largely applies as does to the Embassy and the Consulate; the Commercial Diplomatic will deal with large questions of policy but the Consular offices will deal with local difficulties in which the British firm may find itself.

This is a broad distinction, perhaps too broad; there are many features of interlock between Services or rather of the component parts of H.M. Foreign Service. A Consulate will take up a case locally and, if it exhausts all recourses for reaching a solution, will refer the matter to its Embassy for heavier metal to be brought to bear. Similarly an Embassy and hence the Foreign Office must depend to a great extent for its political decisions on information from the Consular Officers, who cover a wider field. The closest interlocking is of course, or should be of course, in an Embassy where the political, commercial, economic, passport control, consular and other branches have the greatest opportunity of exchanging news and views. Such exchange is invaluable and has recently been greatly fostered by the increasing tendency of senior diplomatic officials to visit Consular posts and for Consular conferences to be held at the capitals; not all diplomatic nor all consular officers have as yet taken full advantage of such opportunities but the newer entry, who terrify people of my seniority by their obvious competence, seem likely to achieve the objects contemplated by the amalgamation of 1943. A vastly improved Foreign Service will result.

For the moment, however, I should be speaking more of the Consular Officer and what he is and does. He is the person most likely in all the world to become a Jack of all trades but one of the persons most likely to be called on to appear to be master of many. Only a priest perhaps, with no distinction between churches, is in the same position. He too has to be, or should be, constantly polite even to people he knows are nuisances and no more; he too has to confront in his own person the problems that confront many. Particularly when he is comparatively young, and in charge of a post he may have to give advice on many subjects to persons who, in their own field, are far more expert than he is. The consular officer is aware of this, only too painfully aware, and all he can do is to learn as much as possible from the more experienced man before him and then, if he can, apply a perspective view to the problem of which the British Subject who has come to him for help can see only the one, expert side. Each person who comes to see him can give him invaluable leads, unconsciously, as to how to deal with some other problem which may meet him later in his career. His mind becomes, inevitably, something of a rag-bag of human experience; the good consular officer will know which rag to bring out of the bag to patch the hole of which a British Subject complains. An experience in China can show him how to deal with a problem in Rome; a victory over a local official about a local tax can show the way to gain a similar victory over a local official about marriage formalities five thousand miles away.

Introduction

Theoretically there are Consular Instructions on which he should base his decisions; but you could as well expect a consular officer to keep strictly to these instructions as to expect a naval officer to navigate his ship on nothing but King's Regulations and Admiralty Instructions. The case is a close parallel; your young officer in each case has superiors on whom he can rely for advice but he must and should frequently make decisions of his own without reference to his superiors and take a reprimand if it is coming to him. There is a definite danger to the Service in the form of too much centralization with a consequent diminution of initiative. Too rapid communications have a tendency to make reference to headquarters too easy to send. This is getting controversial; I'll stop.

I will get back to the Consular Officer; He is always at least a dual personality; he is sure, for instance, if he is any good, to be on various community committees; in these he must be a member and not the leader of the community, unless the committee desires him to be Chairman. Even then he must be Chairman and not Consul, not always an easy task; his committee may decide on a course of action which may lead to official representations; he may then find himself as Chairman writing to himself as Consul asking for assistance. In a capital he may find himself in a more difficult position yet when as Chairman of a Committee, Consul and First Secretary of the Embassy he can see the desires of the committee clashing with the interests of the community and these in turn not agreeing with some policy of the Embassy of which he is an integral part. The tight-rope at this stage becomes a slack, not to say sagging, wire. In a still wider sense he is always a dual personality; a member of the community comes to see him in the morning on the subject of a proposition which the Consul thinks is far from commercially admirable; that must make no difference when the two meet at a cocktail party in the evening. Similarly when he knows that there is urgent work and work that needs concentrated thought in his "In" tray and he has a caller who has always wasted his time and will again, he must still appear to have been waiting for that particular caller all his life: lucky is the consular officer who can close his ears to masses of irrelevant detail, putting in the occasional polite word, and go on thinking quietly of the problems that are really occupying his mind. He should never appear to be busy; that is often regarded by the caller as rudeness.

His individual official problems may have the widest range; most people realize vaguely that he issues passports and visas, some realize that he has something to do with marriages of British Subjects abroad and that people sign things before him. Shipmasters know that he will clear ships, sign on crews and so on. The story of the third class ticket home for the broken gambler in Monte Carlo is repeated in every Consular office in the world even when there are no currency restrictions. But there is far more to it than that; anxious wives in England try to trace their errant husbands believed to be within five hundred miles of his post; a firm manufacturing artificial jam pips wants to know what openings there are for trade in his district; a learned society wants to know whether there are certain fossils in his district. The consular officer is expected to cope; shall I say firmly that he usually does; only the middle example is slightly, but oh so slightly, exaggerated. People ask you to intervene between them and their families, their sons and their fiancées, how to invest their money, which is the best hotel or doctor, to arrange tours for them where no European has been before, to start their stamp collections, anything, just anything.

In the meantime of course you have to deal with the Office, the F.O., the Foreign Office. This is not merely a matter of answering dispatches or telegrams; there is an enormous amount of routine in a Consular office ninety-nine per cent of which would be called by many "red tape" but which is ninety per cent very reasonable supervision. You may have "Query Papers" on your quarterly accounts: there used to be a legend that clerks in the finance office of the F.O. got a bonus for every mistake they could find. You have a staff to look after, with all the clashes of temperament and method that are bound to arise. You have returns to make, you have to remember that stationery, fee-stamps and so on have to be ordered well ahead of time. You have, perhaps, five or six safe combinations to remember and cyphers to worry about. You have repairs to premises to consider, with limits on amounts you can spend without special authorization. Except in the biggest offices you have neither specialists nor personal secretary; you are your own

Introduction

specialist and your own secretary. You have, in particular, little time to settle down to work; visitors, telephone calls and so on see to that.

You have to be a little of everything, frequently lawyer, sometimes an architect when the home authorities are not fully aware of the details of a rebuilding problem, sometimes a financier when people ask your advice on investments and of course a bureaucrat in so far as you are expected by the public to know all about every United Kingdom regulation ever introduced, a father confessor and an office executive, as well as giving a lead to, and a hand with community activities.

If you can do that you are a good Consul; if you can!

The Song of the Second Secretary

(A ditty composed for the use of a second secretary in the Foreign Office in March 1942)

Macao? Macao? Where the devil's Macao?
We're bothered by telegrams all the time now.
By Golly, it's true we did send a Consul
But forgot him the same as we would a lost tonsil.
There he is encocooned like the smallest of larva
The only one left from Siberia to Java,
And, looked at again, from Chungking to Chile.

It's really absurd; the position too silly.
But in they keep coming these bothersome cables
They are filling the pigeon-holes, piling the tables.
Then give him routine this solitary fellow
Alone in an East so fast turning yellow.
"When did you say was his telegram one?
January 1st? Well, it's got to be done
It's only March now; we'll send him a word.
What? Answer his question? Don't be absurd.
Surely by now we've learnt to use phrases
Which leave every question in primeval hazes.
Remember our motto, now how does it go?
"A fig for all Consuls. God bless the F.O."

Chapter I

The Beginning

The unbelievable had happened, the unbelievable inevitable, and Japan had attacked. True enough we had all realized that she would, sooner or later, but I, for one, had placed the attack inaccurately; I had expected it between Christmas and New Year 1941 when, I argued wrongly, the Japanese would expect the foreigners in the East to be concentrating more on parties, and on recovery from them, than on defence.

But Pearl Harbour had happened, as one of the communities had heard on the radio at 7.30 and telephoned to me. The first bombs were about to fall on Hongkong, forty miles away. Two British ships had left Macao for Hongkong at 3 a.m. and nothing could be done about them. One, the SS *Saion* remained and was due to sail at eight.[1] I pulled trousers over my pyjamas and clutched an overcoat. Luckily the car was not suffering from winter sluggishness and I tore through town with my fingers on the horn, earning for myself then, perhaps, the unjustified reputation of being the most dangerous driver in the Colony. I stopped the *Saion* from sailing, requesting the Captain to wireless Commodore Hongkong for confirmation. Commodore's reply was succinct "Stay where you are".

My action and Commodore's confirmation was frankly not popular with certain members of the Community who, very understandably, wished to rejoin families in Hongkong or who desired to aid in the defence of the beleaguered Colony. Hot words were exchanged but I hope and believe that I have now been forgiven for the only action which appeared right to me.

One cadet of the Malayan Civil Service had been recalled to Hongkong the night before.[2] The Governor, who heard of the recall, had said at eleven the night before "This means war". He was right, only too right, but all I could do at that stage was to ask the cadet in question, R.G.K. Thompson,[3] to advise my wife,[4] still in Hongkong for Christmas shopping, to return immediately. The message never reached her and, even if it had done so, she could not have returned; no ships, naturally, could leave Hongkong, already under fire.

The next step was to move all papers from the Immigration Office on the Praia Grande up to my house and Consulate, which was, inappropriately, next door to that of my Japanese colleague.[5] This was accomplished in the morning. One Chinese optimistically applied for an Immigration Office Permit to enter Hongkong. I am afraid his two dollar expenditure was wasted. The Immigration Office, usually packed with a milling mob, was deserted and some of the staff, very sensibly, settled down to play cards. There seemed nothing else to do.

Indeed that seemed the case for all of us for the next three weeks;[6] there was nothing to do. Communication was virtually cut off and no one wanted the services of a Consul who could do nothing. The Fletchers,[7] whose son was in Hongkong,[8] and Mrs. Mitchell, whose husband was second-in-command of the Volunteers in the Colony,[9] reacted magnificently. They were determined to show the Japanese, of whom there were many in Macao, that our little Community was not down-hearted. A round of cocktail parties was organized and some, at least, used to drop in at the Consulate for an eleven o'clock sherry, while the sherry lasted.

For the rest, our feelings were individual in reaction to the sounds of the conflict, plainly heard in Macao, where, indeed, windows would rattle in reply to some particularly big explosions. The wireless was nothing but depressing, bringing unrelieved news of defeat. Gradually friendly stations in the East went off the air and Japanese cackle was all we could hear. Depressing and discouraging it was, but this is perhaps not an inappropriate place to pay my small tribute of praise to the British Community of Macao and its genuine friends, none of whom ever, even in the blackest days, showed anything but courage and faith in ultimate victory. They were at all times magnificent and I am proud to have been associated with them.

The Beginning

Hongkong fell on Christmas Day after a gallant defence in which many lives were lost unnecessarily.[10] It will always be a point of discussion as to whether the Colony was defensible and whether it should not have been declared an open city. One cannot help feeling that many of the men who died, butchered, after surrender would have been saved if the Japanese had not been flushed with armed conflict. Many too of the humiliations suffered by our people might have been spared if the Japanese had taken over without fighting. But, in any case, on Christmas Day Hongkong fell and Macao's long isolation began in earnest.[11] Macao is some forty miles from Hongkong and west of it across the mouth of the Canton river.[12] It consists of five square miles of "mainland" joined to the mainland of the delta by a causeway, and of two islands to the south.[13] The latter are sparsely occupied by fishing villages and it is always of the mainland one speaks when using the word "Macao". It was first occupied by the Portuguese in 1557 and is thus the oldest foreign Colony in the Far East. More than this, during the Spanish occupation of Portugal, Macao was the only place where the old blue and white flag of the Portuguese Empire flew. So the Loyal Senate, the local Governing Council, has this proud motto, "Não haoutso mais leal" (There is none more loyal).[14] I regret to say that in 1622 when the Dutch squadron attacked, and was repulsed, English ships in the bay, in spite of the old treaty of alliance, failed to intervene. The repulse of the Dutch is still celebrated every St. John's Day, the anniversary of the original battle. It [Macao] has survived many troubles and dangers external and internal and was now to face the blackest period of its history, in some ways, too, its most glorious.

Its buildings are a medley of old Portuguese Colonial, Chinese and modern style and there are many who regret the latter intensely. It has, from the very nature of its history, a character of its own, a character which Hongkong, for all its natural beauty, lacks.

Its population is in the very great majority Chinese. The Chinese population had been greatly increased by the influx from surrounding territories as these came under Japanese domination between 1937 and 1941. Whole universities had moved to Macao[15] as well as large numbers of businessmen and their dependents. Normally some 150,000, the population grew during this period to 450,000, virtually all concentrated in the five square miles of the mainland. Before 1937 Macao was the most densely populated area in the world; one can imagine what it was in the war years, and the problem facing the Government which had to feed this vastly inflated population.

This problem was not made any easier by the attitude of the various Japanese Departments, Naval, Military, Gendarmerie and Financial which only refrained from quarrelling with each other in order to put up a united front against assistance to Macao. The problem was dealt with by the Governor, Commander Teixeira,[16] Portuguese Navy, and by Dr. P.J. Lobo,[17] Director of Economic Services, with consummate skill. Despite their efforts, however, reliable information places the deaths from starvation in 1942 at 27,000 when cases of cannibalism were not unknown.

For imported goods Macao had always depended on the hinterland for natural products and on Hongkong for manufactured and tinned goods as well as for processed goods such as flour, tobacco, sugar. These supplies ceased suddenly on December 8th 1941 and the entire economy of the Colony had to be re-orientated. A sort of sales moratorium was imposed for a few days but Chinese ingenuity found methods of selling and some of the richer members of the community laid in fairly large stocks of tinned food. For myself, I did not, partly because I felt any but the vastest stocks would be exhausted in a very short period compared to the probable length of the war and partly because I felt Macao might at any time go the way of Hongkong in which case I was not very likely to survive to enjoy tinned goods of any sort. I had little faith in Japanese respect for diplomatic immunity.

From now on, from December 8th 1941 till V.J. Day, August 14th 1945,[18] for more than 3½ years we were to get no mail, barring perhaps 6 or 7 stray newspapers, no private correspondence and in fact nothing which could not be transmitted by radio. We were to gather vaguely what a jeep was, for instance, but no picture of one ever reached us. By 1945 toddlers in other parts of the world were far better informed than we were; we were to lead a lively but Rip van Winkle existence.

Such then was our setting, such was the overture. The curtain was to rise. We were on stage, practically motionless, awaiting our cues for speech and action.

Chapter II

Getting Going

This state of coma lasted quite a long while broken only by the arrival of SS *Perla*,[1] a Portuguese vessel which was given permission by the Japanese to evacuate some Portuguese citizens from Hongkong to Macao. The Governor, who had issued instructions to that effect, had told me that my wife would be aboard. She was not, owing to the ineffable ineptitude of certain Portuguese in Hongkong one of whom later went into gaol for fraud, as I believe, a fate more than just. The Governor had no little to say on the subject and I was inclined to pity the gentlemen concerned if he laid hands upon them.

With this ship came the first news of the fighting in Hongkong and this gave me my first real lesson in the way in which rumours could circulate in Macao magnifying at every moment. Confusion there had been in the defence of Hongkong, a confusion only to be expected in a Colony attacked without warning; but the rumours which came by the *Perla*, aboard which were one or two very talkative people indeed, gave the impression there had been nothing but confusion. The criticisms of these gentlemen were the more resented in that the critics were undoubtedly of the arm-chair variety. The majority had taken little or no part in the defence of their home Colony. They, however, very thoroughly enjoyed the momentary prominence which lifted them from well-deserved obscurity and gave libertine rein to the imaginations or to their powerful sense of exaggeration. They did little to cheer the spirits of Macao though we soon learned to disregard them.

It was known semi-officially that the Government of Macao was attempting to arrange for mass evacuations of persons of Portuguese race from

Hongkong and some tentative arrangements had been made. When the first large numbers of refugees arrived there was, none the less, complete confusion.[2] Accommodation reserved was grossly inadequate, though, in the crowded state of the Colony it must be confessed that the Government faced a tremendous problem. Feeding arrangements were of the most tenuous and indeed it was not until Mrs. Fletcher and another British lady, Mrs. Wilson,[3] whose husband was in the Hongkong Police, raided the Riviera Hotel for tea and milk, that even children received anything hot and nourishing. The food problem was dealt with, in the emergency, as adequately as possible by the Salesian Fathers who never showed themselves reluctant to jump bravely into any breach which presented itself.

Accommodation was scattered all over the town, a fact which further rendered the situation uneasy to handle. Food inevitably reached the refugee centres lukewarm or cold; medical attention was made more difficult by the dispersal and families were separated. This led in one case to an amusing incident due partly to the frequency of such names as Remedios, Ribeiro and Xavier. It was in fact a Mrs. Xavier who appealed to the authorities (me) for a bolster to put in the middle of her bed. She was told that this appeared to be unnecessary as she was in a double-bed with her husband. The authority concerned was nonplussed by the reply "No; that's my son-in-law".

Nor, at this stage, had any natural leaders emerged. One gentleman was obviously of the opinion that this was his moment. He sat in a room at the Macao Club[4] looking far from underfed and telling any who would listen of the hardships he had undergone and of the immense quantity of jewellery that his wife had lost. Everything, whether ring or bracelet, appeared to have been a metre in breadth and encrusted with diamonds. His ability to gain the fortunes he had spent on this jewellery did not enable him to deal with refugee problems. An airy wave of the hand and the orders to ask someone else were the apparent limit of his administrative capacity.

The "someone else" at this stage was most frequently Dr. Elsa Fernandes,[5] a woman doctor with a private practice as well as her Government Medical Duties to attend to. No praise can be too high for her work. It must be realized that many of those who arrived in the first two mass evacuations were suffering from the results of privation, age, infirmity and sicknesses, which had not been adequately treated for a month or more. For the vast population there were only some ten qualified doctors, two Portuguese and one Chinese hospital, and one or two emergency medical posts. This organization was suddenly called upon to cope with greatly increased problems. Dr. Elsa put heart and soul into the work and dealt with many questions which were far outside the normal scope of the medical profession.

As might well have been the case in England, the general organization was strained to the utmost. The Colonial Secretariat, under whose jurisdiction the refugees were placed, had not the staff to deal with the multitudinous questions which arose. In fact it was some time before even the compilation of a census of refugees was undertaken. A Mr. Rocha finally offered his services for the registration and some order began to emerge from the chaos. Mr. Rocha had a very difficult problem on his hands; the question of nationality was one which had hardly occurred to the average refugee and indeed there were some to whom the question of marriage and its implications seemed to have had little importance, at least from a legal point of view. "Dual nationality" and "master nationality" were mere phrases, phrases which might have been heard but had certainly not been understood. Mr. Rocha himself would be the last to claim that he could decide alone on the subject of a coloured gentleman with a Portuguese surname of supreme Nationalist significance who called himself a British Subject born in Peru. It must be remembered also that the majority of the refugees were without passports or documents of nationality. These, particularly when they showed British nationality, had mostly been prudently destroyed or genuinely lost. The only document common to all was a certificate from the Acting Portuguese Consul[6] in Hongkong to the effect that the bearer was of Portuguese race. The gallantry and enterprise of Portuguese explorers of the past had had some surprising results.

The problem was now complicated by the fact that a great proportion of the refugees were British Subjects without claim to Portuguese nationality as opposed to Portuguese race. Rightly the Government of Macao decided that these were a British not a Portuguese responsibility. The first of the major anomalies of the situation immediately appeared, namely that within refugee administration many were to receive financial support only from the British Government. Naturally, being in Portuguese territory, they were subject to Portuguese law: the question of bye-laws under the Refugee Commission (C.E.R.)[7] was perhaps more difficult. Counting on the undoubted intention of the Portuguese not to discriminate between their own and other nationals under the scheme I would have preferred to have run my own centres for British nationals with my own, very probably inferior, arrangements and discipline.

This solution was, however, impossible since in theory all these refugees were Portuguese and the arrival of others might well have been prejudiced if I had taken too active a part in their administration. In fact it was not till I had asked for and obtained permission from His Excellency that I even visited the refugee centres in a purely private capacity; the visits I think gave hope of better things to the refugees and at least gave them the impression that some interest of a personal nature was being taken in their problems.

The matter of personal interest was an important one to people whose morale was undoubtedly very low. I have mentioned Mrs. Fletcher and Mrs. Wilson of the British Community and I exempt from the criticism which will follow His Excellency and Mr. Lobo, the Chief of Economic Services, whose personal interest in the refugees and their problems was not only strong but sustained. His Excellency showed his appreciation of the work of the two British ladies by his marked friendliness to them on the arrival of the second refugee ship; some Portuguese ladies wished to receive some similar acknowledgement and did a little half-hearted work for a short time; the drudgery was too much for them and they soon desisted. Portuguese officialdom on the whole took little interest in the plight of their racial brothers and seemed indeed, at times, to wish to deny them what small pleasures they could arrange for themselves. The general public of Macao adopted, with some exceptions, a similar view and the term "the refugees" became one of scorn rather than of pity. Some families had relations amongst the refugees with whom they had been glad to stay or associate in Hongkong in the days of peace and of their relation's prosperity; those who were now refugees were not given any effusive welcome by the relations whom they had entertained in happier times. In their defence I confess freely that the behaviour of some refugees, and the ingratitude of many, hardly encouraged the people of Macao to open their doors to their cousins in distress.

Conditions in the majority of the centres were undoubtedly shocking. Sanitary and kitchen facilities were most inadequate or totally lacking; hot water for laundry there was not. A brief description of one centre will suffice. This building, the Macao Club, was, as its name implies, a place of ephemeral entertainment not intended for residence; its cooking facilities were those of a small sandwich bar rather than those of a restaurant; its sanitary equipment was typical of a club with no residential quarters; laundry facilities did not exist. The premises consisted of a theatre and its foyer, a library, a billiard room and one or two small public rooms. Into this space including the stage and gallery of the theatre more than two hundred people were crammed; the theatre, as is common with such buildings, had virtually no lighting or ventilation but plenty of draughts. One family of nine had a space of some twenty feet by ten in the gallery, the floor being in steps where the raised tiers of seats had been.

Many of the refugees suffered from skin disease; in such close quarters spread of the infection was inevitable; in addition lack of boiling water for laundry resulted in the impossibility of ridding clothing of infectious elements, though no cases of verminous infection were reported to me. In fact, in the circumstances it was no less than remarkable that the refugees managed to keep themselves as clean as they did.

Some of the centres were better[8] than the Macao Club but every one had its disadvantages of one sort or another. So much, in any case, depended on the spirit of the inhabitants, but in the early days there was little *esprit de corps* amongst the refugees. It might perhaps have been better if more of those of ages between 20 and 30 had been there but they were mostly in prisoner-of-war camps. As a result the majority of those in Macao were either elderly, and had felt the shock of war and of violent uprooting the worse, or were youngsters in whom a sense of responsibility had not yet time to grow. One centre, however, did organize weekly dances with its own amateur guitar orchestra. These were shortly afterwards forbidden for no reason that was apparent to either refugees or myself. I should emphasize that at this point I had virtually no *locus standi* as regards refugee administration. I could not therefore interfere in matters of discipline or morale except by showing general interest in the problems of the individuals or groups; this was, I fear, a very small measure of consolation.

I remember one occasion when I was obliged to give advice very strongly against my instincts and against those of the people advised, namely a group of refugee youngsters who were being plagued by a more numerous group of Macao "bloods". One of the refugee lads had offered to fight the Macao boys one by one but the local boys refused this offer, relying on numerical strength. The refugees came to me begging for permission to fight on equal terms or against odds. Most reluctantly, in the interests of the name of the refugees in general I refused permission; my decision was, alas, loyally followed.

This chapter closes gloomily when Singapore had fallen, when *Prince of Wales* and *Repulse* had been lost;[9] when the refugees were at their worst from the point of view of morale; when funds for their support were desperately low, when one never knew whether Macao would fall to the Japanese, when one never knew what the succeeding hours might bring. This was our blackest hour in Macao.

Chapter III

"The Situation"

The situation was now not a little interesting. My flag, floating next door to the Japanese Consul's, was the only Allied flag, apart from Chinese, for some distance, west to Yunnan and Chungking over 700 miles, north to Vladivostok 1,800, east into the Pacific some 4,000(?) miles, southeast to Port Moresby over 3,000 and south to Australia 2,700. It was to remain the only one constantly floating until the end of the war when it was described by the press as "The Lone Flag". It is possible that no other British flag has ever been so alone from the point of view of distance to the next.

Some play was made later in the press as regards my proximity to the Japanese Consulate. There simply was no other house available at the moment, in 1941, when I had to find an office and residence.[1] I have already referred to the crowded conditions in Macao but where there were a few empty houses, these were mostly pre-empted by rich Chinese of Hongkong who, astutely seeing trouble coming, had prepared for themselves a bolt-hole in Macao;[2] indeed I secured the Consulate only just ahead of one of these gentlemen, who in the end remained in Hongkong throughout the war to his own enrichment. My Japanese colleague before hostilities broke out, was evidently well imbued with the typical espionage complex of his race. Hearing that I liked Japanese food he asked me to dinner while offering his regrets that there were no geisha in Macao. "But", he said, "you will have seen that pretty Chinese girls come to my house". The dinner never occurred owing to the events of 8th December but it is obvious that he thought I was following his plan of noting all visitors to the Consulate.

Mr. Fukui, my Japanese colleague, was a fine man. The Governor once remarked of him that he ought to be promoted to another nationality. Even after hostilities had started he did all he could to assist, from a humane point of view, activities which could not hurt his country. He was known to have put all his weight into the return of my wife from Hongkong; he was known to have facilitated the dispatch of food parcels to prisoners in Hongkong and he was known to have personally brought letters from prisoners to their families in Macao. He was killed by an assassin hired by the Japanese Gendarmerie.[3]

The other members of the Consular Corps, in so far as there was such a body, were the honorary Consuls for Holland and Thailand or Siam. Neither Mr. Nolasco nor Mr. Fernandes would expect me to say they were overworked with Consular business. The former worked in cooperation with me; even if he had not desired to do so he would have been obliged to since he had no code with which to communicate with his Government. I still remember with horror the coding of such names as Vanlidtegude (or an approximation thereto). Mr. Fernandes' commission was almost unique; he held it not from the Siamese but from the Portuguese Government, a situation which arose when Siam, wishing to have representatives in Portuguese territory, asked the Portuguese Government to choose them. Mr. Nolasco had Dutch interests to protect in the form of the plant, property and ships of the Netherlands Harbour Works Company; these amounted to a very considerable monetary responsibility and to an even greater value in an area where the Japanese were desperate for ships and metals. One dredger indeed was forced from his hands by considerations too complex to discuss here.[4]

For so small a Colony this appears to be fairly strong Consular representation. But it must not be forgotten that up to the nineteenth century virtually all trade with China had passed through Macao. Here had been the headquarters of John Company[5] and of the Dutch East India Company. The former English factor's house still stands, now a museum, and the Dutch Company's tenure is commemorated by the Rua Horta da Compania (Road of the Company Garden).[6] The factor's house, on historical and traditional grounds should have been my Consulate and Residence, my Consulate because the East India Company's factor had been the real fore-runner of the Consul, and residence on the flimsy grounds that having been educated at Haileybury,[7] the old training school for John Company's officers, I was the traditionally lineal descendant of the many Haileybury men who had occupied the house; but a museum it remained.

I have no knowledge of the origins of our own Consular representation in Macao. The Consulate-General at Canton was established in 1843 and was presumably in control and in charge of British Interests in Macao. At some point, I believe in the 1930s, Mr. F.J. Gellion, Managing Director of the Macao Electric Company, the senior British firm in Macao, became Honorary Vice-Consul, under the control of H.M. Consul-General at Canton. In 1940 the post became an independent Consulate in the charge of Mr. H.D. Bryan, a career officer, whom I replaced in June 1941 to, perhaps, Derek Bryan's later relief.

British Interests in Macao consisted chiefly of the Macao Electric Company, which controlled also the Macao Water Company, the latter being a Portuguese registered company entirely financed by the Hongkong and Shanghai Banking Corporation. At the outbreak of the Pacific War we had a fleet consisting of the SS *Saion*, which I have already mentioned, an Asiatic Petroleum Company lighter and a small sailing boat belonging to the Malayan cadets. Another British interest was the general store of Mr. Cassim Moosa;[8] an Indian gentleman whose firm dated back into the middle of the nineteenth century. Apart from this some Hongkong firms, chiefly dealing in petrol, insurance or tobacco, had agencies in the Colony. Of all these the only one which was to cause head-and-heartache was Melco, the Electric Company, particularly as Mr. Gellion was away in America. This is no insult to my very good friend Mr. Fletcher who took over the affairs of the Company in the absence of Mr. Gellion. There were also a number of Indian stores but the majority of these became involved in the Indian Independence League[9] movement and would hardly have had the impertinence to appeal to the Consulate if they had been threatened;

it is noteworthy that none appealed against the threats against them by the I.I.L., which they alleged in their own defence after the end of the War.[10]

British Subjects were few; Mr. and Mrs. Fletcher, Mrs. Wilson, the Mitchell family, the three Malayan cadets, Mr. Borras of the Chinese Maritime Customs,[11] Mr. and Mrs. Lammert, Mr. and Mrs. Galloway and Pat Heenan[12] of the Royal Insurance Company were those of whom one saw the most. The Indian community consisted chiefly of the merchants I have mentioned and of police, both Mohammedan and Sikh in the employ of the Macao Government. There was also a handful of British Subjects of Portuguese race. Needless to say when relief appeared available many others claimed British nationality but their claims could usually be denied either on "dual national" grounds or under a special regulation introduced by which those who were resident before June 1941 but had failed to register were not entitled to relief. It is and probably always will be a sad reflection to Consular Officers that most British Subjects abroad are aware or prefer to be conscious more of the rights than of the obligations of British nationality. In general Consular Officers only see British Subjects who are in trouble; when they are not they have no need to see a Consul: this state of affairs is enough to make Consular Officers feel that there is no British Subject but a British Subject in trouble. Ordinary tourists and businessmen without worries hardly impinge though any Consul would like to know more of them.

The attitude of the Portuguese to the War was interesting. Some were completely in favour of Germany, though not of the Japanese.[13] I remember one in particular, whose moustaches had earned him the soubriquet of "Handlebars" though it might as well have been "Kaiser Bill", had been pro-German in 1914, pro-German in 1918 and was still pro-German; he probably still is. For a person with such unwavering views one had genuine respect. Some were genuinely pro-Allied or pro-British; amongst these I number unhesitatingly the Governor, the then Secretary for Chinese Affairs who on VE day disclosed beneath his waistcoat a portrait of Churchill, most of the naval officers and one in particular, and a certain genial surgeon who only lost his temper with the British when they displayed, in moments of temporary defeat, what was to him an infuriating stoicism. Mr. Lobo may certainly be mentioned as a friend of Britain, all the more valuable a friend for the appearance of strict neutrality he managed to maintain vis-à-vis the Japanese who also regarded him as friendly. Perhaps the finest compliment ever paid to him was by a Japanese; "Lobo is a very good friend of ours but nothing could buy his loyalty to Portugal". I could have said the same but I would have been justified in using far warmer terms. Other Portuguese had a rather petty-minded attitude arising from jealousy but usually attributed to our having allegedly stolen territory (was it Rhodesia?) from Portugal.[14] This group wanted to see Britain victorious but wished to see the lion's tail well tweaked first. One very senior official indeed was reported to me as having said, during the Blitz, "I want the British to win but first I want them to suffer and suffer". Others again were anxious for personal reasons to keep in with both sides and indeed as neutrals they had every right to do so; it was only distressing to know that some citizens of our oldest ally went out of their way to be friendly to Japanese to secure some personal advantage, such as the dear lady who went out of her way to launch a Japanese Family in Macao society and expected us to remain as friendly as ever. Of some others we saw little until D day but their friendship ripened successively as VE and VJ [Days] came along.

Somewhat similar activities led to my resigning from one of the few centres of recreation, the Melco Club; or, to give it its full title the Watco and Melco Staff Club. This was situated on the race-course[15] and consisted of a large hall with a stage, a small bar, changing rooms, two tennis-courts, and a football ground. It had been the centre of social activity but had fallen off as cost of living increased and transport decreased. However, the Golf Section of the Civilian Tennis Club requested Melco to allow its members, who played on a course in the middle of the race-track to use the Club "between rounds", a delightful temporal definition which included evening dances. The Club could hardly refuse this request from another Club with the result that the Japanese, who were the principal golf players, became regular frequenters of Melco Club. I reluctantly resigned, and pointed out to the President my displeasure that a Club run on British money should be opened to the Japanese. He replied, correctly, that in view of the tactics used, he had been helpless.

Before the war the race-course, also, now that I remember, a British concern, had been the scene of very cheerful friendly little race-meetings. There was one arranged for January 8th 1942 but of course it was cancelled. Not to be beaten by a mere war, and in the spirit I have mentioned, George McCaskie, one of the Malayan cadets, and I organized a bicycle gymkhana, which was really successful in entertainment value. At least it kept people's minds from brooding for a short while. Later the actual race-course became a series of Chinese market-gardens; the Chinese are a practical people and presumably argued that where there had been horses there must have been manure and what could be better for vegetables; and it is a fact that they flourished.

George, by the way, was one of the most universal characters I have ever met. So far as I remember he was a licensed preacher in the Church of Scotland, had passed examinations in law and medicine and had acted as third engineer on a Merchant ship. It gave me more than a single pang when I heard that he had died in Free China after surviving all the risks of getting through the Japanese patrols.[16] Charles Knaggs, the other Malayan cadet still in Macao in January also later died of fever in South-east Asia after escaping from the Colony. They were both fine men and were a great loss.[17]

This matter of escaping was naturally very much in the air. Four people actually escaped from Stanley internment camp and arrived by sampan. These four included Pam Harrap,[18] who has written of her experiences, and an American by the name of O'Neill. My memory fails me as to how Miss Harrap escaped from Macao but she made a success of it without my help; at this time I was not yet in touch with the organizers of the later escape routes and could, in fact, help very little. In these early days people made their own arrangements and all got through owing to their nerve and initiative. The only one I really helped at all was Pat Heenan to whom I gave a falsified Immigration Office Permit, describing him as born in Spain, which enabled him, speaking perfect Spanish, to go by a Portuguese vessel to Kwangchowan,[19] a French colony partially controlled by the Japanese, and into Free China.

George McCaskie and Charles Knaggs also made their own arrangements but I still remember Charles doing training walks to fit himself for the journey, most of which was bound to be done on foot. I believe they were confronted many times with the equivalent of a "Trip Cancelled" notice before they got through but they made it in the end by a somewhat harrowing journey. The other escapees from Stanley and Miss Cholmondeley of Hongkong,[20] later also a Mr. Stott, got away by means of their own Chinese connections but the trade had not yet become wholesale as it did later.[21]

O'Neill deserves a paragraph to himself.[22] I have never seen a man so continuously drunk. He was far from lacking in resource, managing on one occasion to smuggle the blankets out of his boarding-house at two in the morning in order to pawn them; in this he succeeded and, by a further stroke of genius, purchased a bottle or two of Chinese wine, fiery and intoxicating stuff. After he had nearly caused various incidents with the Japanese, on one occasion standing outside their Consulate and shouting insults, on another sinking into a drunken stupor in the Japanese Consul's car, I asked the Governor to have him removed to one of the islands where he could cause less trouble. Later the State Department asked me how many American citizens I had who desired repatriation. I gave the number and concluded my telegram with the words "and one under detention at my request". The mild humour of this lies in the fact that I was not then in charge of American Interests.

American Interests in Macao consisted chiefly of the Pan-American Airways property[23] and some agencies of which a later chapter will tell more. There were just a few American citizens, employees of Pan-American, teachers and missionaries some of whom, including Bishop Paschang and other Maryknoll fathers, were allowed by the Japanese to come into Macao from their station. The Americans also had a "fleet", one Pan-American launch in which I spent a blistering afternoon tearing the engine to pieces to make it work. She was something of a menace to navigate, since she was fairly heavy and could never be persuaded to go astern.

Earl Redden,[24] the Pan-American Manager, and Pat Heenan lived a weird existence of their own at the passenger-station. Their experiments were magnificent and ranged from Pan-American stew, through tobacco manufacture to Pat Heenan's beard. The stew was their staple dish; it consisted of all the vegetables and perhaps a bit of meat that they could buy in the market on their very small living allowance put firmly in a pot of boiling water and allowed to simmer till Pat would prod a potato and decide everything was well-enough cooked. Pan-American poison was a threat to civilization but went well with the stew; into one bottle went every variety of firewater available; bath-tub gin paled into impotent insignificance compared with the result. For some time too canvas rolls appeared, redolent of tobacco and molasses, Pan-American plug. A further activity was fishing in the reservoir with patent traps which opened all at the wrong time but caught various interesting weeds. I hasten to add that Pat's beard, dense as it grew, was never used as a fish net. Pictures of the girls from *Esquire* by Petty decorated the walls more than brightly and altogether "Angel's Roost" was a place to visit. Its visitors' book signed by such dignitaries as Marjorie Duchess of Macao, remains a great record of that small band who lived those anxious days together.

On the visitors' book, rather than in it, since it consisted of a board on the wall, the signature of the Commodore of the Allied fleet in Macao, Trygve Jorgensen, master of the SS *Masbate*, 790 tons, Panamanian flag.[25] "Trigger" was Norwegian and his English was doubtful and remained so, though it improved as time went on. He also had a drink of his own aboard of genus akin to Pan-American poison. A cheerful soul was Trigger, worried about one thing only, the fate of his wife, as he called his ship. He was fortunate in having a really loyal Chinese beneficiary owner, Mr. Chang; who consistently refused tempting Japanese offers, sale or charter, for the ship. He was to have his adventures later, as was the ship, but for the moment he lay peacefully at anchor in the outer harbour awaiting what the war would bring and concocting Norwegian hors d'oeuvres from the limited supplies available.

Such, roughly, was the Allied Community, though I must not fail to mention Jean Fay the Commissioner of Chinese Maritime Customs, his wife and his charming family.[26] They were all most definitely Free French and never wavered. They had a hard time throughout financially, but always put a brave face on things.

We were cut off, we were to get on very well, and we were to get to know each other very well. In spite of the nerve and other strain we were to undergo I doubt if one of us really regrets Macao 1941–46.

Chapter IV

Organization

Things soon started moving and we had a foretaste of what was to come when we had a request from the Red Cross for a list of all casualties and internees in our district. Our "district" was by then no small one but we set to work as best we could be questioning refugees and anyone else we could get hold of, including junkmen from Amoy and Swatow.[1] We produced a card-index, on small cards made of cut up envelopes stacked in little wooden boxes: we had no stationery such as to produce a beautiful modern index as we see in the advertisements. Consulates never do see such things; the average Chancery or Registry has a heterogeneous collection of cupboards, sometimes appropriately called presses, filing cabinets of steel and various types of wood, and card-indexes of every variety except efficient ones. Not far from me in my office in Rome I am sure I could find furniture marked V.R.,[2] a tribute if you like to the durability of Office of Works furniture but hardly a tribute to the modern mindedness of those who supply us. British traditional conservatism has much to answer for if our offices are not as efficient as they might be.

That, however, is a *cri de coeur* which has little to do with Macao. There we had to improvise; we had not even supplies of all those forms which are supposed to be dear to the heart of a bureaucrat but which are in fact anathema to him as they are to the public. The first glimmerings of the spirit which was to animate my staff throughout began to make their appearance, a spirit which was later to be crystallized in our unofficial motto, a piece of vile dog-Latin composed by myself with full knowledge of its grammatical shortcomings: "Nihil descendit nos", translated as "Nothing gets us down".

We therefore card-indexed vigorously the many rumours which reached us, checking where we could. Sometime or other while we were hard at it Wilfred appeared. That is really the only way I can describe it because it seemed that one day he was not there at all and the next day he was at a desk card-indexing. I feel sure that he must have asked if he could help but I have little recollection of his doing so. My impression is simply that he walked in and sat down and my improvised staff had begun. He belonged really to Cable and Wireless,[3] was Mauritian by parentage and had come over with the refugees as his wife was Portuguese. Anyhow there he was, making himself useful, a performance he kept up with increasing degrees of usefulness to the end of the War.[4]

I should point out here, to avoid tiresome reiteration, that my staff grew gradually as new work and more voluminous work had to be dealt with, or as new needs had to be met. They were, if you like, as improvised as the office equipment. I have been criticized for not taking on the older members of the communities, for having mostly comparative youngsters except in specialized jobs such as accountancy and teaching, though even my doctors were, when they joined up, far from old. The reason is this, that the job was essentially a young job, a job for people who had had no time to become routine-minded. Policies and methods had frequently to be changed to meet new circumstances. In addition I was myself young and I had to be the boss, not I hope in a dominating sense, but in a way which might not have worked out well if the staff had been composed of men who, by long experience, felt, perhaps rightly, that they knew much more than myself. I do not say that I could not have found older men who would have joined in well; indeed I did find one or two; but I do say that it was better to get young men and to train them for their specific jobs. This policy I pursued and did not regret it.

It is to be remembered that to all intents and purposes, except for the chapter on Nationality, Consular Instructions became on the 8th December 1941 a book of little value to me. It had been one's gospel, but it was a gospel whose preaching had become outmoded in the peculiar circumstances which we faced. Chapter after chapter either threw no light on our

Organization

problems or simply did not fit. I confess also that I was not displeased to have the chance of trying out new methods and my excuse is simply this, that in those circumstances they worked and were flexible, this quality being perhaps their greatest virtue.

The old system of filing, for instance, went by the board and was replaced by a scheme which eliminated card-indexes. We had no cards in any case. Papers were not put away at the end of a year; where a file continued to be "live" it went on from year to year, merely filling more space on a shelf. The last paper was not put on top of the file but at the back; I have an incurable fondness for reading a book from page 1 to page 400 and not from page 400 to page 1. Many papers were not registered in the correspondence register and solemnly given numbers; if this had been done with all the letters asking for relief or an increase of relief seven men with seven pens would not have got it clear. Relief cases were numbered and indexed, the individual papers relating the story were not. Yet we boasted with truth that any paper could be found in five minutes. Medical history cards were alphabetically arranged. Receipts for relief and subsidy had to be devised with always an absolute minimum of paper wastage; this latter was a point of the greatest importance; we did not waste envelopes which reached us; they were cut in half and sent, later, to the Clinic where they were used to issue pills. As little as possible was done in duplicate or in triplicate; there was, remember, a severe shortage of paper. Other forms had to be improvised, identity certificates, certificates entitling refugees to medical attention and even for a while, ration cards, these last having to be organized and issued at twenty-four hours' notice owing to a sudden rise in the price of rice. So it went on and it worked, at times a little creakingly but never incapable of meeting an emergency, never brought to a standstill, and with little waste.

We were and are proud of the fact that out of every dollar that passed through our hands 98 cents went to the refugees directly in subsidy or medicine. The other 2 cents paid salaries, rents, incidental expenses of all kinds including some intelligence expenditure and the expenses involved in moving people to Free China, telegrams, stationery and in fact all overhead charges. We claim that few firms or institutions, non-revenue producing in

Consulate organization

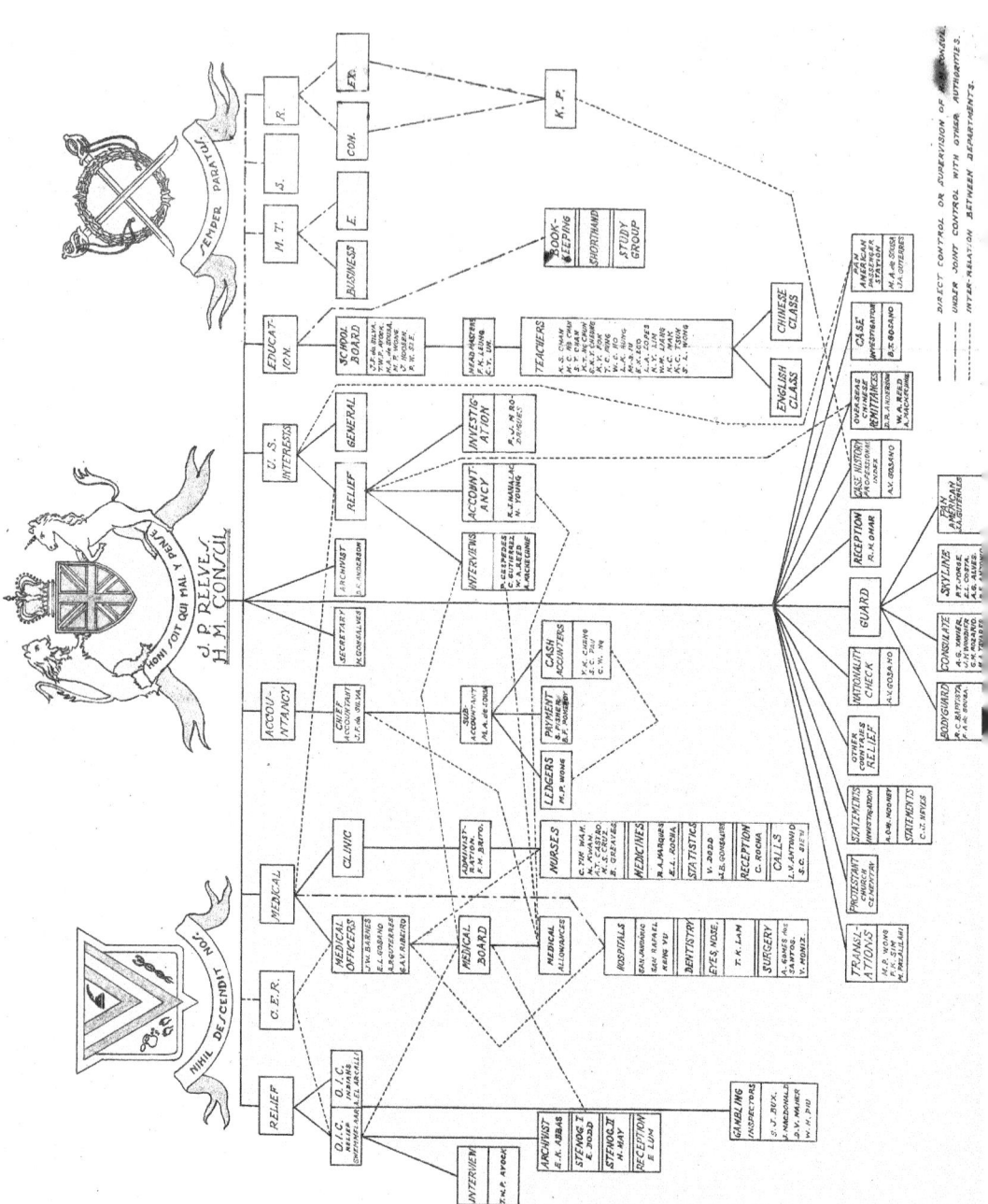

Organization

particular, can boast of an overhead bill of only 2 per cent; and it must be remembered that this was in the face of constantly rising costs for everything from paper to electricity.

It would probably serve a useful purpose if I were to give here a rough outline of the organization which gradually developed; details can be left to appear in the text at moments when they assume significance. The chart, which accompanies this chapter largely, speaks for itself but needs some explanation.

It is headed, you will see by our self-devised coat of arms or shield, representing administration, relief (in a larger form coins are seen falling into outstretched hands from a bag marked "Charity") and the Caduceus for Medicine. The execrable motto has been explained.

Relief was of course much more than half our work though it occupies but a small proportionate part of the chart. To start with I dealt with all cases personally but the volume became so tremendous as the thousands mounted up that I had to call in assistance, even though Wilfred was doing all he could to take the burden off my shoulders. I was fortunate in finding amongst the semi-refugees (for he was obtaining remittance from a film company in America) Dutchman A.A. Swemmelaar. "Swemm" or "Sandy" soon fitted in and undaunted by my 14 points, or qualifications to be taken into consideration before granting relief in any particular case, put his back straight into the work. He had comparatively little connection with Hongkong, having been there only a short time, and, being Dutch, belonged to none of the racial groups composing the refugees; I was confident therefore that he could be relied on not to be swayed by racial or factional prejudice; my confidence was never misplaced.

Later in the scheme of things Mr. Abbas el Arculli took charge for me of the very tangled skein of Indian affairs. Apart from being only normally cognizant of the customs and demands of various Indian beliefs, racial or religious, I was out of my depth in trying to deal with the various factional differences within the Indian Community in Macao; these led to person after person representing himself as the only loyal and reliable man of the community and telling me tale after tale of the disloyalty and unreliability of all but his own friends. Mr. Arculli's knowledge of his own people and his legal brain sorted out many a puzzle. In addition any non-Indian case could be submitted to him in the knowledge that a fair appraisal would result.

Later on again we had L.O.P.A., Liaison Officer Portuguese Affairs; this job was handled admirably by Freddie Xavier who, while appearing slow, was far from it and who had what I can only call an enjoyable obstinacy in defending the interests of his people.

Under "Interviews" appears the name of Ayock; this is in fact Wilfred again who saw most applicants for relief or increase in relief and made his recommendations to Swemm, with whom the final decision rested. In these interviews Wilfred, more, probably, than anyone in the office, had to put up with rudeness or downright abuse. Looking back I think my ex-family will realize that they received great courtesy in return, some of them more than they deserved.

A section which intrigues all those who see this chart is that of "Gambling Inspectors". These gentlemen formed a patrol which circulated about the various gambling houses and reported on any refugees found playing. I took a considerable exception to the use of money given to people for their stomachs and backs finding itself into the pockets of the gambling kings. It must be remembered that gambling was not illegal in Macao and that therefore the refugees committed no legal but only a disciplinary offence in gambling. There will be further reference to this subject later.

Passing to the next section directly controlled by me we reach the Clinic. This again started in a small way but gradually enlarged to cope with the increasing volume of work till it reached tremendous proportions. As was inevitable there were disagreements between medical and lay points of view, as represented on the one side by my doctors and on the other by Swemm and myself. On the whole these differences were ironed out without really exacerbated feelings and certainly with only momentary bad humour. Ozo, Joe, Eddie, Tony, Germano and Ho did a fine job for which I, and I hope the refugees, have a real gratitude.[5]

Accountancy, if Jerry and Micky will forgive me, is a difficult subject of which to write interestingly. Jerry Silva had had many years of it in the

Hongkong Government and it held no mysteries for him. He was particularly valuable in that he knew the Governmental approach to accountancy. Micky Sousa had not been an accountant; he soon was. It is enough to say that when we were demobilised, or demobilising, and wanted to present consolidated accounts Jerry was seriously perturbed to have lost, between January 1942 and June 1946 the large sum of three cents, about a half-penny; about £1,750,000 had passed through his hands.

Departments controlled directly by myself come next; they are varied. My "inner office" team was composed of my Secretary and my Archivist. They were both beyond praise. Derek Anderson[6] had to deal with all documents passing my hands and could always find them. There will be more of him later. Of Micao, what can I say? Perhaps merely that the cold name M. Gonsalves stands for perfection in the world of secretaries.

The various other departments which appear at the foot of the chart will gradually appear as the story unfolds and need little mention here. Look, however, at the names and they will give you some idea of the universality of race of my staff. One hopes that as they worked together with me they will work together for the future of Hongkong, which badly needed such intercommunal co-operation and probably could still do with it.

The U.S. Interests department followed closely the lines of organization of the British side. In the course of the narrative of this account of Macao 1941–46 more will be heard of this department and those with whom it had to deal. I must emphasize that the organization started before I was put officially in charge of U.S. Interests and long before I knew that I would receive any backing, moral or financial from the States.

The educational department started when it was drawn to my attention, Wilfred again, that whereas the Catholic children were receiving schooling, and the Mohammedans were receiving religious instruction, other young brains were being left fallow. From among the refugees we were able to find a magnificent band of teachers from all the schools, except those staffed entirely by Britishers or religious organizations, that had existed in Hongkong. It is not therefore surprising that the standard was high and it was heightened by the devotion of the teachers to their pupils. There were also various unofficial educational groups which met with more or less success, the most successful being the Accountancy School of Mr. Figueiredo. All contributed a real worth to mental rehabilitation and to morale.

There follow three headings in which only the initials are inserted; the retention of the full names of these departments was necessary at the time as they had to remain confidential. The M.T. was a newspaper, the *Macao Tribune* which was controlled by me and was an attempt to get the Allied point of view more prominently placed before the public; the story of its suppression will be related in its place; but I can at least record my appreciation of "Uncle" Gingam, Franco, and the silent (at editorial meetings at least) Talip. They may recognize the style of "Peter", their leader and limerick writer in this jingle:

> It was really fantastic, the way
> The *Tribune* appeared every day:
> The Editor's staff
> Gave the snags the horse laugh
> And, still stranger, they made the thing pay.

"S" covers lots and my collaborators in this can only be given a tribute, none the less real for that, anonymously. It stands for "Secret" and little but its obvious results can be spoken about.[7] Its most spectacular job was "Escapes" but it did much else. But to "Chan", which is not his real name, to a certain Portuguese British Subject and to the man who kept his gun wrapped in newspaper, "Bunny", the best thanks, not only of "Sampan" (one of my many *noms-de-guerre*) but also of those whose lives they saved and protected, the possessors of which have in many cases no knowledge of the work that was put into their preservation.

Finally "R" stands for "Rehabilitation". The idea was that of Mr. J.P. Braga, one of the grand old men of Hongkong; on his death the legacy fell to me to try and translate his idea into action with the constant aid of his son Jack Braga.[8] A Committee was formed of senior Chinese, Portuguese, Indian and Eurasian representatives then in Macao of the Hongkong Community and we did our best to prepare plans for the renaissance of that Colony.[9]

The plans were drawn up. What happened to them, a pathetic story, will appear. This is a brief, though to many perhaps too long, description of our activities. It cannot be said to cover all facets of our work but these will I hope appear in perspective in succeeding chapters.

Plate 1

John Reeves

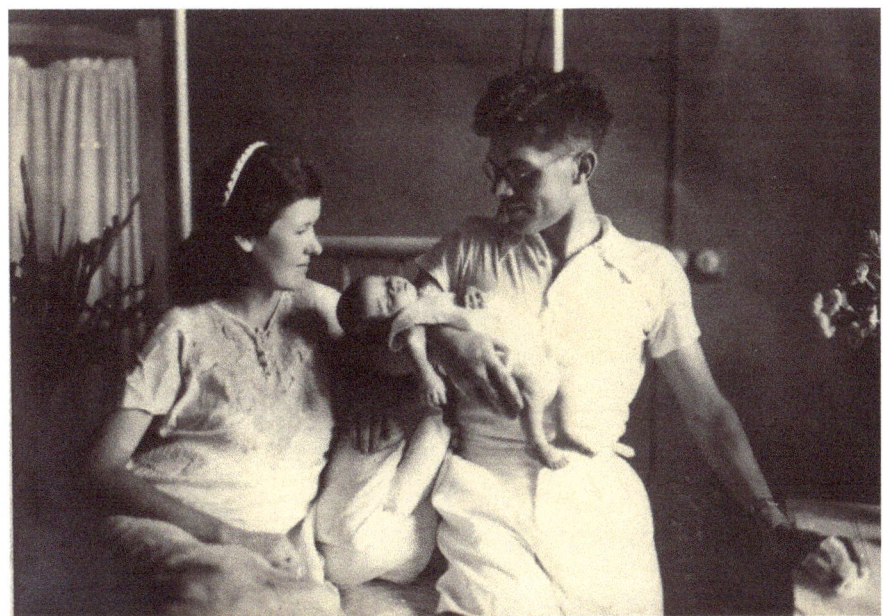

Plate 2

John Reeves and his wife Rhoda with their newly born daughter, Letitia. The photograph was presumably taken in Hankow in 1937.

Plate 3

John Reeves gazing over the South China Sea

Plate 4

A group of friends in Macao on Christmas Day 1941, the day Hong Kong surrendered, but probably before the news reached them. John Reeves is in the back row, far right. The central figure in the back row is believed to be Karl Fletcher. His wife, Marjorie, is second from the left in the front row.

Plate 5

Japanese consulate. This photo was taken after the British consulate had been demolished. It is likely that building was similar in style to this one.

Plate 6

The Macao hockey team, with John Reeves in his Cambridge blazer third from the left in the back row.

Plate 7

The badge worn by British consulate employees in Macao

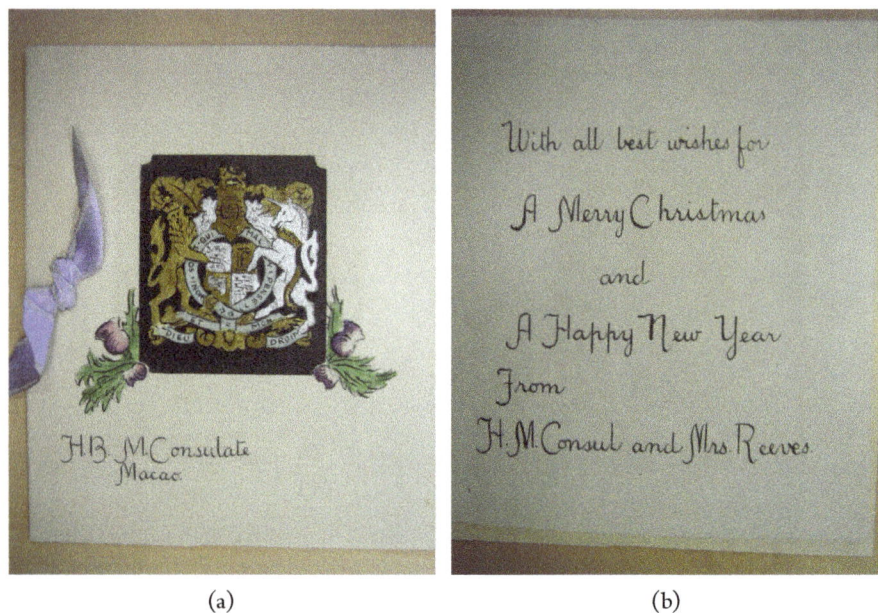

(a)   (b)

Plate 8

Handmade consulate Christmas card during the war years (a) front, (b) back.

Plate 9

Karl Pope Fletcher

Plate 10

Marjorie Pope Fletcher

Plate 11

Thanksgiving service, 19 August 1945

Plate 12

Medals awarded to John Reeves. On the left, that for Officer of the Order of the British Empire (Civil Division) awarded in the New Year's Honours list 1946. On the right the medal from the Portuguese Red Cross for dedicated service.

Plate 13

The Lone Flag, the new Union Jack raised for the first time after Japan surrendered

Plate 14

John Reeves in South Africa

* New Para

While on the subject of money it might be as well to delve shortly into the exchange problem. We had several currencies running, if not all officially, in Macao. There was the pataca, the official medium, at par with the Hongkong dollar at about 15 to the £ sterling (before January 1942 there were more Hongkong notes in circulation in Macao than pataca notes); there was the Hongkong dollar, the Chinese National dollar, and the military yen, this last printed by the Japanese Army without even serial numbers. The pataca remained steady, partly at least because new printing was backed by sterling in the form of my remittances. The other currencies varied almost hour by hour, and wildly; to complicate this, one $100 Hongkong note might be worth one day $110 and another day $60 in Hongkong notes of smaller denominations. At one moment the $10 Hongkong note was only worth about $2.40. and after the war was redeemed, to me incomprehensibly, at par. Some people made a very, very profitable speculation in Hongkong notes! They cannot have been as confused as I was over exchange possibilities.

Plate 15

Sample (Chapter VI, page 59) of the handwritten sections of the manuscript

Chapter V

Parochial

Supposing we change the subject and get right out of the office.

Macao has been variously known as the gambling hell of the Far East or the Pearl of the Orient. Similarly there has been great play on the subject of its opium "dens" almost as, with more modern habits, one might refer to a chemist's shop as an aspirin "den"; the third industry of Macao facetiously, was sometimes mentioned as being prostitution. When talking, as I am, or shall be, of the "amenities" of Macao it might be as well first to examine these three aspects of its life.

Gambling there was; so there is in England. It was run by a Concessionary Company which paid some HK$2,000,000 a year for the privilege. The story goes that on one occasion the usual sealed tenders were to be opened by Mr. Lobo. One only had up to then been presented, that of the Company which had held the concession for many years. At the last moment another envelope was presented, to the consternation of the Concessionary Company who asked for another five minutes, at the end of which they entered a tender for an extra quarter million. Mr. Lobo then drew from the other envelope a blank sheet of paper and blandly remarked that evidently the Company was not finding taxation too heavy. This story at least deserves to be true.

So there was gambling, recognized and legal and by that fact so much the more regulated; in addition it was in the interests of the Company to see to it that the gambling was straight; I do not believe, myself, that it was crooked. It took three main forms, *fantan*, the three-dice game and *Pakapiu*, though I feel sure I have spelt the last wrong. *Fantan* consists merely of pouring out on the table an unspecified number of counters or beans. Betting is done on the probability of the remainder, as the beans are removed four by four, being one, two, three or four. One small room in the Central Hotel was still kept for the benefit of the tourist where the bets were lowered, and the winnings, if any, sent up in baskets on strings. The majority of the gamblers, however, preferred just to play round a big table. My story, to be taken with a pinch of salt, is that I once walked into my clinic dispensary to find the lads playing *fantan* with newly-bought sulphanilamide tablets; far from reproaching them I claim rather to have encouraged this to assure accurate counting. For myself, I gambled on *fantan* once while I was in Macao; frankly games of pure chance bore me to tears so my abstinence from gambling was no virtue. The three-dice game amounted to a complicated form of roulette; three dice were thrown and you could bet on combinations of the numbers appearing on the dice, or on the totals. The most remarkable thing about this form of play to me was the system by which the results were electrically signalled to various floors where large facsimile dice would light up on the wall, for instance, above the orchestra on the dance floor. The third game, the one of whose name I am none too sure, was really pure sweepstake; its inner workings I never understood but I believe it was only too easy to lose more than one's shirt.[1]

The gambling season, though it went on of course all through the year, was officially opened by the Governor once a year when he either made the first bet or threw the first dice. At all other times Government Servants were forbidden to gamble though the prohibition was far from effective.[2] At one other time in the year the gambling departed from its really very humdrum and routine character. This was, I think, at Carnival or Chinese New Year, when gambling was allowed all over the streets; this licence had however in some years during the war to be curtailed for reasons of public safety.

Next on our list of "industries" is opium, which was a Government monopoly; the vexed question of the morality of this procedure is no subject for this book. Even doctors, I believe, agree that opium, <u>in moderation</u>, can do no harm or at least no more than eating drinking or smoking <u>in moderation</u>. One can at least say that unbridled consumption is, to some extent, checked by Government Control.

Parochial

The same applies, after all, to prostitution; there was plenty of it in Macao and it was recognized. Your room boy at a hotel would offer you a girl with as much *sang-froid* as that with which he would announce that your bath was ready. Here I speak from first hand information for I have heard it done more than once; I hasten to add that I never stayed at a hotel in Macao, except in my first weeks when the Consulate Office was in a hotel of great respectability so far as I was concerned. The Government took the familiar line that licensed prostitution is better and cleaner than unlicensed underground prostitution. To this view I personally incline. I can hardly leave this subject without a short note of admiration for the work done for the prostitutes by Madame Gomez dos Santos, wife of the Director of Medical Services, herself a doctor. Her work was too little known and certainly had not enough public recognition.

There were other industries, chiefly dried fish and firecrackers, the latter almost closed up during the war for lack of materials; part of it at least blew up shortly after the war, fortunately on the islands, when materials were again available. Firecrackers could not, in any case, be exploded in Macao during the war without police permission, a very wise precaution; good ones sound too much like shots. The former maintained its redolent self upon the southern quays of the Interior Harbour[3] and spread itself to such an extent across the roadway that at times one's progress in a car closely resembled that of a fishing trawler in a thick shoal of herring.

Amenities and amusements were few. Three or four cinemas operated, largely on films stolen by the Japanese in Hongkong during the war; needless to say the stock was low and even the most ardent film-fans must have found it difficult to see the same film time after time; later hazards were introduced by the playful placing, presumably by "protection" racketeers, of bombs in some of the cinemas; one very good Chinese friend of ours, a Mr. Fong, was killed this way though I do not believe the attack was meant personally. Theatres, except for Chinese theatres were rarely, if ever, open and then mostly for concerts; in this connection I should mention the very gallant effort of Mr. Fernandes and the Melco orchestra who were, competing with great difficulties, making the nucleus of a really good ensemble.

The Portuguese are a musical nation and the Fernandes family was large enough and musical enough to make its own orchestra; musical evenings at their house were a real pleasure.[4] While talking of music one must mention the several choirs organized by, chiefly, the Protestant Schools and Colleges which sang foreign as well as Chinese music; one remembers them particularly at Christmas when they would tour certain houses bringing, to that remote corner of the Far East, some of the spirit of the waits.[5]

The Chinese Universities and Schools were quite a feature of life in Macao. Their students must have numbered 20,000 who had fled from Canton after the occupation of that city by the Japanese and re-established themselves in neutral territory.[6] Some of course were more pro-Central Government than others but I would be the last to dare to say which. One was constantly discovering, post-war, people whom one had mentally condemned as collaborationists or traitors appearing with cast-iron credentials from either provincial or central authorities. It was all very difficult for the simple soul, like myself, to understand.

There were clubs, other than Melco, in Macao, a multiplicity of them; social clubs were, as well as Melco, the Military Club (Gremio Militar)[7] and the Macao Club.[8] One would normally find in each, one or perhaps two bridge fours, very solemn and serious, their games enlivened only by discussions, disputes, quarrels, call them what you will, which led the foreigner to believe that knives would be out and blood shed at any moment. However they subsided quickly and were merely a more violent or Latin form of the post-mortems held at the Unionist Club, Mudbeach-on-Sea. The Argonauta Club was semi-social and semi-sporting; its full activities eluded me.

The senior sporting club of the Colony was, if not by age at least by the reputation it had gained in the Far East, the Hockey Club of Macao of which I was later to have the honour to be elected President, and, after my departure, Member of Merit. At the time of my arrival the Club was inactive owing to the season and it remained dormant for two years after which the two Fredericos, Nolasco and Barros, and Ade Santos-Ferreira got it going again, generously giving me the credit. The hockey in Macao was far from village hockey; touring sides had made a reputation in Shanghai, Singapore and of course in the neighbouring Colony of Hongkong. Hockey was fast, accurate and, at times furious; it was also only too frequently talkative.

Other prominent sporting clubs were the Football Club, two tennis clubs, one civil the other military, the latter moribund and again of course, Melco Club. For the Football Club there was a large stadium which had been built for dog-racing, an abortive enterprise.[9] There was not really a great deal of football as there were not enough teams, and of those there were it was strange that the Police, somehow or other, almost had to win the Leagues. There was at least one virtue in the Police team, a Comedy King, by nickname King Kong, a barrel-chested fellow named, I think, Collaço, "as a footballer laughable, as a comedian lamentable" who could give a beginner lessons in missing open goals; but he always played for Macao; you are right, he was a Policeman. The Civil Tennis Club,[10] situated on one side of the rocky bastion which formed part of the Governor's residence, had three courts and a wall and this was probably the most active Club of all; it was certainly pleasant to sit by the sea in the shade of the Club house watching the energetic hard at work. The Military Tennis Club[11] despite floodlighting and so on simply did not function: it had probably been started with great enthusiasm and, on the transfer of the leading personality, lapsed; this used to happen to many organizations in Macao; there was plenty of enthusiasm but very little staying power. The Civil Tennis Club had a golf-section which played on a nine-hole, dead-flat course in the middle of the racetrack and that completes the list of sports in Macao, with the exception of Melco which also had Badminton and Table-tennis. There were few non-Chinese restaurants,[12] though one was famous for its roast pigeon, known as *Shekki* pigeon, whether these were bred in captivity or not I cannot be sure but they were fed on milk and basted on the spit with soya bean sauce till they were a delight and deserved a place on any gastronomic map of the world. There were many Chinese restaurants of course, one of the best being on a houseboat moored alongside in the inner harbour. For my own part I liked Chinese food immensely so there was always somewhere to eat out, if I felt so inclined, but I will not dilate on Chinese dishes and mention those which sound so odd to foreign ears; it is enough to say, with regard to the divergence of tastes between Western and Eastern gastronomes that many a Chinese dish, served on a plate with knife and fork, has been eaten with delight by the man "who had always loathed Chinese chow, couldn't stick it". The food at the only Portuguese-run hotel was dull, insufferably so; one did not dine there for pleasure.

One could dance at the Central and the Grand Hotels,[13] the former having Chinese dance-hostesses, the latter not; a great advantage of the Grand, during the summer was its roof equipped with a "juke-box" and plenty of waiters with cool drinks. Not being either a good or an enthusiastic dancer I rarely visited the Central, and the Grand I went to purely for the coolness. Both the hotels were Chinese-run.

It was in fact a noteworthy feature of Macao life that virtually all business concerns were run by Chinese; there was no Portuguese tailor, no Portuguese grocer's shop and so on. Portuguese supplied the professions, lawyers and doctors but, after all, the inclusion of foreigners in the professions is prohibited by law in most countries. All one's friends amongst the Portuguese were of the army, navy or civil services, lawyers or doctors; one or two chemist's shops were run by Portuguese but this again was a result of their protection by the necessity for such persons to hold Portuguese diplomas. And, of course, there was the Portuguese Bank,[14] the only foreign exchange and note-issuing Bank in the Colony. It was headed by a gentleman who described himself as a mixture of poet, philosopher and airman; I am told he was a very good poet.[15]

There were, of course, many places of historical interest in the Colony, pride of place in the Portuguese view, going to the Garden and Grotto of Camoens[16] where that celebrated poet is supposed to have written large parts of his *Lusiadas*; some experts, including I believe Major Boxer,[17] cruelly claim that Camoens simply was not in Macao when tradition has him living there; if they are right one of the highest lights of historic Macao is extinguished. There was also the Protestant Cemetery which had claims to attention both for its peace and beauty and for the interest of the graves which included that of the first Protestant Missionary in China, Morrison, and of a relation of Winston Churchill.[18] Apart from that there were many fine

Parochial

churches and buildings, my own favourite being San Domingos[19] and the old Supreme Court, now pulled down. I cannot help but record my genuine pain at the process which in the name of progress, pulls down beautiful buildings which have been shockingly neglected and replaces them with concrete boxes. No one enjoys modern architecture in its place more than myself but Macao's character depends so much on its antiquity and this character is being rapidly lost.

The most prominent landmark of Macao is the Guia lighthouse, the first modern type light ever erected in the Far East.[20] It was to become a symbol of so much.

> Longest of all has shown its double shaft
> Through many years to guide the erring craft,
> Pitied their plight
> The Guia light.
>
> Many a mariner has blest its steadfast gleam
> Showing a haven with unbroken beam
> The gentle might
> Of Guia light.
>
> The gloom of conflict shadows all the East
> Held in the maw of Moloch, god and beast,
> Yet in this night
> Shines Guia light.
>
> When other beacons flicker, fade and die
> Their friendly shaft gladdens no sailors eye
> One alone is bright
> The Guia light.
>
> Long may it shine; a symbol clear of peace
> From war's alarms bringing a sweet release
> To those in flight,
> The Guia light.[21]

Another historical monument was the Monte Fort with its ancient cannon still grinning from the embrasures.[22] At the time of which I speak it was more prison than fort and had a very domestic atmosphere. This, none the less, leads to a mention of the garrison, a company of Portuguese infantry, a company of Portuguese artillery and a company of negro troops. All were tired of being kept in Macao and the negroes simply could not understand why they were not sent home. I knew few of the officers and it would not in any case be reasonable or fair of me to comment on them. The naval air squadron had two or three planes, Ospreys I believe;[23] one crashed in the town and the others, I was told, were demilitarized and exchanged with the Japanese for rice. I append a guide to Macao (Appendix 13)[24] to avoid a wearisome description of other monuments which I have not mentioned; the historically minded will find much of interest.

Have you by now a picture of life in Macao before the war? I fear not since words are so difficult a way of conveying an atmosphere quite unique; the atmosphere of Macao is as untranslatable as the Portuguese word "saudade", a compound of longing thought, home-sickness and remembrance of absent friends. It is a feeling common to those who have been in Macao, even to the refugees who may not have been happy when they were actually there. I think we all miss Macao now we are no longer there, and the friends we made there. We all had much to be thankful for in its mere existence.

Chapter VI

Relief

Let us return to our refugees and their problems and see how they were looked after. Some of them, I am afraid, would deny, or try to deny that they were looked after at all but it is the lot of the public official, all over the world, sometimes to have to take unpopular decisions, sometimes against his own wishes, without being able to point out to the public the reasons for such decisions, whether they stem from superior orders or from his own judgement of the situation. On the whole, apart from the inevitable disgruntled minority, to be found in every community, my family showed their appreciation of our efforts very fully indeed and we are grateful for their gratitude; it fortified us during our difficulties and refreshed us after our labours were over; it leaves to this day, and will till our deaths, leave an aftertaste mentally which cannot be destroyed.

I have spoken vaguely of the C.E.R., the Portuguese side of the relief problem. This was, as I have indicated, to begin with, extremely haphazard and even fragmentary; no definite policy was determined and everything was on a hand-to-mouth basis. This could not continue and a conference was held between Mr. Leo d'Almada Jr. (a member of Hongkong's Legislative Council), Mr. Remedios of the P.R.A. (Portuguese Residents Association of Hongkong) and myself in general terms. As a result of this, Mr. Remedios and I sent in completely independent memoranda suggesting a course of action vis-à-vis the Portuguese refugees; somewhat surprisingly, the two memoranda were almost identical notes; we both suggested a measure of self-government for the refugees and various means, communal gardens, farms, classes etc. to improve morale. Whether owing to our memoranda or to the fact that the problem was now beyond the power of an already overworked Colonial Secretariat, the first part of the programme at least was put into action and the C.E.R. was the result.

I may here not have given enough credit to Leo d'Almada,[1] who may have influenced the course of events more than I knew. But I have at least given credit to Mr. Remedios[2] who later died as a result of Japanese cruelty, as so many innocent men and women were to die.

I must again emphasize that this record is not written with a strict regard for the chronological sequence of events; parallel interlocking developments were too frequent for such a course to be possible. So, if I speak of the C.E.R. as a living entity, I imply that it grew, little by little to the stature that I describe. It had a semi-governmental capacity being headed by Mr. Lobo and Captain Silva e Costa who was known as the Governor's Private Secretary; his actual title was Chefe de Gabinete (literally Chief of Cabinet or Office) which could more or less be translated as Chief of the Governor's Civil Staff;[3] since I have already referred to him as "Captain" this may lead to further confusion but many Civil posts under the Portuguese Estado Novo, New State, the Government of Dr. Salazar, were filled by members of the Armed Forces; the Governor himself was an example.

Under these two was an Executive Committee consisting of Mr. A.A. Lopes, Mr. Eddie Sousa, and Mr. Botelho. The first of these was the President of the Executive Committee, Sousa was supply-officer and Botelho accountant (if there are any inaccuracies it must be remembered that I am writing from memory). All three did a fine job, better perhaps than the refugees themselves know; Artur Lopes used to be blamed for dictatorial methods but thinking refugees realised that strong discipline was frequently only too necessary. It is within my personal knowledge that Artur many times risked his position to help refugees who were behindhand on repayments due to the Commission; if his cash position had been examined at such a moment he would have been dismissed; only very few of us knew the risks he was taking on behalf of individuals some of whom deserved less consideration by far.

Eddie Sousa, a giant of a smiling man, best known perhaps for his comedy turn as a child in sailor clothes, had a hard row to plough. It was far from being a question merely of indenting for all the supplies of rice he required; in the early days rice for one of the centres had to be borrowed from a Chinese hotel which was hoarding without Government action against it. The same applied to meat or fish or vegetables or bread; there was a shortage of everything. In any case a great deal depended on the skill and organization of the individual cooking centre; I would single out for special mention the Armacao centre[4] where the meals, despite the difficulties, were more than just reasonably palatable.

It must be remembered that a Chief of Centre was attempting to feed his people on some £2 per month out of which amount he was obliged also to find fuel and incidentals. Rations could hardly be anything but meagre in a Colony where prices were constantly rising although the Government assisted in such forms as the privilege of purchase of rice at Government prices; this was of necessity; with rice at 28 or 43 cents per catty official price,[5] the person without Government privileges had to purchase at prices which reached $3.50 per catty; at such prices the refugees would frankly have starved. Firewood was a big item and had rocketed in price; I regret that an attempt of mine to get the Government to transport firewood for the centres from the islands, thereby at least halving the price, was a failure; I cannot tell the motives behind this though I have my suspicions; someone after all was making a profit, a large profit, though I do not say this was a Government official; it may have been a Chinese merchant with influential friends.

The general principle was that a refugee could draw either subsidy or rations. I have to be somewhat chary of figures as, I repeat, I am writing from memory, though I hope to get my figures checked from Rome by reference to Macao, but I am almost certain that the rate of subsidy was $30 each for father and mother and for the first adult child, $24 for the next child, $21 for the next, $18 for the next and so on with a maximum of $130 per family. This maximum was later raised to $150 at the insistence of Artur Lopes, who also saw to it that the original practice of lumping in-laws together till a "family" might cover, and did in one instance cover, 13 people still at a maximum of $130 per family, was discontinued. Those of course who lived in centres had rent, light and water free. But in any case the maximum that a family of 5 or over earlier, 6 or over later, could receive was $130 or $150. Artur also introduced the scheme by which some members of the family could draw subsidy and others rations which were valued at $31.50 per head. A family of six would frequently therefore draw subsidy for two, amounting to $60 and rations for four amounting in value to $126 or a total of $186. In addition of course those in the centres were aided by the free rent, light and water which could hardly be reckoned at less per month per head than $15. The family of 6 was therefore getting, at best $276 in cash or benefits, a total of $46 or about £3 per head on which to live. Those who for one reason or another could not live in centres or on rations, and it can well be imagined that these were hardly suitable for the delicate digestion, had £2 a month for all expenses though they were entitled to buy certain goods at Government prices, thus slightly alleviating their situation; but imagine the case of one elderly lady whose husband had spent, in the service of the Portuguese Government, some thousands of dollars on entertainment of official guests: she was now obliged to live on £2 per month, though she could not stomach the rations and at her age and seniority needed more privacy than a centre could afford. I can only believe that she must have been assisted by charitable friends; I was unable to assist officially as she was a Portuguese citizen without any claim whatever on British support. Looked at in any light one shilling and three pence a day is not a lot to live on.

At least I felt that British Subjects and those who had served the British Government in Hongkong at a moment of peril or for many years should receive better fare; and so my own relief scheme was born, though one or two persons were already in receipt of a little help. It may well be asked how, in our isolated position, I was able to finance such relief. To start with it was not easy and indeed I had, in these early days to borrow money from a friendly compradore[6] Mr. Y.C. Liang of Wong Tai Co. who lent me some thousands of *patacas* (Macao currency, in peace-time at par with the

Hongkong dollar) to be repaid, without interest, "when we had won the war".[7] Later the Foreign Office arranged telegraphic transfers via H.M. Embassy Lisbon and I can say at once that from then on every request of mine for funds was met by the Foreign Office with a promptitude, if other departments did not intervene, which would shock those members of the public who think the Foreign Office inefficient or slow. I will mention one specific example; one year I asked on about the 26th August for an increase of $200,000 per month; on about the 4th of September in came not only the increased amount but a lump sum in retrospective payment; and my telegram had to go Macao-Lisbon, Lisbon-London, request considered, approval given and remittance made London-Lisbon, Lisbon-Macao, a more than commercial speed for what is sometimes considered a sleepy department. Time lags there were sometimes, and serious they were to be, but when you are dealing with a Bank, which has been known to take 30 days over a telegraphic transfer much can be expected in the way of delay.

However funds did start coming in and with a nationality check, coupled with investigations into an individual's war or government service we were beginning to discover who was entitled to British support, as well as Portuguese, and who was not. Many were pained to come up against the principle of dual nationality by which those possessing two nationalities, one British, are not entitled to the assistance of H.M. Diplomatic and Consular Officers in the country of their second nationality. This caught out a number of gentlemen who, realising the comparative unpopularity of British passports in Japanese occupied territory since 1937, had taken the trouble to provide themselves also with Portuguese papers. They never quite understood my argument that as with British Nationality, the rights of the citizen or subject involved also certain duties and possibly penalties; they wanted the best and none of the worst of both nationalities. In this, as in all cases of regulations, some innocents suffered with the guilty; some had been registered as infants with the Portuguese Consulate in Hongkong and had never divested themselves of the nationality thus acquired, even if they knew they had unconsciously acquired it. It is a general reflection that the majority of people make little or no attempt, even where there is a possible doubt, to make sure that their national status is unquestionable: such an important point is only too often overlooked.

The arrival of money did not mean that my problems were simplified; distribution is never much easier than production. When Swemmelaar took over, as I have mentioned, I gave him fourteen points all of which were to be taken into consideration when estimating relief for a person or family.

Many of the points were imponderables but they had to act as a rough guide in discriminating between one type, not class, of refugee and another. I cannot frankly remember them all at this time but here are some of them:

(a) behaviour in Hongkong; by this we meant an appreciation of a person's pre-war manner of conducting his or her affairs; for instance if it was known that most of the earnings of a family had gone on the mother's back there was plainly no point in giving that family more than was necessary for actual food and clothes maintained at a respectability but not a finery level.

(b) behaviour in Macao; this of course was easier to check and covered such matters as gambling, a tendency to big dinners on subsidy day before paying the rent and so on.

(c) previous standard of living; that this should be considered at all may come as a shock to some and certainly there were complaints in Macao. But there was a sound and solid reason for such consideration namely that, for instance, an elderly lady who had always had the best would cost us more in hospitals and medicines if she did not have some of the comforts she had been accustomed to than if she had them.

(d) other means available; the main source of other income for a refugee was a remittance from his employers and I may say here that the majority of British firms did as well as they could for their employees who were at this period far from revenue-producing. In addition many firms were not themselves making money and some had the greater part of their assets frozen. Other sources of relief, if not income, were, for instance, the presence of better-off relatives in Macao though, as I have said, this was not always a factor of major assistance. With the non-Chinese such sources of extra income were fairly easy to trace but with the Chinese they were almost impossible.

(e) date of arrival; this again seems a queer thing to take into consideration but there was a good reason for doing so, namely that many remained in Hongkong, making a good or at least a fair living under Japanese occupation for quite a time, and only came over when persuaded to do so by the collapse of their business, the increasing unpleasantness of the Japanese or Allied bombing of Hongkong. On the other hand many, in the early months, abandoned all that they had and came to Macao some at least with the intention of volunteering for further service. The latter plainly deserved more sympathy. My graphs of refugees coming under my care showed, incidentally, a marked increase after each Allied bombing of Hongkong.

(f) service during the war in Hongkong; I am not going to say that the majority had not done what they could in the defence of the Colony; but there were, none the less, those who could have been in the Volunteers and had preferred a billet with Food Control. This was always a difficult point to adjudge.

(g) in the case of Government servants both length of service and importance of service had to be considered; a man for instance who had been called in during the war period, from 1939 on for an important executive post in the metals control had to be assessed against a man who had been a Treasury clerk for twenty years.

h) the question of dependency was also difficult; someone would take under his wing a nephew and niece whose parents had remained in Hongkong; in Macao the two might be regarded as dependent on the uncle; but the parents might be making money in Hongkong though refusing to remit or unable to remit.

(i) capacity to earn; I was anxious whenever possible to get my refugees to work for themselves but there was virtually nothing for them to do; it can well be imagined for instance that import and export business was far from flourishing. With this policy in mind we took off any refugee's subsidy half the amount, and not the whole of the amount he managed to earn. On the other hand we passed as tax-free any amount he was earning in the service of his fellow-refugees; this again was necessarily only a rough and ready guide; that is to say that where a refugee earned sufficient to maintain himself reasonably well he got no subsidy.

(j) capacity to repay; on the 15th January 1942 I had posted a notice to the effect that all sums received from my office were in the nature of loans from H.M. Government and repayment could be claimed; but it was clear that a Public Works Dept. junior employee with ten children and a normally ridiculously low salary would be unable to repay as much as a doctor with a practice he would be able to resume when Hongkong again became ours. We could therefore lend the former less than the latter though in such a case, if the doctor were a bachelor, he would get less than the government employee.[8]

The mechanics of granting relief were of course at first somewhat haphazard, inevitably when we knew neither how much money nor how many people we would have to handle. Bit by bit however the matter became systematized and then it ran roughly like this.

A refugee on arrival would apply for relief giving the particulars of his family, personal particulars, and a brief life-history, including, which was a key point, his history during the hostilities in the Colony and thereafter. This statement in application for relief had to be countersigned by two people known to us who could be presumed to know the facts. This countersignature followed a statement that the guarantors realised that they were liable to prosecution if any of the statements were found to be untrue. One group fooled us completely. They organized a scheme by which any of their crowd was met, on arrival in Macao, by an agent who provided wife and a few children with whom the applicant could be photographed. He would thus draw subsidy for three or four or more and after presumably sharing the spoils with his "wife and family" would live very well. And incidentally quite a number of coolie women thus received hospital confinement at my expense. This racket was finally broken by the initiative of some of my staff who, with the knowledge and consent of the Portuguese Police raided, late at night, the area where most of this group lived. I wish I could have gone on this raid myself. By the time it was well under way there were frantic husbands saying their wives were staying out for the night, that the six children had gone to the cinema, others careering the streets to locate, or even identify their "wives" or to warn their friends and so on. In the end we had signed confessions of fraud from ninety per cent of the group. I wish I could finish this little incident with a spectacle of dishonesty meeting its just reward. Alas, with the signed confessions in their hands the Hongkong authorities saw fit to re-employ all these men. It is not for me to question their judgment but I feel that men who could organize such a fraud are not necessarily the best policemen.

To return to the application; with this in hand the applicant would probably see Wilfred who would question him adroitly to see how far he had strayed from the strict truth. One gentleman, for instance, who claimed an income of £100 a month as an exporter and importer turned out to be a shop assistant at more like £5 a month. He probably broke down when told that plainly he could not yet have exhausted his savings in Hongkong and could live on those for a while. Wilfred would put his recommendation on the case history and pass it to "Swemm" who would O.K. it or discuss it further with Wilfred or with me. We attempted to obtain uniformity in the end by having a scale which would theoretically cover most of the physical points I mentioned earlier in this chapter. The four of us, Arculli being the fourth, will remember the afternoons we spent going over every case and readjusting it to the new scale. We will also remember the number of exceptions that had to be made. The task may be gauged when I say that by the end of the war we had 4,118 cases (families) on our books.

Once the application was approved the recipient was given an identity card with the date marked on which he would receive his relief and a medical identity card which had space for the doctors to mention any visit he made to our Clinic, the diagnosis and so on. All he had to do then was to come on his due date and receive his money or what was left of it. This may seem an odd remark but deductions were enforced in certain circumstances. We found, for instance, that many refugees were getting dental and optical treatment which they would probably never have afforded for themselves. The usual ad hoc methods had to be adopted and we found that refugees could let their teeth go on without treatment for quite a while if ten per cent of the bill were deducted from their subsidy for the next ten months. Similarly in certain circumstances clothing allowances were granted and deducted at ten per cent per month; "robberies" of clothes became far less frequent when this regulation was brought in.

For the refugees the story finished there except that, not unnaturally, many would write in or call to ask for extra relief. Most of these cases were genuine and we did what we could to meet them; but it was always hard to convince a refugee that we couldn't dig money out of the garden and many did not realise the difficulties we were facing except when owing to late arrival of a remittance we were unable to give more than half-subsidy in a month. Another reason for such a cut might well be a sudden influx of refugees since I could plainly not estimate and ask the Foreign Office for funds which might be needed but might not. It is true that the £1,700,000 remitted to us during the war was a drop in the bucket of our overseas expenditure but it was a drop and one had to avoid adding another drop to it. We therefore ran constantly on a very narrow margin.

Other considerations were religious festivals; the Mohammedans had to have money in their pockets for the end of Ramadan and the Christians for Christmas; this involved payment of large sums in relief in advance and sometimes embarrassed us. The mechanics of payment gradually evolved through the initiative of my accountancy staff until each refugee's pay packet was made up the night before, work which involved long hours for the staff. However this meant that the refugees receiving subsidy could be very rapidly dealt with and if my memory serves me we got the timing down to 70 payments an hour. We did not go in for duplicates because of speed and because of paper shortages but on one sheet any refugee had his total receipts and details of any refunds he had made so that when the relief scheme finished it took us not too long to present the bills.

Other behind the scenes mechanics included the counting of the money; the bank would receive from the gambling houses bundles of notes purporting to be, say a hundred dollars. These bundles would be passed to us without having been checked by the bank, which when I drew a cheque for $10,000 would presumably have in its books "Received from gambling house $10,000" and "Paid to Consulate $10,000" and this should of course have balanced the books. At least 50 per cent of the payments to us were inaccurate apart from containing false or even half notes. I would then write a note to the Bank to say I had received 100 dollars less or more than the 10,000; they would pay out or receive the difference and I have always wondered where this went in the Bank's books. On one occasion the Bank paid me 15,000 on a 10,000 cheque; the guard collecting the money realised when he was half-way to my office that he had been overpaid and took the balance back. Frenchy was too honest! My money counters had a laborious job counting masses of small change to find out the differences, which were always honoured on both sides, and $10,000 in 50 cent notes, as once happened, take a lot of counting.

While on the subject of money it might be as well to delve shortly into the exchange problem. We had several currencies running, if not all officially, in Macao. There was the *pataca*, the official medium, at par with the Hongkong dollar at about 15 to the £ sterling (before January 1942 there were more Hongkong notes in circulation in Macao than *pataca* notes); there was the Hongkong dollar, the Chinese National dollar, and the military *yen*, this last printed by the Japanese army without even serial numbers.[9] The *pataca* remained steady, partly at least because new printing was backed by sterling in the form of my remittances. The other currencies varied almost hour by hour, and widely; to complicate this, one $100 Hongkong note might be worth one day $110 and another day $60 in Hongkong notes of smaller denominations. At one moment the $10 Hongkong note was only worth about $2.40 and after the war was redeemed, to me incomprehensibly, at par. Some people made a very, very profitable speculation in Hongkong notes! They cannot have been as confused as I was over exchange possibilities.

To end the behind the scenes working of relief let us have some straight statistics.

We handled 25,000,000 dollars (Hongkong). We were out 3 cents on our accounts and Jerry was broken-hearted. Our administration costs including all non-refugee expenditure but including intelligence, salaries, rents, telegrams, stationery and so on were $330,000, less than 2 per cent. There were 4,118 cases and 33,000 papers concerning them apart from census forms, registrations, medical cards and so on. In one typical month taken at random Wilfred saw 560 people apart from those seen by Swemm or myself. Daily there were 70–100 callers for payment. Inter-office memoranda on relief, not included in the above figures, which crossed my desk in a month amounted to 170 apart from those sent to me, minuted and sent back. This is all exclusive of consular work and such things as clinic and school papers. And the administrative staff could be counted as fifteen. Call us lazy who dares!

Chapter VII

Medical

The Clinic had a hard career. It moved so many times that I was never quite sure till the end where it was. And it started, like everything else, almost by chance.

It was obvious from the beginning that the Government medical service could not possibly cope with the problem with the best will in the world. It must be remembered that there were not many doctors and these were only part time Government officials; when they were not on duty they had to earn their livings by private practice and one period or the other would have been swamped by the refugee clientele who had not normal health on the whole. The Governor therefore consented to the import of medical practitioners from Hongkong and permitted them private practice feeling that the refugee practice alone could not support them. This procedure was not strictly legal as not one of them had taken the tropical medicine course demanded by the Portuguese laws for doctors wishing to practise in the colonies; the wife of the Director of Medicine for instance, though herself a doctor, was not permitted for a long time to put up her plate in Macao. The Governor was, no doubt, not acting strictly according to instructions but no one could in the circumstances, when medical aid had to be found somewhere.

To start with Dr. Ozorio came over to be followed by Gosano, Ribeiro, Guterres, Barnes and much later Ho Asgoe.[1] They were given a small salary by the C.E.R. and permit to practise privately to supplement their income. The first office was tiny with just two of them hiring their own staff and having crowded hours during which they saw the C.E.R. patients. It is important to note that they were, at this stage, only concerned with C.E.R. patients who numbered some 2,000. They had, in fact, time to make extra income outside their official work, and the arrangement went along fairly smoothly except for their difficulty in getting from the Government services the medicines which they felt they needed for their charges; I had evidence of this when a resident of Macao was given a similar atropin prescription to that given to a refugee; the resident was told to wait while the refugee was told there were no stocks; the resident's prescription was then filled; my informant by the way was the resident and not the refugee. I am of the opinion that a lot of this sort of thing went on and I am supported by Swemm who, before joining my staff, was trying to sell patent medicines in Macao. He saw, with his own eyes, large stocks of medicines for which a prescription would meet with a bald *esgotado* or "Run out". Very many drugs were in terrifyingly short supply particularly anti-epidemic vaccines and inoculations. (I am sure by the way to make many mistakes in medical phraseology; I was only Dr. Reeves *humoris causa*.) What would have happened if a real cholera epidemic had broken out I hesitate to think; in those crowded streets half the population would have been swept away. It was owing to the vigilance of the Macao Medical authorities that this did not happen and they deserve great credit for this fact. We did our little bit about epidemics by insisting on regular inoculation of the refugees; no compulsion was used but a refugee could not get his subsidy until he produced his immunization certificate; this worked well. I am sure that the Governor, a devout Catholic, felt that much was done by Our Lady of Fatima under whose protection the city was put in a moving ceremony;[2] who is to say that he was not right? No one, for instance, who has been to Lourdes can deny that miracles occur whatever the agency. We had a little cholera; what city in China does not but it never spread. Its presence however made me issue one of my most unpopular edicts, no swimming in the Exterior Port;[3] but the drains from the cholera wards emptied into the port and I could take no risks.

Gradually the refugee medical picture changed as non-C.E.R. refugees began to be the more numerous. This necessitated a gradual re-orientation of the organization; what had been the Clinic of two or three doctors now became the Consulate Clinic and the doctors who had been receiving a set fee from us for each non-C.E.R. patient agreed to accept a salary which, though large by Portuguese standards, was less than that they were earning by the individual fee method and far less than we would have had to pay if we had had to give individual fees to the Portuguese doctors. The amount of payment they received did not further endear them to the Portuguese Government doctors and it is regrettable to have to state that there was considerable friction between certain of the local doctors and mine; I do not say that the fault was entirely with one or the other. Attempts to get a real working agreement failed, one bone of contention being attendance by my doctors on their patients after being put into the Government hospitals. We came to lean, for non-C.E.R. hospitalization, more and more on the Kiang-Wo Chinese hospital.[4] It is symptomatic of the situation that when certain Chinese offered an operating theatre to the Kiang-Wo permission was refused because Chinese doctors, fully qualified, were to operate. It is not unreasonable to suppose that had this come about many rich Chinese would have been operated on in the Kiang-Wo and not by the Portuguese surgeons. My doctors were never permitted to operate nor even to attend operations, except in the Kiang-Wo, though they were anxious to do so. The most serious operation done in my clinic was therefore pneumo-thorax (collapsing of the lung) an apparently fearsome but actually not dangerous performance.

The Clinic was really born near the San Rafael hospital,[5] then moved to a building near the hockey ground, coming to a final home on the Praia Grande at the Eastern end where it remained until it was demobilized. In all its premises its equipment was primitive. Up-to-date sterilizers and so on were unknown to us; water boiled on a charcoal native stove had to do instead. This had its advantages as I always demanded a cup of tea when I arrived at the Clinic, as I usually demanded a glass of water at the Relief office. Nor were there proper examination beds and so on; native couches had to do duty instead. Neither my doctors nor the nurses were daunted by this sort of thing. How well they succeeded was proved by the fact that the refugee death rate was less than that of London before the war and it must be remembered that the refugees neither arrived in a good condition nor had much opportunity of improving it. The magnitude of the task faced by the doctors is shown by these figures: in 1945 the average monthly number of Clinic consultations was 2,241 and cases treated including these consultations amounted to 5,527 per month. It can be seen that my doctors had no time for private practice and therefore had to be put on an adequate salary.

The supply of medicines was also a problem divided into two parts, prescriptions and stock. The matter of prescriptions was a permanent problem and wherever we bought them we were bound to be accused of favouritism. When the contract became a big one and the sums involved similarly large we had our doctors write out a number of more or less routine prescriptions and we asked some of the chemists to tender; we naturally accepted the tender which came out on average about 25 per cent less than the others. We still had complaints of course and some were at least partially justified but we always had satisfaction from Mr. Nolasco's pharmacy[6] which served us to the end. Of course Mr. Nolasco made money, why not, but he gave us better service at a lower price than was offered by the other chemists; that was the yardstick. May I say too that his prices and quality were checked, the latter by the Government analyst; he knew this and welcomed it. Cod-liver-oil was one of the big problems, necessary as it was in particular for the "borderline T.B." cases. There was frankly a constant divergence of opinion between the doctors on the one side and Swemm and me on the other about this. The doctors, rightly, thought predominantly of their patients, Swemm and I of our costs. Frequent memos went to the doctors begging them to use plain cod-liver oil rather than expensive proprietary brands of halibut oil and so on. At one time we even toyed with the idea of establishing our own shark-liver oil refinery but we could not reach a satisfactory financial agreement with the promoters and the idea fell through; but this detail shows what avenues we were obliged to explore.

Stock medicines were of course all those which we purchased and kept for issue ourselves without the intermediary of a pharmacy. It was incidentally noticeable that the Government pharmacy was usually *esgotado* of any medicine we were known to have but as a measure of humanity we gave to Portuguese, with the approval of the Foreign Office, who should have been served by their official pharmacy, exactly as we gave to British Subjects. At times in point of fact we probably had a larger store of drugs than the Government itself. The price became more astronomical as Hongkong and Canton stocks became exhausted and we had to buy from smugglers; at one moment we were paying about 12/6 for one sulfathiazol tablet and using not a few.[7] These large and very valuable stocks were looked after and carefully checked by the Clinic Administration staff and I can say at once that I was lucky to have at the head of this branch two men of outstanding probity, Johnny Gonsalves and Freddie Britto, both of whom guarded these stocks not with their lives but with such concentration of effort that the former, to my intense regret, developed a nervous breakdown. I cannot say that we never lost a pill or an injection; but I can say that the amount broken or mislaid was infinitesimal. Patients signed on for the medicine they received from stock and a careful stock book was maintained. I was pained that we had taken so much trouble when I later realized the extravagance, in this regard, of the forces.

The issue of these stocks was always a bit of a bone of contention, as I have hinted before, between the doctors and ourselves of the administration side; I would write minutes and memoranda begging the doctors to substitute prescriptions wherever possible for expensive and rare proprietary medicine; the doctors would say, no doubt with justice, that only the proprietary medicine would do the job in certain cases. The important thing was that refugee health was never as low as it could have been expected to be in the difficult circumstances.

We had to experiment of course, by which I do not mean that the refugees were guinea pigs, but that when we were desperate we had to try anything which we knew could do no harm while it might do good. For instance at the beginning we were bothered by contagious skin diseases among the refugees in the crowded centres where, I repeat, the opportunity for washing clothes in really hot water simply did not exist; all sorts of salves and ointments failed to cope but someone had a bright idea and injections of carrotin [carotene], concentrated Vitamin A, were tried and worked to the extent that we never had a serious recurrence of this trouble, luckily, for our stocks of Vitamin A were never too high. I can never remember whether sulfa guanadin (even if I have spelt it right) is the cure for amoebic or for bacillary dysentery; but I do know that towards the end of the War we were using it for both with quite remarkable results. I would have liked my doctors to have written full reports on the various purely medical aspects of the refugee problem but they will be the first to acknowledge that they disliked writing quite intensely; written answers to memoranda, even, were difficult to get and depended largely on whose turn it was to do the writing for the month. This refusal to write has, I feel, done my doctors a bad turn; a considered report from them on the medical aspects of refugee care in peculiar circumstances might well have earned them considerable favourable notice in the circles of their own profession.

Disease incidence was interesting to watch and my graphs, now I suppose never to be finished, kept a careful eye on this aspect. One could expect T.B. and near T.B. to increase in winter and gastric troubles to increase in summer when the children particularly would not be fussy about the origin of the drinking water but the item I kept the closest eye on was avitaminosis as I felt that was almost a personal reflection on me as relief administrator. I am glad to say we had very few cases and they were nearly all recent arrivals from Hongkong, or people who would spend their subsidy on a few tasty and hearty meals at the beginning of their "subsidy month" and half starve themselves for the remainder. In any case our record in this regard was not one to be ashamed of particularly when I realize, as I do now, that comparatively well-off people can suffer from avitaminosis in a country well off for food by buying the wrong foods and relying more on taste than on nutritive value. In some cases, however, avitaminosis had to be fought with diet allowances and this is where the Medical Board came in.

This was really instituted to curb the incurable kind-heartedness of the doctors in the matter of diet allowances, special medicines, cod-liver oil and so on; like anybody else they found it very difficult to say no to a

Medical

refugee that they thought deserved sympathy. Medical and diet allowances got out of hand and the medical board, the doctors and Swemm, came into being to review and check the findings of one of the doctors, of any one of them. Their meetings were not, shall I say, grossly hard work and in fact the members got a good deal of fun out of some of the more confirmed beggars, who might easily have been suspected of making themselves up, if greasepaint had been available, to look as haggard as possible. Loud and persistent coughs shook the building, coughs which disappeared in the centres where they would have roused the fury of the other inhabitants; people would totter in who, in the excitement of a baseball game, had been positively dancing in the bleachers in the afternoon; old ladies whose constant flow of conversation drove everybody mad would complain of shortness of breath and so on. Our medical allowance bill went down very rapidly; besides refugees knew which doctor was likely to be the most kind-hearted and would flood him with work; in the end we were obliged to limit the patient's freedom of choice as regards doctors and assign him to the doctor who had the least work; this was unpopular but necessary.

Each refugee had, as I have said, his medical identity card; I should add that some refugees who received no money from us were granted medical aid only. Armed with this the refugee would go to the Clinic where he would wait his turn in the waiting room; we had two types of trouble over this, patients getting to the doctor ahead of turn and overcrowding. The first was difficult to check in that the doctor concerned might have given an appointment and also in that the receptionist had to make a snap judgment as to whether a patient really looked too ill to wait long before seeing a doctor; there may have been abuses but I do not think there were many; it must be remembered that my staff were refugees and that the community was restricted so that things could have been made very unpleasant for any who abused his authority; they could have been made very unpleasant even for me and I had a distinctly privileged position. The other aspect was, as I say, overcrowding. Many of the refugees seemed to regard the Clinic as a sort of Club and it was rather a matter of one member of a family being ill and the others going with him to see if they couldn't get some medicine too. This state of affairs was periodically, not very effectively, corrected by slapping on a purely nominal consultation fee of 20 or 50 cents which also helped, of course, towards the expenses of the Clinic. Similarly much against the doctors' will I sometimes imposed a house visit fee to discourage not so ill patients from calling doctors at all hours of the night for an attack of, as the doctors would have put it, rhinitis, the common cold. Incidentally transport for the doctors was never easy as bicycles supplied by the C.E.R. collapsed or were withdrawn; however rickshaws provided the lack; later on I was to see one or two of them travelling around on the carriers of bicycles in Hongkong, pedalled by energetic but dangerous coolies who hired themselves out this way owing to the shortage of rickshaws.

The Medical Board was also the scene of Homeric struggles on economy of medicine and so on and in point of fact on any point where the layman, Swemm or myself or both, and the doctors disagreed; we would all speak firmly, emphatically and at times acrimoniously but these very frank exchanges of views cleared the air and really made us all feel a lot better. I hope I have not given the impression that we were constantly quarrelling; nothing really could be further from the case; I merely defy a layman or body of laymen to run a Clinic without occasional disagreement with the medical staff; on the whole we got on very well together and I, at least enjoyed every moment of the experience.

The dental problem was always difficult; there were practitioners in Macao some good, some not so good, amongst the latter to be included the gentleman who was using lead fillings in teeth. And most were expensive and their tariffs difficult to control; the medical board and the ten per cent charge reduced dentistry bills considerably but they were always high. We finally found a woman dentist who really did very reasonable work and our patients were sent to her because her prices were as reasonable as her work; but I think I should emphasize that any refugee was entitled to go to any doctor, surgeon, pharmacy, dentist or oculist he liked except that if he went outside those included in our scheme he would have to pay for it himself.

On the optician/oculist side we were luckier in finding Dr. P.K. Lam who deserved well of the community; much of his profits went to the free treatment of coolies, fisherfolk and all sorts who needed his attention but who could not pay, and for them as for the refugees he did nobly as he did for the richest in Macao. Our relations with him were always good and we were thankful to have him around.

I cannot close such a chapter without mentioning the nurses and the rest of the administrative staff. Both worked selflessly and magnificently in circumstances of discomfort and difficulty. In saying this I know that I shall have full agreement from the doctors, one point on which I fear absolutely no opposition. I should also mention with the very deepest appreciation the way they all looked after me; they kept me going whether I was well or not and I was far from an ideal patient. They suffered much from my impatience and poured gallons of glucose and vitamins into my veins so that I couldn't feel it. I have a strong feeling that I would by now be something of a tired wreck if it had not been for their devoted care.

Thanks for everything!

Chapter VIII

Other Countries' Interests

The biggest individual group of nationals was, not unnaturally, the American, apart from the British; the majority were from the Philippines or from Hawaii though there were a few continental Americans divided between the religious denominations of missionaries and Pan-American employees of whom there were only two. The leading missionary was a Mr. Davies and there were also Miss Lowry and Miss Bond amongst those we knew best; for a while also there were a group of American Roman Catholic priests under the leadership of Bishop Paschang but they soon left us for the wider pastures of Free China.[1] Davies naturally took the lead and we started telegraphing the State Department for assistance for the American citizens stranded in Macao. I think I am right in saying that we started on about the 16th January 1942 and went on till October without a reply when some genius suggested we should mention that the daughter of Vice President Osmena of the Philippines was in dire straits;[2] coincidence or not this worked and we got US$5,000 from the American Red Cross. This helped but it was far from enough as were all the sums we received from America. In the end, in fact, the American Government owed us 800,000 Hongkong dollars, about £50,000. Perhaps this was used as reverse lend-lease.

Davies finally left, of which more in another chapter, and took with him a number of Philippine seamen. These had been the subject of considerable telegraphic correspondence with Chungking who were urging us to send these men through. Our end of the exchange of telegrams finished when we sent a wire which referred to those sent by Chungking and added crisply "Using what for money query". A certain comedy level invested much of my correspondence with the State Department who once asked me how many Americans desired repatriation. I was obliged to reply, as I have mentioned in an earlier chapter, that one was under detention at my request. I similarly had some difficulty over a beautiful form called 430 which was headed something like this "Affidavit in support of application for pre-investigation of national status". I felt that this was hardly a real proof of nationality being merely an affidavit by a Chinese that he was born in the United States. However I was told to accept this for purposes of relief; I kicked when people started coming in who had not been back to the States for twenty or thirty years (one had left in 1895) and obviously had no real intention of maintaining their American affiliations. So I wired the State Department and suggested, mark you, suggested, that a time limit be set to the validity of these documents. The reply was that no one knew where I had got the idea that there was a limit to the validity of these documents. I gave up and merely did my best to check the photograph and identity of what had been a ten-year-old when he left America with the strapping fifty-year-old now applying for a hand-out of American dollars. There was really very little we could do about it except to get guarantors but I have already pointed out that, as regards the British side of relief at least, guarantors were not always reliable. The Americans also wanted everything in quadruplicate and this strained our paper resources to the utmost. We dutifully complied and I can only hope that the mountains of forms have been found useful.

Davies had organized an unofficial committee to gather information and dispense relief but after his departure and when I was put in charge officially of American Interests I felt that a democratic experiment would be in order and in the spirit of the times. I accordingly called a meeting for the election of a committee and held a secret ballot. When the results came to be counted it was only too clear that some of my constituents had learnt some of the less pleasant aspects of lobbying and had learnt also the universal pre-election promise fever habit. After some three or four months I had to get rid of some of the Committee, as elected and put in instead members of my own staff. Nathan Young, Pablino Cespedes, Manalac and Warren Wong remained of those elected and invaluable they proved to be to the end, except for the last who went into Free China with the paper parcel which concealed an enormous revolver; I have every reason to know he needed one and not because of American relief problems either.

The American relief roll finally reached 940 but it would have gone much higher if we had not made it clear that those who crossed the border into Japanese occupied territory for their own purposes were to be struck off the roll. The problem of trading with the enemy was different in the case of the Americans from that presented by the British refugees; it must be remembered that most of the American Chinese were residents of territory which had been occupied by the Japanese since 1938 and that they had therefore had far more opportunity to escape the clutches of the hated invader than those who were caught in Hongkong in 1941 and who thereafter had their comings and goings controlled.

One American Chinese deserves a special line or two; he was serving in an American gunboat in Manila when that city was invested; he served in Corregidor until the gallant island fell, and then escaped. He worked his way to Hongkong in a Japanese ship and thence came by junk to Macao where he reported for duty. I hope his loyalty has met with reward.

In general the American system of relief applications and so on was the same as ours and worked about the same way except that the numbers were so much smaller. The only difficulty was the matter of funds; the Foreign Office on one occasion when the American debt had grown large told me not to go on using British money for American support but I am afraid I replied that I could not let these people starve and went on using British money though on a greatly reduced scale. In fact I contracted with an eating-house to supply so many meals daily and gave out no money. This was far from satisfactory as it left the way open to abuses on the part of the restaurant but it was really all I could do.

The Philippine boys, most of whom were dance band players, had in general a source of income playing in bands at the Central, the Grand and the Riviera.[3] But they will be the last to deny that money with most of them was easy come, easy go and that even those drawing salaries were never far from the rocks with a heavy onshore wind blowing. One of this community on being discharged from hospital said he could not get out of bed because he had no clothes; I gently suggested he could use those with which he had entered the hospital; he countered with a knock-out blow to the effect that he had had these taken away and pawned to gamble on a number in which he had faith; clothing allowance and ten per cent per month refund.

There was also a fuss about the appointment of an American doctor, a Philippine. This gave rise to such current and counter-current of internal politics that frankly I would prefer not to embark on the details. It was a distasteful affair.

On the whole however we saw pretty well eye-to-eye and had no serious differences, and none which did not arise from fundamentally differing points of view, both sides having their good and their bad ideas, but we reached a compromise and it worked more than adequately. What more can one ask? The badge given me by the American relief committee is displayed in my present office and it would not be if my memories of American relief were in any way unpleasant.

American commercial interests were centred in the one institution, the Pan American Airways property consisting of a wireless station, a passenger station and a motorboat. The wireless station was sealed and guarded by the Portuguese authorities and I had nothing to do with it. The passenger station was on the Exterior Port and I put my own guard in it as there was valuable equipment there; we also used it as a place to go to get some breeze in the evenings and very pleasant that was, except that the breeze was sometimes laden with the odours from the sampans which were hauled ashore nearby, and you must remember that a family of six or seven may live in one twenty-foot sampan as well as the owner's hens and so on. The building was somewhat damaged in an American air raid on Macao but that is another story. The motorboat really only reappeared once more in the history when I got weird orders that she was to be stolen and conveyed to Free China but I was not to appear in the matter; since she was by then ashore in a cradle in the Portuguese Naval Yard[4] without an engine the orders were marked N.F.A. for "no further action" and could have been marked W.P.B. for "waste paper basket" except that my files had to remain complete.

From the point of view of value on the spot the Dutch had a far greater property in Macao than the Americans; this included dredgers, hoppers, lighters, railway track and engines and all the material which is put into the field when the Netherlands Harbour Works take on a big job.[5] The value of the stuff ran into millions of dollars and was a distinct worry for Mr. van Woerkom the manager, Mr. Nolasco as Dutch Consul, and myself. One of the dredgers was sold to the Japanese under pressure; I would not like to go into the rights and wrongs of this as I was never in possession of all the facts.[6] What is clear in my mind is that Nolasco had no codes so that his telegrams were forwarded by me; to code a name like Vanlidtergeude, as I have mentioned, was a headache, and with the complexity of affairs we could never just telegraph "Following for V". Woerkom and I discussed the vessels and their safety; we were, after all, to have a beautiful example of a cutting-out expedition later. The result of our deliberations was that all the remaining Dutch floating equipment was brought to the inner end of an open dock in the Firecracker Factory area (52 on the [original] map);[7] how it happened I would not of course know but an hour or two later one of the biggest lighters sank at her moorings at the outer end of the dock, by sheer coincidence right across the channel. She would have needed twenty-four hours of pumping to lift and Admiral (*humoris causa*) Reeves went and had a glass of beer with Van Tromp's successor in a state of considerable satisfaction. There was little we could do about the stuff on shore but it was mostly heavy and the water alongside was only shallow, as I was to discover later, so there was no really serious danger. The most serious danger to these premises probably was constituted by the very fine and fat poultry bred by the Woerkoms.

Trigger, whom I have mentioned, the Captain of the *Masbate*, was our Norwegian interest, though there was one other Norwegian, a refugee who came, I think, under the Portuguese scheme but got some remittance from Europe. And Trigger was always an interest whether anchored in the harbour entertaining lavishly, sailing under charter to the Portuguese Government with two unsuspected Japanese aboard (this was a slip of mine; I should have suspected them), lying at anchor near Green Island,[8] getting bombed by the Americans or living ashore in the Villa Lille Norge at the foot of the "Russian mountains".[9] Trigger and a dull moment were contradictory. When he first arrived he knew little English but later on his "All alone, waiting for the Japanese", though a phonetic spelling of his way of saying this defeats me, and his absolutely Norwegian form of *Ai de nie* (*Ers av nid*) were constant joys.[10] Trigger was mixed up in one of the groups of cloak and dagger boys, unless I am incredibly mistaken and if his reports were not anglicized by someone else's secretary, I should have loved to have read them. We always teased Trigger and were all fond of him. He won't mind if I continue the habits.

His ship was a Panamanian interest, one of those queerly arranged affairs with Chinese beneficiary owners, Norwegian registered owners, and Panama flag serving the China coast ports. Trigger used to refer to her as his wife but others have married plain girls. As I have said she shifted anchorage two or three times to avoid being cut out[11] by the Japanese and did avoid that fate though her Allies, as will appear later, treated her far from kindly. But she survived and was, I suppose, the only decent size Allied ship in the Far East not to fall, sooner or later, into Japanese hands. Far East, by the way means to me Singapore and eastwards and does not include India.

French interests as such there were none. But there was one French family, the Fays. Jean was Commissioner of Chinese Maritime Customs under the old organization of the Customs by which foreigners held many of the key posts, this being because a loan to the Chinese Government by various powers was guaranteed at least in part by the Customs revenue. Jean, his wife and family arrived only just before the war in the Far East broke out, to replace an American. I had no doubt of Jean's sympathies; he was definitely Free French and I had pleasure in putting that opinion in writing; I am convinced that the fact that some Customs equipment went to the Japanese was not his fault but rather that of a doubtful Chinese doctor who was convinced that he, and he alone, could arrange the peace of the world. He went so far as to ask me to get him appointed as a delegate to the peace conference but I had to tell him I was not quite that powerful. Jean always had a few friends round on Bastille Day and always gave a short speech; I am no lover of speeches but I confess that I looked forward to Jean's; he always said the right thing and said it well. Naturally the family was not happy; they had not only national but personal troubles to worry about as they had at least one son in Paris. But everything, so far as I know, worked out well in the end.[12]

There were of course citizens of quite a number of the Allied nations in the town and all came to me as I had the only Allied brass plate up; but I could do very little for them. I did prepare, and smuggle through, lists of the nationals of some thirteen Central and South American republics but nothing came of this unless some of them got remittances privately. I at one time suggested that I should be put in charge of the interests of all the Allied nations but I can quite understand that this seemed unnecessary to the authorities at home or in the capitals of these nations. The odd Swede or Dane could be assisted individually after reference to his Government and the American Republics seemed to be suspicious of their own passports; I understood later when I heard that Central Europe was a flourishing source of forged or falsely issued passports of this sort. In most cases I am sure that the appeal to me was a try-on; they were nearly all made by Chinese who had settled in Macao many years before and who had virtually forgotten the country whose nationality they now claimed.

Financially, apart from the purely British side, our biggest turnover came in the end from Chinese in the States remitting to their families in Macao. We were asked if we would take on this job and did so, refusing the offer of extra staff which was made to us by the Chinese Embassy in Washington. This was typical of the keenness of my boys; when the request came in Derek Anderson and Willie Reed[13] took the job on in spite of having full time employment already and were quite indignant at the idea of taking on extras. Handling this was far from easy; by the time the family in the States had put their relatives' names into European spelling and those and the Portuguese addresses had been telegraphed to us "Lin Luk Wan, 15 Avenida Almeida Ribeiro" would come out as "Lee Tik On, 150 Avenida Bebida Rempiro"; this would be followed by a figure showing the number of dollars deposited in the U.S. Later on they were given code letters according to the cities in which the relatives lived and a serial number so we spent hours checking over laboriously SAN 3 (for San Francisco) POR 8 (for Portland) and so on. To be quite frank if the war had gone on much longer I think we should have had to ask for extra staff as the volume of remittances increased monthly.

Tail piece. Circular to H.M. Consuls in China "His Majesty's Consuls may give advice to foreign nationals in time of need but such nationals should apply direct to their own Consular authorities for more active assistance".

Chapter IX

Morale

This is a difficult subject to tackle but obviously needs a chapter to itself since it plays such an enormous part in the well-being of refugees. It is, further, entertaining in that it covers so many facets of existence. Imagine yourself as a refugee arriving in a place that is strange to you, where you have few if any friends, where there is no real organization to look after you, where you are left largely to your own devices. Before long you will get tired of doing nothing but cooking skimpy meals, making your bed, doing a little laundry and so on and spending the rest of the time staring out of the window. If you discover a friend to play chess with, this is the beginning of the return of your morale which has been upset by whatever made you a refugee; a bridge four is a further step, a study group another and so through perhaps amateur theatricals or organizations for other people's welfare as much as for your own you get morale really going and you become a community.

When the refugees arrived they were very depressed as was only natural when many had lost members of their families, or their homes, and all had undergone the hardships of war followed by a violent uprooting and a pitchforking into conditions at which they could only guess. Morale was inevitably low and was not raised by the quality of their reception in Macao nor by the conditions in which they found they would have to live there. Mrs. Wilson's and Mrs. Fletcher's actions and the Governor's immediately felt warm humanity at least gave a spark which could catch alight; but on the other hand when some centres organized dances they were discouraged by a certain section of officialdom. However things did get going and shortly there were concerts in the centres. Easter 1942 saw one in the Sergeants' Club,[1] which was a centre excellently run by a woman, a Mrs. Xavier. I was asked and gladly went, as I always did when I could, to show that I was not merely an official but a person of some flesh and blood. This centre was mainly composed of Portuguese nationals but I regret to say that when the anthems were sung at the end of the performance they knew "God save the King" better than they did their own national hymn. To show how careful one had to be I will mention here that I requested that "God save the King" should not be sung because I was present; one never knew what the Japanese might consider to be a provocative gesture. It occurs to me only now that the prohibition of the singing of the British national anthem may have been thought by some refugees to have been an unnecessary order by the Portuguese Government; if so I am glad to put the matter right by taking the blame on my own shoulders.

Another highly successful concert was one at the Armacao. In this there took part a youngster of ten or so who had all the provocativeness of Carmen Miranda and I confess that I blushed even through my normally sanguine complexion at "I like your lips and I like your hips" directed with every possible ogling glance straight at me as guest of honour. I venture the opinion that the Governor, the day before, carried this situation off with far greater aplomb than I did. Anyhow I always enjoyed these concerts for there was an amazing amount of talent among the refugees although I suppose it is not really surprising when you consider how musical a race are the Portuguese. I frequently felt impelled to learn the guitar but laziness prevented and the knowledge that years of hard work would be needed to get me to the standard of a competent refugee twelve-year-old.

One might have expected a full orchestra to grow up but I imagine that very few of the refugees could make room for instruments in their meagre baggage allowance. Nor were plays attempted perhaps because of the sustained effort needed to put on a good show; long rehearsals would certainly have put a strain on never too high vitality, and, of course, there were no books.

This business of having no books was a serious matter both in leisure time and at the various schools. The Loyal Senate library[2] was excellent but with a very scholarly bias and permission to take books out to read had to be withdrawn after the privilege had been abused; the Macao library was small and the Macao Club library was shut and of course we could not import. I never quite fathomed how the San Luiz Gonzaga school, or my own for that matter, got the books for teaching but after all mine was not the only office or institution in Macao which scraped along on a very short shoe-string.

That, of course, was the whole problem, how to occupy leisure time; in the average centre apart from those told off for cooking fatigues and rice cleaning, in which every grain was theoretically hand-picked, most families would finish off their chores in about four hours.[3] The rest of the day was free except for mothers with large families whose housewifely work never finishes in Macao or anywhere else. So much leisure time was really a bad thing and organizations gradually grew up, sometimes based on refugee, sometimes on non-refugee initiative. One that grew up into a very sturdy child was the Bridge Club, under the aegis of Antonio Maria da Silva; it had its troubles with regard to premises and to a group that wanted to play much too high stakes but on the whole it flourished and the two or three tournaments it organized at the União Nacional were very greatly enjoyed, even by those who, like Leo d'Almada and myself, never seemed to have any card in our hands above a knave.

On the whole the click of mah-jonng tiles was louder than the flap of cards and this was annoying because this game virtually demands stakes; you can play bridge for love but hardly mah-jonng and I have never heard of mah-jonng drives or tournaments. So gambling came in again and in a form almost impossible to check since the game was played in private houses or in centres where no one would inform on the gamblers who would anyhow probably have said they were playing for matches. It is no use denying that this problem had us stumped and we could only act when we chanced to get really good evidence that stakes were high. I must emphasize that I considered a gambling game where skill counted, as far from reprehensible so long as the stakes were really low; at low stakes mah-jonng, bridge, poker or hearts could be regarded as occupational therapy; they occupied minds and kept them alive.

I have mentioned the cinemas and dance halls of Macao. I had no objection whatever to my refugees going to these places of amusement and only tried to control that they did not thus spend large sums of money. For that matter I had no objection to refugee girls acting as dance hostesses to earn extra money; I could not see that their morals were in any danger in this employment and in any case if their morals were weak there was no need to be dance hostesses to be loose in their activities; there were plenty of other chances for that sort of thing as the birth of illegitimate children showed. As a matter of fact I think the general moral standard of the refugees was very high indeed though there were bad examples; you will find them in every community of ten thousand. In any case boys will be boys and girls girls and no amount of regulations are going to stop flirting. A certain discouragement of going beyond flirting was made by refusing extra support for illegitimate children, who were, after all not British Subjects; and any new case of venereal disease had to pay for his or her medicines out of subsidy; I am aware that many such cases went to other doctors than mine but there they had to pay too so the same object was attained although of course this led to a gap in my medical statistics.

Morale depended on, amongst other things, cooking and this was far from simple in those centres that had kitchens which might have to do for two or three centres; the corollary to this was that the non-cooking centres tended to get their food cold; this could perhaps not be helped and resulted at least in a saving of fuel, payment for which had to come out of the money allowed for food. I have eaten centre meals more than a few times and the difference in tastiness between those in different centres was amazing. I must give the palm I think to the Armacao whose ingenuity in the use of the money available reached a high level. They even managed here, for large periods, to produce extra broths for the youngsters and special treats for everyone now and then. In this centre at least the day's purchases and the prices were always put on a board in the hall for all to see and any head of family had a right, and was invited to inspect the accounts whenever he wished to do so.

In all centres, as good chiefs were found for them, cleaning and cooking fatigues were taken on in turns, and anyone who refused to take his turn might get expelled from the centre or in extreme cases, from the C.E.R. altogether, a punishment of which I voiced disapproval since it left the person so punished without any means of support, if he was not entitled to any help from me, and put an extra burden on my finances if he was.

Some centres had an immediate basis for good morale in their position or the form of the building. The Bela Vista,[4] for instance, built as a hotel, fairly high above the sea over which it looked, invited cheerfulness. No. 3 Praia Grande, on the other hand, a deep building with no windows whatever at the sides and few enough at front and back, was depressing in the extreme. Chácara Leitao[5] had a beautiful position but everyone in it got malaria. It is true that whereas the Bela Vista would put on a good show of some sort for Christmas or New Year the Praia Grande centre might remain completely without decoration because nobody apparently felt like decorating. Every detail counted, visits by the Governor or Lobo, the existence of the nucleus of a harmonica band, a semi-professional humorist in the house and all sorts of other considerations including, of course, the weather. Much, very much indeed, depended on the Chief of the Centre and his assistants who had to have a blend of tact and firmness and sympathy that it is given to few men to possess. Too much liberty and the centre became a madhouse; too many restrictions and the centre became bad-tempered. Jealousies and resentments flourished, that one person got a better ration than another, that one family had larger living space than another and so on. Let us be frank about it; the Portuguese were not particularly good at pulling together; they tended to complain to their centre chiefs, to the C.E.R. or to me much more than the other communities whether they were in centres or not; in many ways they took things worse than the other communities, and the strength which comes from individualism becomes a menace when the individual has, willy-nilly, to live as one of a close knit community.

The Portuguese did less than the other groups to organize clubs or welfare outfits, or study groups; the inspiration for such things nearly always came from the outside and had to be fostered from the outside, whether that outside influence was the C.E.R., the Church, the Government or my office. They had the advantage of being centralized but this was perhaps neutralized by the disadvantage of being crowded together; their Latin blood made them sometimes the most cheerful community but sometimes the most fretful. I think they themselves will acknowledge the justice of what I say and I hope they will not take it as hardly meant; I knew their difficulties, they were members of my family and I was genuinely very fond of even the worst of them while in the main they earned my admiration and respect.

Those in the centres formed more or less homogeneous groups and were comparatively easy to deal with but the "extra-murals", those who did not live in centres, were far more difficult; they had no rallying point. On the other hand they had the advantage of a certain privacy which did keep spirits up. Being crowded does not help morale and never did.

As regards the morale of the youngsters amongst the Portuguese I must again and more fully, pay tribute to the Irish Jesuit fathers. There is a quarter in Rome called after Macao because it was a Jesuit property at the moment when the most successful Jesuit mission was in that outpost of civilization. I venture to think that no better work was done in those days than was done in 1942 and the succeeding years. I really care little for the scholastic success of the school though that was, no doubt, considerable; the important thing was the change in the attitude of the Portuguese lads when S. Luiz Gonzaga opened. A fine spirit was fostered and maintained and spread throughout the community. The fathers were always ready with help and advice and I feel sure that no one in future will ever be ashamed of having been a pupil of Macao's short-lived San Luiz Gonzaga school.[6] For the girls there was the Little Flowers of Mary. I knew little of the work of this purely refugee organization though I went to any displays or bazaars that it initiated and one felt that good work was being done.

Among the non-Portuguese refugees the children had more of the individual and compact attention of the parents to offset the advantages of being organized as a community. The Chinese largely went their own individual way and showed little community spirit. Their children were later in the day cared for by the Consulate school, the M.S. school. The letters M.S. really meant "minimum subsistence", but no one was at all ashamed of that. It grew to, as I remember, 471 pupils of all sorts of races and creeds; complete freedom of religion was the guiding principle with the proviso that any pupil could take any form of religious teaching that he liked from Confucian to Catholic. The school was extremely well run by a board, largely of my staff, and a very devoted band of teachers who produced an astounding scholastic standard. The headmasters managed their heterogeneous subordinates and pupils with great patience and skill and all who were connected with the school were tireless, including the physical training instructor; one display given by the school was described by the Governor as the best he had seen in Macao. In one test of general knowledge amongst pupils they were asked what the initials "B.C." meant. All replied unhesitatingly "British Consulate". Could one have a fairer flattery?

The Indian and Malay community, for the two merged into one while in Macao, developed a high sense of community life and even, from their meagre resources, started a welfare centre where the children of the communities, could, once or twice a week, get a scientifically arranged meal of high vitamin content. The woman who ran this, a Mrs. Perry I believe, made the most of what was available and the children benefited enormously. I must add that I had no part in this whatever. How she produced a meal which appeared to have thousands of calories and vitamin units for every cent she spent I have no idea. Unfortunately this was located in an area also occupied by Public Enemy No.1, a Chinese gangster employed by the Japanese and my security advisers would not permit me the frequent visits I would have liked to have paid there.

So much can be included under the heading of Morale that this chapter may be top-heavy. But the individual aspects would not constitute chapters on their own and so the risk must be taken. One of the main factors in morale building was of course sports, but unless the result of every game was given there would hardly be enough for a chapter of any reasonable length.

Our sports and games ranged widely; I have mentioned the Bridge Club at the sedentary end of the scale. At the very other end was miniature football which is precisely what its name implies, smaller field, smaller ball, smaller goal and smaller teams, seven a side. The game was exceedingly fast and gave real enjoyment to the spectators who were never lacking. The only disagreeable feature of the league which grew up was the organization and within the organization the refereeing. The former was always suspected and I think rightly so of putting too great a share of the gate into its pocket. In normal times this might not greatly have mattered but when the refugee teams depended on the gates for purchase of shirts and shorts and shoes it was a very serious matter indeed. The refereeing was only too often beneath contempt. I have mentioned that the Police team was always expected to win but I have never seen such completely cynical disregard for impartiality or even for the rules as the referees' methods of obtaining these results. I was on one occasion constrained to leave my seat of honour and leave before a game was ended as a mark of protest; I who will not even leave a cinema before a bad film is over in case someone's feelings are hurt, even an usher's. Another thing I disliked and against which I inveighed in leading articles was the immense amount of betting on the games. Many of the spectators were more interested in the money than in the football and I particularly consider that members of the committee of the association should not have betted; such actions could only lead to a suspicion that the refereeing was not unbiased. However on the whole the game served a good purpose, it got people into the open, it gave them something to think about and aim at and it aroused a very healthy sense of competition. On at least one occasion it gave rise to a moment of some embarrassment when a Canton Police team came down to play the Macao Police in a charity game; at the time of the kick-off no ranking Portuguese official was on the ground and it fell to me to kick-off and be introduced to the sides; I therefore found myself shaking hands with eleven members of the Japanese-employed Canton police all of whom were, at least in theory, my deadly enemies.

Hockey naturally was popular, being as it was, the game at which Macao traditionally excelled as I have said. There was some difficulty over equipment and the ground,[7] in peace time reserved for hockey alone and carefully tended, had suffered from neglect, football and softball, but we soon had games going again and at our peak had a senior league, a ladies' league and a junior league. We also had "interports", Macao versus Hongkong and the alacrity with which Macao allowed me to play for the Hongkong refugee side may have had something to do with my standard of play. These games were always hard fought and great fun with no quarter asked or given. Frederico Nolasco was one of the hardest hitters I have ever seen and it will be a long time before I forget stopping one of his shots for goal, illegally, with my ankle; I could have sworn it nearly splintered the bone. My own office team played regularly; we called ourselves the Valentes (Valiants) and the initial enabled us to wear a red white and blue V on white shirts without being accused of propaganda; that is, in fact, why we chose the name. We never won a league or an interport but we always had very very good games.

The next biggest draw was softball a version of baseball with the same rules, more or less, a smaller diamond and a larger but softer ball which is pitched underarm. Here again competition was remarkably keen and supporters young and old were ready to shout themselves hoarse rooting for their side. One particularly vociferous young man was known as Donald Duck and his first utterance was enough to tell you why. Only advanced medical science could have explained why he did not burst blood vessels in his throat. Barracking was, in the best traditions of the game, loud and continuous; my only objection to it was that it varied so little, phrases like "a slice off the old apple" and "give him a basket" recurring too frequently; I cannot help feeling that a little originality would have been more effective as well as more amusing. The girls had their own league and very good indeed they were. I seem in particular to remember one pitcher of remarkable speed and accuracy, and "Hellcats" and "Spitfires" would probably have given their brothers and cousins a good game. The barracking at a girls' game had to be heard to be believed.

For the older, but not exclusively for the older, members of the community there was bowls, lawn bowls. This was made possible by Melco Club who opened four rinks which were, during the season, continuously in use. Another good thing about this, apart from those advantages offered by every sport, was that on the green there was more mixture of the senior members of the residents and refugee communities. If, in fact, the greens had been earlier opened I feel sure that many of the misunderstandings which arose between the two groups would have been ironed out around the jack; a peaceful game bowls, and one conducive to gentleness, though I hardly showed enough of this when I opened the greens by bowling the first jack which disappeared at an alarming speed into the far ditch.[8]

Net- and basket-ball were also played but they affected the community less, being apparently on a semi-professional basis. They became particularly strong towards the end of the war and certainly did not lack spectators but I confess I took a smaller interest in these activities because they had less exclusively refugee character.

There were of course facilities, or rather courts and so on for tennis and badminton but the equipment went up so much in price that none of us could afford to play. Golf continued but, for the same reason, few could carry on; in fact the Japanese became the predominant golfing group; it was perhaps fortunate that I was far from keen on the game; I agreed with my father who used to say he would "take up golf when he was too old for croquet which was a faster game". I did however play one historic round just before the war broke out with Carlos da Silva, secretary of the Golf Section; he beat me by one hole over the eighteen and I had only played twice before at intervals of five years.

The part played by the Churches in the building of morale is a difficult one to discuss since they depend for this sort of thing far more on the men concerned than on the institution. There were of course, two sharply defined groups; nearly all the Portuguese were Catholic whereas the Protestant Church was wider in scope, the Eurasian Community being particularly strong in this regard. When I said morale depended on the "men" concerned I created a misapprehension as the affairs of the Protestant

Church were in the very capable hands of Deaconess Lee[9] a tireless and good woman. Since there was no other pastor of this community the Bishop of Hongkong called her to the interior of China and ordained her as a priest so that she could celebrate Communion.[10] This, as can be imagined, caused no little stir in orthodox Protestant circles and after the war she reverted to her rank as deaconess. She remains however the only known example of a woman having been a fully ordained priest of the Church of England, or, I believe, of any other of the more conforming religious institutions.

As regards the Catholic Church let me get the worst over quickly by saying that I do not see eye to eye with those who turn a ten-year-old girl from the Communion rails because her sleeves are not long enough in the knowledge that it is not easy for a refugee to dress herself at all and that all material is costly. And having got that off my chest I can turn quickly to Father Granelli.[11] This enormously tall Italian ex-cavalryman was the parish priest in Hongkong of many of the Portuguese who had come under my care. When he arrived in Macao he came to see me and we decided that, though technically enemies, we would forget all that and work together; he became S.O.I.C. (spiritual officer in charge) and I shall always be grateful for the help and advice he gave me. We only had one fight; he was getting ill simply because he would give away even his food so I practically ordered him to take liver injections; the first one put him on his back with a high temperature; when he recovered he came in and said he had thought he could rely on my word that we were not enemies but here I was doing my best to kill him; but the twinkle was in his eye. The matter of Granelli's giving things away was serious; when, one Christmas, public subscription bought him an overcoat we had to make him promise on his word of honour to keep it; otherwise it would have gone straight on the back of someone with a plausible story. He was magnificent all through and I am sure every Catholic refugee will join with me in thanking him for what he did for us all. It was some time before the refugees had "their own" church but in the end the church opposite the Macao Club was lent to them by a Confraternity and became the refugee church.[12]

At one moment there was trouble even over this. An article appeared in the press that the refugees had put obscene matter in one of the collecting boxes and hinting that the church might be closed to refugees. I was annoyed and asked to see the obscene matter and for proof that a refugee was responsible. The latter I did not get, the former consisted of a few pages from a geometry textbook and a highly respectable picture of a professional dancer cut from a staid Hongkong paper. I mention this merely to show how some people considered that any stick served to beat the refugees.

But the church served as a great rallying-point and I doubt if any of us will ever forget the poignant and moving experience of midnight Mass there. You must remember that Hongkong had fallen on Christmas Day 1941.

On the whole morals and morale were good. In every community of ten thousand there are likely to be good and bad and my family was no exception. We had our looser members, our prostitutes, our thieves, our scandal-mongers, our liars and so on. But through and through I would challenge any other average group to do as well in the circumstances as did my refugees. One of the proofs is that, as far as I know, less than a dozen ever were called in by the police. Another, perhaps even more striking, was my family's self-discipline vis-à-vis the Japanese. I had asked them all not to cause any incidents; and when a Japanese leans on your table in a café, grunts offensively and makes the thumbs-down gesture, it is easy to lose your temper; none of the family ever did (the Governor told me towards the end of the war that he had heard of no incident involving Japanese and refugee) and that I consider a clear sign of self-restraint; and for such restraint you must have strength of morale. I throw them this little bouquet with genuine feeling and if any of them ever read this I hope they will know that the Boss remembers them with affection and real respect, however he may here and there chide them a little.

Chapter X

Thrills, More or Less

There were times when I was, as it were, half buried; that is to say that part of my activities were underground while the rest were open for all to see. There was quite an atmosphere of espionage and counter-espionage in Macao, some of it purely comic opera and the rest in deadly earnest. This work is difficult to remember as incidents came so fast and the course of events was sometimes so rapid that a proper order is almost impossible to make sure of from memory. I will do my best but I wish I had the guidance of that grand bunch of fellows who more than helped out, they did the work and a great job they made of it. That will transpire as I try and describe what they did.

Of course the Nips were active too, incredibly active; I nearly asked them to send me copies of all the photographs they took of my house, my car, myself and probably of my laundry. I took a very dim view of their enquiries as to where I bought my food. I prefer any flavouring to that of arsenic.[1] They were at it before the war, they always are, it's in their nature somehow. They must in any case have been extremely suspicious of me as for some totally unfathomable reason the first published news of my arrival appeared in the Hongkong papers with a Moscow date-line of all things; this almost made it look as though I were in the inner councils of Russia as regards Manchuria, from which I came. Before the Japanese war started, Fukui, whom I have mentioned as being my Japanese colleague and next door to whom I had my residence, once asked me if I liked Japanese food. I said I did and he promised to ask me to dinner one night. "But", he said, "there are no geisha girls in Macao; I expect you have seen though, that very pretty

Chinese girls come to my house." He evidently thought I was watching every visitor to his house as he was undoubtedly watching every visitor to mine. To tell the truth, and to use a phrase I learnt after the Japanese surrender, "I couldn't have cared less". It was the Japanese method to gather in chaff as well as corn and hope that one good ear would be winnowed; their intelligence was good though and not to be under-rated. I am reliably informed that their maps of Hongkong were far better than ours and I well believe it. And a certain Japanese barber must have heard a lot in one of the best-liked hairdresser's in Hongkong.[2]

We on the other hand started the Japanese war as regards Macao, so far as I know, from scratch. True two apparently harmless businessmen from Hongkong who had visited Macao for varying periods had confessed to me that they were secret service agents. Of course I do not know if they put any organization in Macao on a wartime footing. Maybe they did; if so it was one thing we did not later find out, though we did find out a great deal and much was simply forced on our notice by ineptitude.

There came into the field fairly early in the party an army aid group; I am sure, particularly since meeting its chief,[3] that it did really excellent work; why I think of it first, as it was also to be my last contact with this sort of work, is because through it I had communicated to me the cypher that I was to use throughout the war, a wonderfully clever thing which you could keep in your head. Clever as it was it gave me endless anxiety; what you have in your head can be forced out of it by the delirium of torture and I was under no illusions as to the sort of treatment I could expect if the Nips laid their hands on me.[4] Good men, men of really iron nerve, had broken down under torture in Hongkong, not consciously, I am convinced, and had given away much; I knew I was just as likely or more likely to do so. I tried therefore to drive into my sub-consciousness a story about the cypher, which I hoped would form the basis of any "confession" which might be forced from me. I once was accused of that truly frightful thing, compromising the cypher; but I believe the blame was not ultimately mine and was put where it belonged.

The group had a coordinator in Macao.[5] I was not quite sure what the title implied or what the holder did, at least not until a little later when one just couldn't help noticing mysterious visits and their frequency and hush-hallo meetings. There was a good deal of false-beard complex about the group's activities in Macao; but so there was about some of my own people so I suppose this attitude is generic to the trade, or rather to its less expert operatives. Later on, as a matter of fact and common sense, a certain liaison was established against, I believe, the superior officers' wishes on both sides.[6] It was none the less obvious, or so one would have thought, that these activities should be coordinated; the duplication and triplication and quadruplicating and every other order of multiplication which ultimately made itself felt and even seen in Macao towards the end of the war was fantastic with British groups, yes, in the plural, and American groups and Chinese groups all operating in concert or opposition or on parallel lines and never quite meeting to pool their knowledge. I know of one man who went into Free China and offered his services to the Americans;[7] they accepted on the condition that he would tell nothing to the British; he wouldn't play and went to the British; they accepted on the condition that he would tell nothing to the Americans. He became a freelance but it is to be noted, savagely,[8] that he was reliable and both were willing to employ him. Never mind, he made himself generally useful in the end.

With the Chinese I was able to work in close liaison; I was unable to help it in any case as I knew they were the only people who could run a shipping line out of Macao. When one party went through under the aegis of the Chinese the then group co-operator came to me, which he shouldn't have done according to his orders, and begged to be given the credit. The Chinese and I willingly gave in to his request, without being priggish, because it was more that we were tired of this bickering, the thing was to get the job done and be damned to the credit. Anyhow Chan, of the Chinese side, and I never knew his real name till the very end, nor was it Chan, was a grand chap who if he said he would do a job did it.[9] Nor was he obvious about it; as chief of a service he was one of the most inconspicuous people in Macao. I am not forgetting his chief Portuguese aide and collaborator; I never shall; I hope they will realise that some forms of appreciation go deeper than words, written or spoken.

This matter of co-ordination in an intelligence service is quite incredibly difficult. Never having been in such a service I do not know how it is worked out but the chain system, with each agent knowing only the agents directly on each side of him in the chain, appears on the whole to be accepted; this or the cell system by which five or six agents know only their immediate chief who belongs to a cell at a higher rank. The difficulty is to decide at what level coordination should come, complete coordination with all cards on the table. Let us pose this not too hypothetical question. A who is working for Group I in Hongkong becomes aware that Mr. Loo Yuan-shia is working with the Japanese and is constantly in and out of gendarmerie headquarters, has an official pass and so on. A thinks something should be done about it and Mr. Loo disappears. Group II thus loses agent B (Mr. Loo) one of their best contacts. True enough that assassination is not the normal duty of an agent but such things have been known to happen. Even if it does not go thus far Mr. Loo may have been vigorously reporting the activities of A in the Japanese propaganda service while A was equally vigorously reporting on the activities of Mr. Loo. There is bound to be, at the least, an immense waste of effort, paper, couriers and so on as well as increased risk of discovery. At what stage in the organization should someone know that both A and B are agents? In Macao I was the arbiter for my own groups but the other groups did not know my men any more than I knew the less obtrusive of theirs. And I fell into the same old trap so far as my own people were concerned; they constantly reported on each other and my files filled up alarmingly.

Let me make the position clear however; I do not think that what I was up to could be regarded as espionage. My main objective was to collect information about individuals which might, after the war, be useful to the British authorities, particularly in Hongkong. I was neither spying on the Portuguese nor on the Japanese when I collected information on a Eurasian British Subject who later appeared in court on grave charges of assisting the King's enemies. I was neither spying on the Japanese nor on the Portuguese if I collected information on the reliability of certain persons who might get to hear of a flight from Macao of some of my people. I do not consider it as spying to collect information which might in the future lead to some person or other finding himself not permitted to land in Hongkong. I do not consider it spying to have tried to find out what quantities of wolfram were passing through the Colony,[10] by whom they were being handled and to whom they were going; this is surely commercial intelligence which any Consul of any country should gather. If in the course of all this one sometimes came incidentally on information of importance, or if I passed on information given to me without any reward being paid I still feel that I was not indulging in espionage. Someone will perhaps be able to tell the difference between keeping your eyes open, collecting normal information of interest, indulging in intelligence work, and espionage. I do not know where one starts and the other finishes.

In particular I was not operating actively in Hongkong. I once sent a message to Stanley Camp[11] but I did so under orders. I used, naturally, to ask newly arrived refugees about conditions in Hongkong but here I was only collecting information which would anyhow be the talk of the town in a day or two. We did thus stumble over things of importance and passed them on; the Sino-Portuguese group with whom I was in touch may twice at least have passed on information which materially altered the course of the war; more credit to them.[12] I feel sure though that if my activities had run counter to the wishes of the Government to which I was accredited I would have heard about it in no uncertain terms from the Governor. Incidentally he knew, for I told him, that our groups were running an illegal radio for contact with Chungking but he never objected.

Finally I consider that gathering information as a result of which my own existence was prolonged hardly struck me as espionage but rather as common sense.

How much the Japanese really wanted me removed I have never known.[13] I know the reward for me once went up to £4,000 and one immediately asks why it was not earned. The answer is not too far to seek; in this sort of job the Japanese were working through Chinese gangsters and these somewhat low types were aware that they were unlikely to live to collect in view of the way I was armed, of the fact that my bodyguard was always with me and that I was normally shadowed by one or two Chungking gunmen. And the Japanese could certainly not be trusted to pay a widow.

Another question that arises here is that of determining why the Japanese did not take Macao itself. My own idea is that they found it useful for obtaining wolfram, and for espionage and, perhaps more important for getting foreign exchange since they needed only to print more and more unnumbered military *yen* to buy Portuguese currency which they could remit to Europe; and there must have been precious few places where they could get foreign currency as easily as that.[14]

Three more or less specific attempts were made [on Reeves' life]. On one occasion my people spotted someone at night putting something into my car but when he realized he was spotted he ran away throwing something into the sea; on another occasion someone fixed my ignition in such a way that all electric wires under the dash and bonnet went white-hot and switching off made no difference; I pulled my gun and ripped it across the wires and then retired to a safe distance till all was cool.[15] That incidentally was the only time I used my gun in anger though I probably wore it more even than any member of the armed forces since it went on with my clothes in the morning and came off with them at night every day for three and a half years. I liked that gun and felt quite lonely when I finally discarded it. The third attempt was no little abortive; someone lost his nerve and placed a time bomb just outside instead of inside the garden or house. It went off with a bang which was heard half-a-mile away and blew an expensive watch, the timing device, to pieces; but it might have been serious since less than a quarter of the charge actually exploded. Another try never quite came off. Mr. Rodrigues, the president of the Portuguese Red Cross was murdered by shooting on the way back from a funeral;[16] the reason was never clearly known to me. As he was an official personage I was naturally going to attend his funeral. I was already dressed for this when I was telephoned to the effect that the idea was to get me on the way back from Rodrigues' funeral. I did not go. This spoiled a succession of similar events as the further idea was to get the chief of police on the way back from my funeral and so on. I interrupted this sequence, a typical product of the Japanese mind.

Thrills, More or Less

On another occasion the laugh was on me and my bodyguard. Firecrackers were prohibited for the duration of war but it was a trick of fate that what I feel must have been about the only one let off in three years was let off just behind my bodyguard and myself in the main street. We whirled round, guns half-out of their holsters and gave the Chinese population a good laugh. But it was serious all the time, however much one laughed it off, to know that at any moment one might be on the wrong end of a shot from behind; in restaurants I sat with my back to a corner, on my own verandah I kept away from the window at night and so on. My bodyguard and I were in constant danger; none of us was within ten miles of breaking down under the strain. In fact I think we rather enjoyed it and I wonder sometimes who was the buccaneer in my ancestry.

At times we mobilized really fully; those were the occasions when it was believed that actual armed attack on the Consulate was possible or probable. Do not be surprised that we considered such a thing as possible or probable; later you will hear the lurid story of the *Saion*. But when we really mobilized the Consulate became an arsenal with fifteen or twenty Chungking strong-arm boys from the roof down. Every half-hour I went my rounds, which meant not more than ten minutes sleep at a time, and this might go on for two or three nights. Many during the war of course had more tiring times but this was tiring enough for me. Besides I had a tendency to forget the password, and to find a gun jammed in my ribs round a dark corner. My "Hi or any loud cry" fortunately always worked although Chinese gunmen are notoriously trigger-happy.

For quite a while a large and heavily-armed junk lay about 100 feet at sea off the Consulate and since its muzzle loading cannon[17] were practically poking in at my window I took a very dim view of the situation; and all enquiries met with the most evasive replies.[18] It was only later, in fact after the war that I was told by my Chinese friends that the junk was friendly and was meant for kidnapping me and removing me to Free China if the Japanese took Macao. This was well-meant but I could never, naturally, have persuaded my superiors that I had not deserted my post so I would not actually have been well served. However it is doubtful whether my staying would have been more than a gesture; one of my people came in one day and said he had learnt the Japanese plans for me if they caught me. They started with my being whipped naked through the streets; at that point I stopped him, thanked him for his no doubt accurate information and said I felt I could do without knowing the rest.

And so to the story of *Saion* night;[19, 20] and what a night; I am not now sure of exact times but it must have been around eleven o'clock that all hell was let loose in the Colony. Then I was telephoned. The Japanese were taking the *Saion* away from the wharf with seventy refugees aboard. One of their own ships was berthed astern of her and from the wharf were pouring armed men. Heavy machine-guns had been mounted ashore and were preventing all approach to the wharf; even the police armoured car could not get through. I 'phoned the Governor and he ordered me not to leave my house as I had intended. It was not anything but sheer luck that enabled me to phone; the Japanese had immobilized many phones by ringing up on the automatic exchange and then leaving their own receivers off; this prevents calls in or out on the phone rung up (try it on your friends, they will be so amused) but they had forgotten my private number; but the Governor's action was as well for me personally.

I learnt later that the Japanese had a bunch of gunmen stationed fifty yards either side of my front gate. By this time tracer bullets were flying all over the place and even the Governor was immobilized. Orders had been given not to fire on the ship as she went out very slowly past the Barra Fort[21] where artillerymen are said to have wept because they were not allowed to fire. I can understand orders not to fire on the ship itself for fear of hurting the refugees aboard but she had one tug ahead of her and one alongside and she passed less than a hundred yards from the fort. The tug ahead could well have been immobilized. She came slowly alongside the channel in front of my house; by now I was lying with my head just over the edge of the roof dressed in dark clothes; I had no desire to be conspicuous. I could see the tug ahead and the dark bulk of the *Saion* passing down the channel. The other tug was hidden behind the *Saion*, secured alongside but off-shore. But I could hear her and this is of importance. She was a tug, which was frequently in port and she had a leaky condenser so that she could be recognised by sound alone from her characteristic periodic whistle. She took more than two hours, did the *Saion*, to get out through the narrow channel to sea, and no one thought of putting even a junk in the channel to stop her. She was last seen with a Portuguese launch looking almost like an escort as she left territorial waters. It is a strange story isn't it? And was it stranger yet that the puffing billy tug was back in Macao a day or two later and no action was taken against her? My refugees were not hurt; four lads in fact in the end escaped from her and got back to Macao after a dangerous swim from ship to shore in Hongkong. My young Chinese office boy Ah Chiu who was aboard was tortured by the Japanese and his health, I fear, will never recover. The ship herself was fated to tragedy; after the war she went back into service and was burnt alongside the wharfs of Hongkong with passengers trapped between decks, a great number of whom perished in the flames.[22]

Another exciting time was had by all when the Americans started raiding us. One lone plane, unidentified, had laid mines by night in the channel and three small Japanese craft went up without noticeable regret being shown in the Colony; the last victim unfortunately was the Portuguese water boat and this roused a certain amount of indignation. But on January 15th 1945 we had our first real raid. Let us confess immediately that the reclaimed land with the Portuguese Naval Air Service hangar and slip-way looked like an aerodrome;[23] on the other side it must be acknowledged that, as we learnt first-hand, the pilots had not been told there was any neutral territory around, and did not know the Portuguese colours or badge. So we were startled one day by the roar of engines, the rat-tat of machine guns and the explosion of small bombs or rockets; not knowing what was happening on the reclaimed land we were out in the streets on the water-front to see the fun expecting to see the Americans claw a few poached eggs (our name for the Japanese flag) out of the sky. We went back in when we saw the sea close by furrowed with bullets. When there was a lull I went out to the reclamation as some of my staff were living in the Pan-American passenger-station there. They were unhurt and far from upset. So Swemm and I strolled onto the grass to look at the bomb or rocket holes. While we were there, there was another approaching roar. The Portuguese who were around very sensibly took cover. Swemm and I decided we would be British/Dutch and show unconcern. We did and did not realize till afterwards that we thus became a target; others told us that bullets were only about four feet behind us. It would have been ridiculous to be hurt by our own people. However, this lot went off to have their lunch and we came to the conclusion that all was over. Not a bit of it, in the afternoon they were back and this time they scored hits. Two hundred and eleven bullets were later picked out of the Pan-American passenger-station and others from the Pan-American radio station. The Governor's car was burnt out and Lobo had to take a quick dive from his into a ditch. And finally the hangar caught it and some 1,500 gallons of petrol went up in a nice black cloud of smoke. I should have known the fuel was there but I didn't; I am also told it was going to the Japanese but this of course in no way justifies the attack.

There were consequences of this raid; for one thing we were very unpopular, as many officials and the more irresponsible members of the Portuguese Community came to the conclusion we had asked for the raid to get the petrol burnt. In parenthesis I may say that could have been done without aircraft. Offensive posters appeared on the walls of the Lyceum and the Valentes were greeted with cries of "yellow spies" when they took [to] the hockey-field. I was obliged to complain about this puerile campaign and it stopped; but no one can tell me that the teachers of the Lyceum, government servants, failed to see the posters, which incidentally were directed against "our friends" the British, not against the Americans.

A second consequence was the abrupt shutting down of the *Macao Tribune*, my newspaper, owing to a tactical error of mine. The Editor 'phoned me and read me what he intended to print, a purely factual account. I approved this and it was printed. We were therefore the only paper not to talk of "barbarous and uncivilized attacks" and so on. The Governor immediately suppressed the paper on the ground that it had almost seemed pleased. I of course could not interfere as I had officially nothing to do with the paper, but this incident shows the power of Government over the Press

Thrills, More or Less

in some countries. I sometimes wonder what would have happened if the *Tribune* had completely ignored the attack. I made representations through the Lisbon Embassy that the livelihood of some of my refugees had been taken from them and on those grounds the paper was restarted in a different form. But we never regained that very happy *Tribune* atmosphere.

The third and most difficult consequence, not of the raid on Macao in particular but of the raid in general, was the arrival in the course of the next twenty-four hours of one single and one group of three American airmen[24] who had been shot down in the sea and brought in by sampan. In each case as soon as I heard about them I sent them instructions to sink their uniforms in the harbour and come ashore in anything else they could procure and grim sights they looked on arrival in my house one, at least, barefooted. There was quite a party that night; after all they found themselves out of either a watery grave or the hands of the Japanese and we were seeing our first visitors from "outside" for three years. The bathrooms were in considerable demand and in the end four very presentable young men emerged. After a day or so I had to tell the Governor and I told him the truth, adding however that my story was that they were road-engineers from China cut off by a Japanese punitive column. H.E. very sportingly said he would not intern them but asked me to get them out as soon as possible. This in any case became imperative as the Japanese had not been fooled at all. So they had to get out of Skyline,[25] Gellion's house where my wife was staying with the child, in a hurry; this was done and the four members of my staff who most resembled them spent a lazy day on the lawn being watched by Japanese field-glasses. Now the boys were no longer in my hands but Chan and the English Portuguese I have mentioned had taken over and away went the four flyers not without diversionary activity at one end of the wharves to draw the watchers' attention while they went off in a junk at the other end. It was a very pretty piece of work indeed and they arrived safely. They were never, during the war, allowed to tell the whole story of their escape. I wonder if they have now. They were grand chaps all of them and we would willingly have had them with us for the rest of the war; I think we shall all remember the efforts to turn the words of a popular song from "I've got two pence" into "I've got tuppence".

This escape was, of course, perfection, the result of much experience. The first lot who went, Portuguese volunteers, had the trip put off because of a rumour that the Japanese were onto it and then got away more by luck than good management. More Portuguese got off in a second group and then I was told to discontinue sending them; and this was odd because I met an officer after the war who had had these boys under his command and who said he could have done with many more. Another delayed sailing involved the secret sending by sampan of stores to a junk in the harbour packed below decks with British Subjects. I have mentioned the Filipino seamen and Davies; once in, the latter started some quite incredible rumours about financial responsibility for the trip but I think this was cleared up in the end. It was, parenthetically, my normal practice to spread the story in Macao that a party was safe in Free China long before it was; this discouraged Japanese pursuit but we used to pass some anxious hours waiting for confirmation from the Interior. The biggest party was the Fletchers, Wilsons et al. and was cluttered up with excessive baggage of one of the party. This attracted the attention of the bandits and the whole of the party's baggage was lost. O'Neill, the drunken American, whom I have mentioned, was Shanghaied onto this trip; he behaved perfectly till Kweilin, then in Chinese hands, and then again went on the booze; as a result he was arrested and flown to India while the sober members of the party kicked their heels for weeks before being taken on. Maybe there is a moral in this. All told the organization took through more than 300 without losing a man, for which I consider they deserve high credit which, so far I know, they never received; and maybe there is another moral in this.

It will perhaps give an idea of how careful one had to be when I mention that Father Joy,[26] a magnificent Irish Jesuit from Hongkong was arrested by the Japanese pretty well solely on the grounds that he had met me in Macao. Fortunately he was clever enough to confess to meeting me once in full view at the Riviera Hotel when, he said, he had talked over relief problems with me. He did not mention the other times when to make sure the meeting was safe I had people posted all round the meeting-place who would have given me the tip, if I were being followed, by dropping a handkerchief. He had a bad time in Japanese hands but emerged to continue as the man whom half Hongkong would like to see canonized even before his death which I hope will be very long a-coming.

One never knew in this part of the game who was saint and who sinner, who was friend and who foe. There was for instance a mysterious German doctor who was always on the verge of producing the most terrific bit of news if a little cash was forthcoming; but the news never came. There was the proprietor of a restaurant who suddenly disappeared from Macao and went into Free China where I believe he was arrested as a spy. There was the curiously helpful Portuguese policeman who definitely was arrested by the Chinese and who is still, in 1949, in detention on a charge of spying for the Japanese. People like these raise the further question of how much one should use people who are probably working for both sides. I was frankly frightened of this type and did my best to avoid them. On the edge of my knowledge were a very different type, that devoted band, chiefly of Chinese and Eurasians who worked for others than me in Hongkong and the French port of Kwangchowan.[27] They would not like their names mentioned but they will know who I mean; more than one went through torture and came out to risk the same thing all over again; such cold-blooded heroism is a thing I wish I feel I would have in similar circumstances.

We had more American raids and in one what can only be described as a miracle saved an enormous casualty list. If you look at the North-West corner of Macao you will see the Bairro Tamagnini Barbosa (52), the *Tungwei* berth (50), the *Masbate* berth (49) and the 28th May Houses for the poor (48).[28] The *Tungwei* was a Customs hulk which was packed with refugees and refugees were packed into the Tamagnini Barbosa and the 28th May. A stick of bombs came down; the first dropped just north of the 28th May and the last in the mud between the basin and the Tamagnini Barbosa, this last damaging a Catholic school for the poor. If the stick had been a bit south the 28th May would have caught it, a bit north the Tamagnini Barbosa, a bit east the *Tungwei*. As it was only the poor old *Masbate* was hit.

Trigger (Trygve) Jorgensen nearly lost his leg and was wounded in the head and his cook and dog were killed while the ship was badly dented. This, mark you, was an Allied ship in a neutral port being attacked by American planes. However so far as I know the compensation paid[29] for this and the petrol I have mentioned more than satisfied everyone concerned.

The *Masbate* figured in one other adventure when she went to Indo-China under Portuguese charter and colours to bring back coal for the Colony. She had Allied and Japanese safe-conducts and carried out her mission slowly but surely. When she was about to leave for the second time the safe-conduct was withdrawn and I believe I know why. I found out later that the Portuguese signed on two Japanese as signallers under Chinese names, knowing perfectly well that they were Japanese. This rather childish piece of deception was evidently discovered by our people and she did not sail again until after the Japanese surrender. I wonder whether the full charter hire was ever paid. Incidentally the beneficiary owner, a Chinese, could have sold the ship a dozen times over to the Japanese and it is very much to the credit of his loyalty that he never contemplated doing such a thing though he could easily have made out that he had been forced to do so. He, the manager of the China Travel Service and the local agent of the British American Tobacco Company were three Chinese who lost much when they could have done well by at least appearing to work in with the Japanese. They all constantly refused. Of course there were many others who did likewise but these happen to be the cases I can vouch for personally. I hope they have been rewarded. There were others, some of great prominence, who were certainly not punished for their flirtations with the enemy.

There were of course constant minor thrills. We were having a party at Pan-American one night, for instance, when Micky felt it was as well to make a little patrol round the building with a gun. Sure enough dodging behind a tree was a shadowy figure. Micky crept forward ready for action only to hear in Cantonese "All right Micky we are here to look after the boss". It was a Chungking man.[30] Chungking gunmen were always at hand; there were always one or two rickshaw coolies at a stand near the house

Thrills, More or Less

who did not seem over keen to take fares but whose thin garments bulged at the hip or below the shoulder. One of my house-coolies, Ah Yu, was handier with a gun than a mop. On two occasions bodyguards and more official guards were thicker than ants in an ant-heap. One occasion was a wedding in the family of a Chinese millionaire. Melco Club had been taken for this and I was amongst those present; now a millionaire in China is good thing to kidnap, in fact this one later was taken off for ransom and returned, so the story goes, with a little off one ear. But to return to Melco Club; apart from police in uniform and plain clothes who stood at or in every window the place was surrounded by gunmen of every allegiance in such numbers as to resemble a thickly planted border.

On another occasion I went to see Lobo just as the Japanese Consul was leaving. Round the door of the building stood my own bodyguard, the Chungking auxiliaries, the Japanese bodyguard, Portuguese police and one or two others who may have been there to look after Lobo. There would have been a glorious scrap if anyone had made too sudden a movement. Another good one was at a Charity dance when a drunken Japanese tried to force the Portuguese-Philippino band to play nothing but Japanese tunes. He got more and more threatening till he remarked "We have thirty armed men in the Hotel; you had better do as I say". At that moment he was tapped on the shoulder by a Chinese who said "Our Consul is here, we have forty". The Japanese left but our guns were loosened in their holsters; we did not know for certain that the drunk would not bring up reinforcements. We were always on the edge of trouble like that; how it never came to a shooting war I have exactly no idea.

Mention of armaments leads in natural sequence to mention of the Japanese employed gangsters. The first to attain any prominence was a gentleman called Yeung Yuk-Kwan; he, I believe, was disposed of fairly early in the party but he was never really dangerous. I used occasionally to be asked "Do you want anything done about so-and-so?" If I said "No" he would be left alone. If I replied "It's nothing to do with me" the chances were that something nasty would happen to the subject of discussion; Yeung was a case in point. In view of the way legal processes have failed to catch up with many who were in the eyes of all but a court guilty of assisting the enemy I say without shame or regret that I wish that I had used the second phrase more, much more frequently. We were fighting a ruthless enemy and I wish I, at least, had been more ruthless.

It is interesting to quote here the remark of the Japanese Consul to the Governor after V.J. [Day]: "When we conquer a country we regard every man, woman and child as our property. Now that we have lost, however Reeves decides to dispose of me he will be right in the Japanese view." Law, in the Western sense, was outlawed by this mentality. Have they changed?

I have strayed a trifle from the Japanese mobsters. When Yeung faded from the scene there arose a far more sinister character by the name of Wong Koon-Kit. This man, a pirate by profession, threw in his lot wholeheartedly with the Japanese. He was so powerful that he was able to turn his house in Macao into a veritable fortress, machine-guns and all. The Portuguese police could do little in view of the people who were behind him; they had their revenge in the end. On one occasion, when he was wounded in a frontier fight and taken to a Portuguese Government hospital gravely wounded, he none the less escaped from Macao in spite of armed guards posted by the Portuguese authorities. Bribery or policy? Just one of those unexplained incidents. We couldn't know everything.

I will go beyond the war period to tell what happened to Wong. After the war was over two F.B.I. boys came into Macao and the hunt was on. I had very little part in it except to help with a little information. The hunt involved such things as Q-junks on the lines of the Q-ships of the 1914–18 war manned by the Navy and Commandos and under the general direction of a resourceful and daring officer Commander Jick (I think I have the name right).[31] These operations drove Wong ashore and into the hands of the Chinese Communists. They sold Wong to the Portuguese and now that the war was over he had no protectors. He was promised to Gray and Farrell the F.B.I. boys, for questioning but perhaps he knew too much; while being transferred by car from one police station to the other he "attempted to escape" and was shot. Our side did not, repeat not, get the chance to question him. The story does not end there; his widow carries on. "The female of the species is more deadly than the male." This dear lady was tough; she came into a gun fight once with a forty-five pistol in each hand and her shooting was accurate with either hand. She was even teaching her young child to be quick on the draw. So far as I know Widow Wong is at this moment in control of the pirate gang and doing very well indeed. What an ally she would have made. I am sorry we were not on the same side; I am sure we would have got on admirably and she certainly would have worked well with the American Chinese I have mentioned whose pseudonym "in the game" was Bunny.[32] Those two together could have conquered half China.

We had an exciting time; I loved it. When I got back someone in the Foreign Office said they were expecting me to look tired and ill. There was only one reply and it was truthful and spontaneous "But I kept my sense of humour".

Chapter XI

Odds and Ends

Naturally various things happened during these years which do not exactly come under any of my chapter headings. So this chapter will be what service signallers would call "unclassified".

There was, for instance, the Milk Board, started by my wife to try and get the children adequate supplies of milk. For this, since it was chiefly the Portuguese children that benefitted, H.E. generously put up the money. It was organized on a group system and various volunteer workers looked after the groups. It was in the centralization of this that Argentina Gonsalves[1] and Alfred Mooney joined us both to become invaluable personally and officially. The main trouble was that in a few, a very few cases the mothers got fat quicker than the children and rules had to be brought in to the effect that the milk went into the child in front of the group supervisor. The stocks of tinned milk dwindled, the children began to get better fed and the Milk Board, I believe, gradually faded out, though not before the d'Almadas had put in some very useful work.

At least two of the years we ran big charity drives for the refugees and collected quite respectable sums of money. The refugees themselves did most of the work in the form of providing entertainment, organizing dances in centres, organizing lotto, housey-housey, whichever you like to call it and so on. And the sportsmen in the later drives put on exhibition games. This way we raised quite considerable funds. I would have been happier if they had been quicker spent but I believe there was still money in hand at the end of the war from the first drive.[2] The last drive was the most spectacular, which we ran in conjunction with the Commissioner of Police, and for the poor of Macao in general. After we had given poor Chinese and all refugee children in the centres a good Christmas feed and when we were planning distribution of clothes and so on the Commissioner had the funds transferred to his own name and I do not know to what Charities he gave them. The war ended before I had the chance to ask. But even if these drives had not earned a penny they were good things as they gave my family the boost in morale which comes from working together for a common end. Incidentally one refugee came to me for extra subsidy on the grounds that he had lost his money at lotto. When we started reproaching him for gambling he came back with the reply that he had only been gambling "for the boss's charities".

In the chapter on Organization I briefly touched on the Rehabilitation Committee. It was I believe the first committee in the hundred years of Hongkong history on which the various communities had equal representation, only the British having less than any. I sat as Chairman and there were two from each other community. We chose key-post men from the refugees for the various departments, police, sanitation and so on and they, sometimes with small sub-committees, worked out detailed plans for the various departments. How detailed they were can be shown by the fact that drawings were even produced, with an estimate of necessary materials, of hand propelled funeral carts. At the broader end of the scale we suggested the continuance of the Japanese district bureaux at which all births, deaths, changes of residence and so on had to be registered; I am still of the very firm opinion that this would be advantageous in such an over-crowded Colony in Hongkong both for police and immigration purposes.

An enormous amount of hard work was put in and, which is important, in an atmosphere both of frankness and of cordiality. I am afraid our plans were pigeon-holed and that the spirit of the Committee somewhat lapsed when the members returned to Hongkong. The work done deserved a better fate, though one can see that the H.K.P.U. (Hongkong Planning Unit),[3] to join which we sent Leo d'Almada home before the war ended, being an official body formed in London, had to take precedence.

Odds and Ends

From Government policy to servants, James and Joseph, Ah Wong, Ah Yu, the amahs and all. James, then our No. 1, left us and went into what was then Free China, Kweilin specifically where he opened a restaurant presumably on capital "earned" when with us. I cannot vouch for the story but I believe he was among those who lost a great deal when the Chinese authorities came to the conclusion that a lesson should be given to the inhabitants of Kweilin. The story went that the inhabitants of Kweilin, a walled city, showed an obstinate reluctance to evacuate when told to do so; that the authorities one day sounded the air-raid warning and the population took to the fields and hills—and on their return found the gates of the city shut and had to go westward with virtually only what they had on. Anyhow Joseph took over, a Catholic with good English, some French and I believe a little Russian. Joseph was a tower of strength; remember how dangerous he could have been and note that he was constantly checked on by Allied intelligence groups; nothing, absolutely nothing, was ever even hinted against his loyalty and discretion. But it was perhaps on mobilization nights that Joseph was at his best; he never panicked in the very least and endless streams of tea and coffee left his kitchen for the troops who would go off at about seven in the morning; by eight the house was again neat and tidy and Joseph carried straight on; I don't know when he slept on those days and nights. Ah Wong was a great heavy chap whose chief claim to fame was his one word of English and his way of saying it, "Boiling" in a sort of deep sing-song. Ah Yu was the extra bodyguard; he had been a guerrilla for some years before being posted to me. They were all good people; Joseph, the admirable, was in tears, open tears for two days before I left; and I was not far off them at leaving such grand people.

While we are on the subject of the household I may as well mention the ducks and chickens in the bathrooms being fed on virtually everything. They were sick birds from the farm and most of them recovered, except for Crazy Maisie who, to the end of her days, walked in small circles and never got anywhere. The farm started as a cooperative among the staff, started by my wife, but the cooperative aspect faded out, for reasons I never enquired into; it was not my business. There were two original plots, one by

Ilha Verde for vegetables and one near the Harbour Office for poultry. The former produced chiefly an extremely gelatinous vegetable[4] whose name I do not remember. The latter was a distinct success in a disused brick yard and at one time we had over a hundred birds,[5] turkey and ducks and hens; they kept us reasonably supplied with eggs and poultry; and here is the only thing I know about turkeys;[6] the young ones are too lazy to eat off the ground and troughs have to be provided to bring the food up to beak-level or near it. The mainstay of production was, not unnaturally, rabbits: these lived in tiers in the backyard of the house with one or two very fancy hutches; I do not believe they were an economic proposition owing to the tendency to buy semi-Agoras or similar expensive bucks and does "to improve the breed" and to the other tendency to regard the beasts as pets rather than as meat producers.

At one time also there was a pig, which boarded out in the garden of Toni and Freddie Xavier; with supreme lack of imagination the thing was called "Porky" and some subterfuge was necessary when he had to be killed to avoid floods of tears from my daughter. But in the meantime the animal had become legendary for its alleged jealousy of attentions to other animals and its other alleged capacity to weep if thwarted. One refugee by the way, A.P. Rozario, a guitar player who also operated an instrument which <u>by name</u> has no wires, made quite a good thing out of pigs and turkeys; I wish more refugees had had this type of initiative.[7]

Occasions that were always great fun, from all but one point of view, were staff dinner parties. We had them at least once a year and on any occasion which seemed to warrant a celebration. On these nights we "let our hair down" and formality went by the board. They got us all together from our various offices and rank did not exist. This makes all the difference to a staff when the feeling of friendliness is genuine and I am sure we all went back to work refreshed, if not on the morning after, then on the morning after that. The disagreeable feature? Speeches made about me and my reply. I look back with some nervousness at these gatherings; one or two well thrown bombs would have caused no little chaos. It is because it was too

Odds and Ends

dangerous to get everyone together in an open space that I have no photograph of the whole staff; this I regret intensely.

A word about Macanese, the language of Macao spoken also largely by the Portuguese community of Hongkong.[8] Remember that Macao was for a long time the only channel of trade with China and that Dutch, British, Indian, Malayan and virtually every nation then in existence traded in larger or smaller way through the Colony. I never made a real study of the language but I can assure you it is incomprehensible to most Portuguese and it has elements from all the races that have touched there. I do not consider that I am completely silly about languages but I never got further with Macanese than two words *Gong-gong* for a flying cockroach and *Tok-tok* for stupid; of the etymology even of these two I have not the faintest idea. It was a queer habit of those who spoke this tongue to add a plural "s" to many words in English which normally go without it, such as "furnitures" and "informations". It was Eddie Gosano who was bringing in a new one: "hell of a" not followed by a noun but by another adjective; thus, "it was hellova good". I am not certain whether anyone has made a real study of Macanese; the study would be difficult because of the rapid assimilation of words; it is still adding to itself and later etymologists may find such slang as *prang* in the tongue and think it is of Malay origin. It is not a dialect; it really is a language.

Ceremonial occasions were I suppose no more and no less frequent than in other parts of the world, and no more and no less tiresome. The year always started by our all going to shake the Governor's hand at the palace. When I say "all" I mean it; everybody went from us bigshots of the *corpo consolare* to the visiting fireman. Before Fukui was killed he was dean of the corps but even after his country had attacked us he always used to try and wave me in first and as a rule, so as not to block proceedings entirely, I went first. After his death I became dean anyhow so the situation was eased.

I seem to remember a Foreign Office circular in the early days of the war which told us that if we found ourselves inevitably in the presence of enemy colleagues we were permitted to "bow coldly". This of course conjured up a glorious vision of H.M. Diplomatic and Consular Officers busily practising the "cold bow". In point of fact at one of these receptions some time after the Pacific War (a glorious phrase, to rank with "cold" and "shooting" wars) had started Fukui leant across and whispered in my ear "Difficult getting whisky these days isn't it?" If journalists had been present and had seen one warring Consul whispering in the ear of the other he would probably have hit the headlines with "Peace Talks Begin?"

Poor H.E. had to stand and shake hands with hundreds of people four or five times a year and I feel sure he didn't enjoy it much. He, like me, was happier in an open-necked shirt. Between January 1st and 6th there was a mad riot of card dropping in which I did not fully participate. One was supposed to drop cards on everyone; the result, of course, was that everyone dashed madly around, dressed up to kill, in cars and rickshaws noting who else was out on the round and calling quickly at the houses whose masters had been spotted to be "out". Maybe this served some purpose; I wouldn't be knowing. On one occasion I had the tables turned on me; when the Mocedade Portuguese,[9] a para-military youth organization once paraded past my house I dipped my flag to their standard; there was no acknowledgment and I let it be known that I thought this was impolite. The same afternoon I went to the Loyal Senate for some official show and walked between the ranks of the Mocedade drawn up to receive the Governor; they came to a smart salute, I looked behind me to see who the salute was for, walked on—and failed to acknowledge the Mocedade's salute to me.

We also had a lot, of course, of church occasions. Fortunately you were not expected, when in uniform, to kneel; you sat or stood. Even so I had to keep a close eye on my neighbours to see that I got the drill right. There was a moving ceremony when the colony was put under the protection of Our Lady of Fatima, patroness of Portugal. There was a less moving memorial service when the bishop's cords came untied and trailed redly a corner or two of the catafalque behind him while Lobo stepped smartly forward and stopped a candle from igniting one of the palms. And there were processions in which we all walked through the town behind a statue and the bishop. I did not like these processions through narrow streets with high and crowded buildings; one small bomb could have made a horrid mess of all the senior officials of the Colony. However, it didn't happen.

I was not always on the receiving end of church services; I on some occasions read the lesson and even preached sermons in the Protestant Church, but never more than 3½ minutes in length. I was a popular preacher! The one that made me most nervous was the Memorial Service for the Duke of Kent which we held in the Protestant Cemetery in the open air.[10] At the end of my short valedictory my voice broke, largely from nerves though naturally also from emotion; to the Portuguese it was pure emotion and they were very greatly impressed.[11]

A very pleasant little ceremonial really belongs in the post-war period but it will fit here as well. On the King's Birthday in 1946 I asked the Governor if he would care to visit the M.L. then in port.[12] He consented and the skipper had his vessel looking like a flagship of the Home Fleet at a Royal Review in peacetime. Full honours were paid and H.E. went all over the M.L., engine-room and all and wound up for a drink in the tiny wardroom. He was pleased and touched at the gesture and we were pleased to have had him aboard. He always made people feel relaxed except I imagine those of his officers who incurred his displeasure, although on parades and so on he was a figure of great dignity and of rigidly correct naval bearing. He had also great personal courage; on one occasion troops[13] in barracks refused duty, in fact mutinied; H.E. walked in alone and unarmed and settled the matter.

Another very pleasing ceremony, which also really belongs to the post-war period, was that of homage to H.E. by the various communities. This started off, I felt incongruously, with an exhibition hockey match in which, of course, I played and got my usual crack (I find it difficult to play chess without breaking or straining something). I limped off the field at a half double, retired to a nearby house where a room had been kindly put at my disposal and limped back, resplendent in white sharkskin to take my place among the bigwigs. Community after community presented its thanks and some token of esteem, usually an illuminated address. The speeches had all to be translated which made a somewhat wearisome succession but there was real feeling behind them, deep feeling of gratitude from all of us to the man who had done so much for us. I knew how much, more than most, and I was intensely glad to be present when this tribute was paid to him. It was so richly deserved. There was the usual touch of comedy when the fireworks didn't go off quite as was intended but that really completely failed to detract from the occasion.

An exploit worthier of the race from which sprang Henry the Navigator was that of the *João de Lisboa*, Commander Amerigo Cabral, the guard-vessel at Macao when the Pacific War broke out. Her displacement was of a mere 1,091 tons but she had, of course, come out under her own steam via the Cape. She was now to face a still harder task. By 1942 the stocks of oil in the colony had become so low that she had to be sent home or remain completely immobilized. Useful as she was as a wireless contact with Portugal the decision was made that she had to go and she got the necessary safe conducts from both sides and then arose the problem of charts. She had none of the Pacific. The not entirely apocryphal story is that the navigating officer, one of the youngest in the ship, went to the captain and said, approximately, "How can I find Honolulu with a schoolboy's atlas?" The captain is reported to have replied "Our ancestors found Macao; you can find Honolulu". Anyhow she sailed with, amongst other things a cracked cylinder head and a few parts left in Hongkong. And she is said to have sighted Pearl Harbour dead ahead at exactly her estimated time of arrival. No mean feat. After the war we had two or more sloops at various times and one remembers particularly Sam Vieira, later to be acting Governor, and Commander Ferreira, that Gargantuan among naval officers. One always gets on with naval officers and we certainly got on with these.

A little while after V.J. [Day] there appeared the *Lourenço Marques* of the Portuguese merchant marine. The story goes that she carried 6,500 tons of cargo of which 3,500 were wine and the rest olive-oil and *baccalao* the famous dried codfish. Every house had now its 20 litre glass jar of wine, housewives looked up their recipes for *baccalao* and olive oil sputtered in the frying pans. I enjoyed myself and I still think the Governor's recipe produced the best dish I met. After staying for a while the ship sailed again taking with her many of the officials whose leave was overdue. The embarkation—she was lying outside the breakwaters—was fantastically mismanaged with women and children having to wait hours in broiling sun, luggage piled high in the grossest confusion and so on. I went down to the wharf but left again before long—this was good-bye to too many good friends. As a result, also, of these imports a Portuguese Restaurant was opened near San Rafael Hospital (and it is strange that I cannot remember its name as I spent many happy hours there, perhaps the happiest I shall ever spend).[14] Dinners there tended to be distinctly enlivened by a gentleman with a guitar who, when he could be persuaded to play rather than talk, played magnificently.

I have mentioned that we had troubles of the Macao Electricity Company—Melco. The Portuguese said that the Japanese would not provide oil for the Company unless they took it over. Roughly we fought for some written guarantee that the Company would be returned when the emergency was over but that we could not get. Meetings grew stormy, protests flew and this was perhaps the worst moment of Anglo-Portuguese relations throughout the war. Our efforts were totally unavailing and the Portuguese took over; we had a good deal of justification in our displeasure at the way this was done by junior officials who adopted a hectoring, bullying, and gloating attitude. We had some measure of apology for this. I will quote one example; Ber Fernandez[15] refused to work with the new company preferring to remain loyal to Melco whatever happened. One official told him "If that is your attitude we shall see to it that you starve on the streets". All the sound and fury which seemed so important to us in Macao did not in point of fact affect the issue which was settled at a much higher level than ours in Lisbon and London with Freddie Gellion in San Francisco, and the Company came peacefully back into Melco's hands after the war. I am sure, however, that Freddie, Fletch and Ber will agree that the Portuguese regime over the Company was efficient and in some respects beneficial, under the guiding hand of Lieutenant Correia Barcos Portuguese Fleet Air Arm. Here was an officer of absolute integrity and, when he was sure he was right, of inflexibility; he was one of the rare types, however, who was willing, if contrary evidence was produced, to acknowledge the rightness of other arguments and come round completely. For some time the Diesels were being operated on an entirely weird mixture of peanut-oil, resin and heaven (and the Irish Jesuit who tested the mixtures) knows what else; I am not sufficiently an engineer to know how difficult this was but it sounds exceptional.[16]

As over Melco, so over more important issues, those in Macao were sometimes lamentably out of touch with home policies. I remember the furious telegrams sent home by the União Nacional, the ultra-nationalist body, when Australian and Dutch troops entered Timor.[17] The mildest expression used was "unprovoked aggression". These were published in the paper and a general whipping up of Portuguese public opinion followed. It was a disappointment, and some people must have felt a bit foolish when Dr. Salazar's own masterly speech on the subject reached Macao and it was found that there was no violent word in it. I confess that when I heard the Timor news I burnt a lot of paper; I thought we were in for it immediately. After the war Silva e Costa flew down there, a very frightening trip it was, and reported to the home government. I understand the Portuguese have as little reason to love the Japanese as have others.

I had one curious little scrap with the Bishop.[18] An article appeared in a Portuguese paper saying amongst other things that Freemasonic Charity was the cloak for the venom of the serpent, or words to that effect. I wrote, strictly privately, to the Bishop and told him that as a Freemason not exactly unknown for charity in Macao, this hurt me personally. An interview was arranged and we had a frank and to me at least enjoyable conversation. He pointed out that many Catholics, in Portugal amongst other countries, had suffered terribly from the actions of Freemasons of the political type. He realized that certain Constitutions of Masonry were non-political and non-sectarian but he could hardly, in preaching against the wrong sort of freemasonry, say every time that of course he accepted certain sorts. "You know", he said, "that we public officials sometimes have to make public announcements with which we are not in complete agreement". We parted the better friends for this talk.

I have not really said enough about the "odds and ends" in the office, these including the non-official activity of the *Macao Tribune*. Exactly how

Odds and Ends

it started I am not sure but I suppose it was again one of those things where someone said "What about it?" and I replied "Why not?" Anyhow it did start, first as a small weekly and then on to a four-page daily. This was tightrope walking with a vengeance as we dared not be anti-Japanese and had to be watchful not even to be too openly pro-Allied. I wrote the leaders and the limericks, and leader writing was not easy when you could not touch on the war, nor on civic affairs. In early November 1944 I wrote a leader called "Twenty-six years ago"; in it I never spoke of the 1939–45 war nor of the Far East; I merely referred to the state of Germany in November 1918; I prepared a second leader and I was right; "Twenty-six years ago" was struck right out by the censor. I did none of the hard work; the editorial staff did that as regards the make-up and so on and a business staff collected the advertisements and attended to all that side. Anyhow when we were suppressed we were just even on the debit and credit side, which was not bad as, of course, we had no subsidy. It was a short life but a very enjoyable one.

Most of the departments in the bottom line of the diagram[19] have already been dealt with but one or two need the extra word. I have mentioned the Protestant Cemetery from a historical point of view but it played quite a part in our wartime life as a place for open-air services, on special occasions, and the regular Sunday services. One high wind unfortunately blew down an enormous tree, which was perched on top of a wall in an extraordinary manner. It unfortunately smashed several tombs and we had no money to repair them as our money was in Hongkong. The "new" cemetery,[20] which actually contained some of the oldest graves, was too big for our needs so I leased half of it for a Catholic cemetery (five years burials and five years exhumations) the municipality in return guaranteeing to keep the whole in order.

And so to the guard. They will forgive a little dig in the mention of the eleven shooting accidents which happened though one was really Wilfred who put his finger over the muzzle of an air-gun to see if it really had enough compressed air; when he pulled the trigger he found it had—and a slug. Georgie put a bullet up his arm when cleaning a gun and this was—luckily—our most serious accident. Someone else let off a Mauser pistol in the guard-room and the bullet went through the ceiling, through a hardwood table, through a second ceiling and away. The table was next to that on which my daughter was having supper. It can well be imagined that when I was offered hand-grenades to strengthen my arsenal I refused. Seriously though I know all of them would have fought it out with the Japanese with the greatest of pleasure and any one, I am conceited enough to think, would willingly have stopped a bullet meant for me. I shall always remember Frenchie going a pace or two ahead at the corners to have a look round and sometimes warning me against anything he thought was too risky. Thank you, boys!

Reception was in several hands before it got into Ramsay Omar's. This was in many ways the most difficult job in the office, mine, relief, or clinic, as everyone calling thought that his business should come first and usually that only I could deal with it. It was reception's job to sort them out and to do it tactfully and often in the face of rudeness. I could not have stood it for a week; how the lads managed to do so is and always will be a mystery to me.

The professional index was intended to help in orderly repatriation as each refugee was indexed under his pre-war position, bank-clerk and so on and under his war-time job, volunteer, police-reserve or telephone-operator. In the end it did not help much as repatriation became largely a *sauve qui peut* but the idea is none the worse for not having resulted in anything.

A very small activity was the registration, without promise given, of claims for property destroyed during the War. Few took advantage of this but one lady put in a claim for "One trained tortoise £200". Tortoises being long-lived and not very nomad I hope she and her pet are now re-united and that the latter is still in form.

There must of course be other "odds and ends" of more or less interest. But I left Macao in the summer of 1946 and now it is the beginning of 1949; and I have now no-one to consult in Macao. So if the participants in events which they feel should be in this chronicle are hurt by my forgetfulness, will they forgive me? I have done my best but my work in this book, as in Macao, is inevitably far from perfect.

Chapter XII

Post-War

I had a nice new big flag.[1] I had let it be known that this flag would go up only when Victory was confirmed, by which I meant when the B.B.C. announced it (and that is the way the whole population felt; "If the B.B.C. says so, it is so."). And then at 7.45 Macao time came the announcement that at eight the Prime Minister would speak. I guessed. I heard the first words "Japan has surrendered" and I was on my way downstairs. The flag went to the mast-head, made-up, at its usual time. But when the flag was broken at the mast-head it was the new big flag. The war was over.

And then materialized an amazing phenomenon. You can imagine how the Chinese felt after eight years of war. You can imagine how my family felt all ten thousand of them. Yet when the Government asked that there should be no celebrations for an unspecified while there were none, at least in public. The Governor had taken a wise step; he wanted tempers to cool; he wanted no incidents amounting maybe to a massacre of the Japanese still in the colony. I took perhaps a greater pride in my community than ever; in this hour of triumph they remained as self-disciplined as ever; they had, under great provocation, caused no incident during the war; they caused none now; they loyally obeyed the orders of the Government which had given them refuge. H.E. would agree with me.

Four hours later there was another materialization.[2] Out of the mist came a grey shape. H.E. and I were at Miramar where was the Government radio station (no. 10 on the map).[3] H.E. was privileged; he was half way up the radio mast. Then a flashing light saying roughly "Request permission to enter and send boat ashore". My glasses focused on—the White Ensign.

It was too much; glasses or no glasses my sight was blurred. It was the greatest—except for one other, purely personal—moment of my life. We had felt so particularly alone, more than ever after V.E. [Day] when, no doubt unjustly, we had felt forgotten. Later we could see a boat coming in; and the Ensign grew till it filled the whole horizon. Do not ask me to recall whether there were official visits or not, nor in what order they were. The emotional tension was, thank heaven, broken by sheer comedy. A signal was received ashore. Would H.E. and I dine aboard H.M.S. *Plym*.[4] Would we? H.E. had served in co-operation with our Navy in the last war; I had been brought up for the Navy till my eyesight went suddenly. Meanwhile the duty-boat's crew had been entertained; among the crew was one man who was quite a local hero as he had played football in Macao—and they were royally entertained. When H.E. suggested we should go out in our boat I suggested that perhaps—; H.E. smiled and called one of his own launches. Our boat preceded us but steered such a wavy course and the crew showed signs of such discomfort for sailors on a glassy sea that H.E. felt it more tactful to pass her and go ahead. The duty-boat had meanwhile signalled the ship on a walkie-talkie "Governor coming aboard does not like red meat?". This had caused a panic. "Is he a Mohammedan? Is Spam red meat? Break out some sardines." However all went well when a correction arrived from the duty-boat, "For meat read tape". This, I consider, ranks with the best signalling stories. And it was so. H.E. introduced himself as "Commander Teixeira, Portuguese Navy, at your service", and the party went informally and most, most cordially. H.E. was not allowed to drink but this one time he had a gin or two and a whisky or two and damned the consequences. It was a great evening whether in the cuddy or the wardroom. I remember particularly the strange impression given me by the fact that I was surrounded by English voices and every kind of English accent. It was some years since that had happened to me.

Around this time, a little before this time, Hongkong had been retaken for us in one of the most daring actions of the war. Mr. Gimson who had been Colonial Secretary of Hongkong for about two days before the war started, without a gun and without any armed force whatever calmly led his key men out of Stanley and told the Japanese he was in charge. He also sent me a message by junk which I wired home via Chungking and this was the first news to reach London of the liberation of Hongkong. Two enthusiasts even hoisted the Union Flag on the Peak but this was taken down for a day or two until our ships, under Admiral Harcourt, came in, for fear of provoking incidents. I wrote to Mr. Gimson and my letter was broadcast in Hongkong. This resulted in the unexpected comment by Antonio Maria da Silva that he did not know Englishmen could be so eloquent. If any should wish to judge this "eloquence" it appears as Appendix 1.

From now on of course my family began to dwindle, by official and unofficial repatriation and in every craft available from steamers to sampans. Few said good-bye to us but who is to blame them for that? They were very home-hungry even though they knew that their homes might have been ruined. Some of course stayed on and we had to put a time-limit on the extension of aid, after which we had to demobilize ourselves, no easy task, of which more later.

Here I must insert a story which is based solidly on fact though I will not vouch for it in detail. There was a lady of a certain age who had once decided, in the office, that she was Christ. She stood with her arms outstretched and exclaimed: "I have always been a good girl, now I am Christ." (She was, by the way, less alarming by far than the person who developed all the symptoms of cholera on the office premises—and died of it.) She was removed and after a while shed her divinity and returned to normal. On the wharf, as she was about to get into a lighter for repatriation, she was off again, determined she was Christ. Someone asked me what to do about it and I replied, "If she's Christ it's only 48 miles by sea to Hongkong; tell her to walk". No more trouble.

This is not to say we were inactive. There was still plenty to do in all sorts of ways and visiting ships and parties became nearly a full time job. My wife and child left in H.M.S. *Fremantle*[5] for America and home at the end of September and we moved out of Skyline and returned to the Consulate itself, which became a focus of unofficial and official visits.

The Lone Flag

But to start with first things; after four days the Governor lifted the ban on rejoicings and similarly that on firecrackers. The town immediately went mad; strings of firecrackers were let down from the roofs of buildings, hung from poles fixed in windows and let off. "Strings" of firecrackers needs perhaps a little explanation; they are actually hundreds of what look like small cartridges for sporting guns threaded onto a long fuse with, every now and then, along the line, an explosive box so that the continuous small explosions are punctuated by quite respectably large bangs. The noise of 400 thousand Chinese celebrating this way has to be heard to be believed; and we contributed a string or two ourselves. Meanwhile the Salesian orphanage brass band started practising the British and American national anthems just behind the house and an occasional message had to be sent to the effect, for instance, that the first phrase of "God Save the King" is not repeated. All this led up to the official celebration by the Chinese community. A stand was built on the waste-ground and there was an attempt to keep a more or less free space in the centre of the ground. I arrived, very protocol, a few minutes early all dressed up in white uniform with sword and white helmet with a spike on top. As I fought my way through the potted palms up the steps to the platform the Salesians let loose with "God Save the King". I snapped to the salute my arm in its upcurve shaking the palms till it must have looked like a jungle with a herd of animals passing through and shaking the foliage. I had relaxed and mounted another two steps when the Salesians were off again, this time with the American anthem; again a salute and this time palms, gathered in the stiff bend of my arm were tickling my ears and neck intolerably. I reached my place without further incident and was sitting down to recover when the Governor arrived and the Portuguese and Chinese flags were raised; more national anthems and saluting. One final salute to H.E. as he reached the platform and I really could relax during a long Cantonese speech. Then came my turn and here I confess to a certain deceit; realizing that I would have to speak I had looked up a few quotations from Confucius and scattered them through my discourse; I had also taken care to have my own translation made, which the interpreter read when I had finished the English version. The quotations caused quite a stir and gave the quite unjustified impression that I really knew my Confucius. This was my first experience of having loud-speakers booming my own sentences back at me from two or three hundred yards away; I did not like it.

Celebrations naturally succeeded each other with no little rapidity.[6] Perhaps the biggest and most successful was the Inter-Allied Celebration at Melco Club. More anthems and speeches of course but I sometimes wonder whether Macao realized in those days how lucky they were that the two chief speech-makers, H.E. and I, were invariably brief. The Portuguese have a phrase for a speech, *Duas palavras* (literally "two words"), which tends to mean nothing less than twenty minutes but neither H.E. nor I as a rule went beyond an outside limit of three minutes. But in any case this was the first time the refugees had really been able to let themselves go for years and they did, indeed they did; when I finally left I was nearly torn to pieces and I was embarrassed by what I believe to have been genuine warmth towards me (Appendix 2).[7]

Another really great event was the arrival of a large party of Hongkong Volunteers to see their families. These lads had fought hard and during their time as prisoners-of-war had behaved in a most exemplary manner. There were large plans for their reception including a march past H.E. and a march past my Consulate. H.E. and I dodged the official committee, went down to the wharf, H.E. spoke very shortly in welcome and that was that, they were free to go off with their families. No one could have blamed them if they had shown a good deal of rowdiness during their visit. But they upheld the reputation for excellent discipline which they had already earned. They presented me with a scroll done by one of their Sergeants-Major and I am particularly proud of this because it was done by the man who, in camp, had added greatly to morale by his illustrated programmes and so on. I believe no one ever found out quite where he got his colours in camp.[8] (Appendix 3)

Other communities too were good to me and gave parties for me. It would look too conceited to rehearse here what was said on these occasions when I was the recipient of more compliments than I deserved. Reports will be found in the Appendices (3, 4 and 5). I suddenly, in fact, found myself being treated as a V.I.P. a treatment I neither expected nor was accustomed to. The newspapers had done their worst, not just in Macao and I found myself, for a short while, famous. For instance when ships started leaving papers ashore for me I picked up a *Daily Sketch* and found a front page, right hand, I don't know how many point headline "He kept the flag flying for four years". I felt I must read about the evidently interesting person and found it was myself. (Appendix 11)

Divine of the Keensley Press[9] was responsible for that one; my old friend Graham Barrow of Reuters was responsible for a lurid story of my playing hockey with a gun on my hip; this was exaggerated; I always gave my gun to a bodyguard as I went on the field. We had many other newspaper correspondents; one I remember well though I may not spell her name right was Dixie Tighe from America. Bob Shaplen who later had me into *Esquire* and the *Nieman Reports* [10] was another and I have been in correspondence with him since. I suppose such a thing is impossible but I none the less feel that correspondents might send you the stuff they write about you.[11] But that would swell my appendices alarmingly; one American paper went so far as to say that the Chinese wanted us to keep Hongkong partly because of my activities in Macao during the war. Incidentally Divine was the first man in. I think he came in the same sloop as Barry of the Hongkong Government Rice Control. He was immensely interesting to us as he had been on virtually every front from Dunkerque to Tokyo and it was a thrill to get more than the straight facts, something of the background; I am afraid we wore him out with our questions.

Talking of Barry reminds me that H.E. immediately after the surrender offered to share all his Government's food stores with Hongkong and did so to the utmost of his ability. I helped where I could by sending across medicines. It seems silly but around that moment I had more medicines in stock than the whole colony of Hongkong. Later there was another commodity we sent over, money. This went by Otter, an amphibian plane of which we saw much and with very much pleasure.[12] This led to a slightly odd incident; it was realized that the Otter was unarmed and that with five million dollars (£300,000) aboard and more or less pirate-infested sea for 48 miles;

after all even an Otter can come down. She had to have arms aboard and a civilian asked his staff to get a couple of Tommy guns and an assortment of smaller weapons. There remains a photograph of H.M. Consul handing guns into the plane. Civilian officer!

These Otters played quite a part in our lives in all sorts of ways. Twice I remember at an urgent request they brought over medicines which did not exist in Macao and which were needed in emergency. We played this one with a certain amount of drama; I would be waiting at the slipway with my car and would rush the medicines to hospital. Another time in the course of a lunch hour medicines were flown across from Hongkong for me. We had a trying time once; someone rather important had flown over and the Otter was on the apron ashore of the slipway. There arrived on the slipway an American amphibian whose wheels folded gently beneath her so that she subsided on to her hull; we then spent a jolly three hours in broiling heat pushing twelve tons of aircraft gently down the ramp; our V.I.P. got off in time but I was not in a fit state to be seen and did not stay to say goodbye. As a coolie fine; as a Consul, as usual, doubtful.

On another occasion an Otter arrived with white streamers and a white horseshoe daintily disposed about her struts and bracing wires. She brought an R.A.F. officer and his new bride. As I drove them off in my car the pilot, one of the Jimmies I think, came down so low over us that I swear he took some paint off the car roof. "I can't really talk", said the groom, "I am the chap who took a Sunderland under Sidney [Sydney] bridge." Another memory is of Jimmy Blair when things were not working quite right just sitting[13] in the pilot's seat tapping his jaw with his flat hand; just that. Peter Woodham insisting on my putting on a Mae West; and turning up later, by a reversal of the usual process, with a beard, in Rome as stage-manager for Fay Compton. It will show my then abysmal ignorance of the services that when I got my first telegram (sorry; signal!) signed "Nabcatcher" I wondered what sort of a bird this was. Only much later, when I dared ask, was I told that this stood for Naval Air Base "Catcher". They lived, I believe because their Commanding Officer thought it was good for them, not in a requisitioned house but in tents on Kaitak Aerodrome in Kowloon, which could be quite incredibly muddy. In contrast their R.A.F. opposite numbers had a very comfortable house as a mess and I was asked (flying by Otter) to their house-warming cocktail party. The party was grand but my then hosts will perhaps forgive me if I say that my even greater pleasure was when Japanese prisoners the next morning came to tidy up and saluted every time they passed my chair.

The Japanese surrender brought a semi-funny story.[14] When, finally, my "colleague" was told to hand over to me his Consulate, he asked for an interview and got back a polite but curt note telling him to call next day.[15] I had told my boys not to make any demonstration but when the Japanese came in he was as white as a Japanese can be. Borrowing shamelessly from Marshal Foch I asked him what he had come for and he replied that he had come to surrender his Consulate. I said I would take over next day with my Chinese colleague and told him he could go. I then thought I would find out why he had looked so frightened. There had been no demonstration but every man, at the door or in the General Office had had a gun in full prominence. My colleague must have thought he was about to be killed. One or two Japanese did commit hari kari in Macao; the rest we sent gradually to Hongkong to internment in Stanley though one or two were in Macao at the time of my departure; they, no doubt, had financial backing, as well as political, from ex-enemy friends. The Consul, incidentally, had destroyed everything in his office except telephone directories and dictionaries. I regretted this; I particularly would have liked to have had his flag as a memento.

I would also have liked to have had a bit off a Japanese plane which landed in the Colony by mistake and was interned; I never enquired about the pilot because some of our lads might have dropped in some day and I wanted a precedent for having them left free. The four who did come, you remember, landed out of uniform and so could be handled as civilians anyhow. I kept the Japanese Consul in Macao longer than I should have done; I knew he was on short commons. When he finally got to Stanley however he wrote and thanked me for the courtesy and kindness with which he had been treated. Japanese property in Macao was a headache particularly as by the time I received orders to take it over with my Chinese colleague, lawyers had been earning good fees drawing up transfer documents so that it all now lay safely in neutral or Chinese names. This applied equally to real estate and to property like ships and wharves. That, I think, disposes of the Japanese story in Macao except to say that the Japanese who left for Hongkong gave a very different impression from the one they had given when they thought they were on top.

One final, totally undignified story; a little while before the end of the war José Lima and his wife Janet, who was British by birth, were visiting us after dinner; we must have been in high spirits as we put a telephone call through to the Japanese Consulate, insisted on speaking to the Consul personally and then said one sentence, "How are your battleships?" Childish but we liked it at the time.

Naval visits were frequent; big ships could not come because of the shallow water but we had sloops, corvettes, B.Y.M.S. (I think these are British Yard Mine-Sweeper), Air Sea Rescue launches and M.L.'s (Motor Launches; I believe they were classified as H.D.M.L. which I guess stands for Harbour Defence Motor Launches). The latter were our most frequent visitors and I think I knew their wardrooms as well as I knew my own sitting room. It did not, repeat not, surprise me much that they always had to come into port from patrol at weekends, carnivals, Easter and so on.

After a while we could talk to the M.L.'s at sea as I was provided with a set and an operator on the veranda. Apart from Official communication with Hongkong and Canton, whose American operator usually replied "Going to PX" (their canteen), we used the set for calling up the M.L.'s and suggesting parties. Hughie's joyful "Drunk or sober, I shall be there" often preluded a hectic evening.[16] My second operator, from the R.A.F., was called Horne, inevitably "Trader". One evening I tried to teach him fencing and, over-confidently, left off my jacket. Either my defence was bad or his methods unorthodox; I still have a four-inch scar on my right arm to prove it.

There were two main incidents connected with their visits which will be long remembered by the participants. One was a night operation in a big way. A dinner was being given for me at Skyline and in the middle of it we had a 'phone call that a British naval vessel was on the exterior breakwater.

Hughie Roskill commanding H.D.M.L. 1105 and I leapt into my car and even Hughie acknowledges he was scared by the way I drove; so was I. After that it was my turn to be scared. There was, sure enough, a British naval vessel on the rocks; she had been the property of the Governor of Macao, had been used by us after the war for piracy control and was being sent to Macao for return to the Governor as a good-will gesture. The gesture never came off; the youngster in charge of her had no maps which showed how far out to sea the breakwater ran, harbour-lighting had not been renewed, the breakwater was awash, and he ran head on into it. We were manoeuvering in the small space between the breakwaters and in point of fact bent a propeller and stripped some planking on them. Hughie was rowing or swimming to get the crew off the wrecked craft, at one moment our lights went off and someone managed to reverse a pump so that it looked as though water was entering the M.L.[17] There was also a fairly heavy sea running. In fact we were having fun; the trouble was that the young sub did not wish to leave the ship, his first command; in the end he realized it was hopeless and came aboard us where he was warmed up with a particularly vicious concoction of Hughie's known as a "Hongkong Telegraph". The ship shortly rolled off the breakwater and was never salvaged. The story, so far as we were concerned, finished the next morning with an incident which typifies the warm-heartedness of the Governor. The sub and I were on the wharf when H.E. arrived and the sub wanted to present his apologies to H.E. I went to the Governor and told him; he replied "Tell him not to worry; as a naval officer I know how such things happen easily; I too have put a ship aground". The last phrase was, I suspect, untrue but was added to make the sub feel better.

Another much calmer expedition was with Chris; an oil-lighter, a big one, was ashore opposite Melco power station after unloading. She was broadside on, bumping and the sea rising. All the necessary formalities to establish a salvage claim were completed, request of master for assistance and all, and off we went on a sunny morning, round the end of the breakwater and north past the reservoir and the Netherlands Harbour Works and then a creep round the corner into shallow water. I had gone along as self-styled "expert on local waters" and the M.L. drew 5 ft. 9 in. but we had her in 4 ft. 9 in. before we finished. No. 1 went across in a sampan and took the tow rope with him; he made fast and we went ahead the screws churning up the sand, praying there were no hidden rocks. Once round the corner and going south we relaxed and a bottle of whisky appeared magically to rest cosily in the voice-pipe. Then I discovered something; Chris was a poet and we had a lovely session swopping verses in the sun. The session was rudely interrupted as with a twang the tow broke just when we were turning in to approach between the breakwaters. There were visions of the lighter and No. 1 drifting into the China Sea never to be seen again but we passed another tow and were able to signal "Finished with engines" without further mishap. I should say the lighter was then, from rarity value, worth some £75,000. I believe the crew of the M.L. finally got about 2/6 each by the time Insurance Companies had negotiated and the Admiralty had taken its whack. I got nothing but you don't find a much more than competent poet every day.

These were the only two major incidents but we saw one M.L. or other almost every day and could never have too much of them.[18]

One story of a very unfortunate engineer lieutenant known to all of us as Rigor Mortis, a piratical type. One very crowded day in my sitting-room he was talking to a four-ring captain and was saying how pleased he was that by the expenditure of a couple of bottles of gin he had managed to avoid a passage in an uncomfortable trooper. The senior officer heard him out and then remarked bleakly "I am Captain (A)" or Administration, in fact the officer who had ordered him to go home on that trooper. I think Rigger was nearer living up to his nickname at that moment than he will ever be in his lifetime.

The Air Sea Rescue launches usually brought V.I.P.'s like Admiral Harcourt, then Governor of Hongkong, or General Festing[19] the G.O.C. that tower of a man with red hair and always a walking-stick for which the word stout was hardly adequate. These vessels of course had a fantastic power and one could see the immense V of the bow-wave coming over the horizon long before one could see the vessel herself. The other thing which used to surprise the Colony was that if a signal was received saying "arriving 1300 hours" that was the exact moment that she tied up.

And from the sublime in motor-driven craft to the slightly ridiculous, my own boat. One rainy day a party of officers including Commodore, Hongkong, arrived at low tide and had to come ashore from their launch in a sampan. As Commodore stepped ashore in the rain I remarked that this sort of thing could be avoided if I had my own motor boat. Whether the remark was operative or not the fact remains that a day or two later a landing-craft arrived and there was my sixteen-footer. She was not elegant then but I put her in the Portuguese Naval Yard and she came out "proper tiddly" in all the glory of new paint, with the Consulate badge each side of her bows and collapsible awnings fore and aft. She sailed out, still noisy, but resplendent with a Consul's flag (blue ensign with the Royal Arms in the fly) forward and a red ensign aft. She was useful in many ways. I handled her myself and she was beautiful to handle. Naturally trips in her after office were also popular and we had great fun with her and one somewhat shattering experience.

One night about midnight I found twelve seamen on the beach with their ship sailing next day at six in the morning. Their ship was lying well out beyond the breakwaters. So we piled aboard and off we went and in spite of a long rolling sea we made it in about an hour and came smartly alongside. The troops piled out and then the engine failed, absolutely dead. It was a stroke of luck for us that at this moment the ship's boat arrived and gave us a tow. But, right between the breakwaters, with a good sea running and a heavy wind from the west, her engine also died and that was two of us furiously fending ourselves off the breakwater, I even trying to make sail with my awnings; by the way the breakwater was no nice smooth bit of masonry; it was rocks piled irregularly on one another and they stuck out with sharp corners in every direction above and below sea-level; we were just where the Governor's launch had hit. Fortunately my "acting engineer" who was skipper of an M.L. had told his vessel to come out and look for us if we were overdue. She arrived and towed us in. Time about 3 a.m. Very unpleasant, but I liked it.

On another occasion my boat was extremely useful; I happened to be at San Januario hospital[20] when I spotted an American launch standing in at a dangerously high speed. I rushed down and got aboard my boat just as the American, by a miracle, got in through a small gap in the southern breakwater wall; the gap itself was small but the helmsman cannot have known that half of it had a wall below the surface to within three feet of that surface. I guided her to safe anchorage and went alongside to find aboard, of all people, Mr. Joeselyn, who had been American Consul-General in Hankow when I was there.

Another American vessel which came into our area was a much unhappier story. She was a landing craft loaded with kerosene and butter. Her crew took the ship out of Hongkong, sold the cargo and then sold the ship, which was later blockading or helping to blockade Macao. Their commercial transactions finished they decided to see life in Macao but by now signals were flying. I caught up with them in the early hours of the morning and warned them that unless they took the next boat back to Hongkong I would have them in a Portuguese prison. Three frightened boys took the next boat back and I heard horrific, but perhaps untrue, stories of their punishment.

Yet another American officer caused me some confusion. My staff merely announced "Captain Jones (or Smith)". I was busy and did not look up till a smart click of the heels raised my eyes to a very fine salute—by a woman. Remember we were not used to women in the Services. We had not seen such a thing before. An American admiral also turned up and I offered one of my staff to help him shop; he was anxious to refuse but I insisted politely saying frankly that I did not want markets spoilt by American "damn the price" buying. The admiral saw the point and very decently allowed himself to be shepherded.

Another "foreign" visitor was Admiral d'Aubignan of the French Naval Forces.[21] He arrived just as H.E. and I were on the cathedral steps waiting to go in for some celebration. So the strange solution was made of H.M. Consul deputizing on the wharf for the Governor of Macao. Looking back on it perhaps H.E. will not mind my saying that this incident reflected the close personal and official relations between us. My deputizing for him did not seem incongruous.

Another party was a group of midshipmen from *Duke of York* who sailed a pinnace across. I received a telegram from Admiral (now Lord) Fraser asking me to "keep a fatherly eye" on them.[22] I wired back that I would do my best but "prefer term brotherly". The midshipmen duly arrived including, I should think, the tallest in the navy; how or if he had slept during the night afloat I don't know. We gave them a Chinese meal and they were then more than ready for bed. They went off again next day and arrived safely in Hongkong though I was more than relieved when I heard they had rejoined their ship. Pirates, after all, were not inactive and ransom has been asked.

The largest single official party to come over was the party to open the N.A.A.F.I.[23] leave centre. The Hongkong press has it that this was General Festing's idea and I know I told them so. But a later perusal of my files showed me a very much earlier letter from me to Hongkong putting the proposal forward. Anyhow it doesn't matter whose was the credit. H.E. as usual was a tower of strength and owing to his intervention we secured the Bela Vista, once a hotel, then a refugee centre, now again a hotel, finer than ever before.[24] H.E. was unable to be at the opening but Madame Teixeira unveiled a notice-board recalling the age-old friendship between the countries and what I believe to be the only leave centre in a place where we had no troops stationed, was open. It got off to a slow start but it was soon in the fullest swing owing to the untiring work of the W.V.S.,[25] of an excellent cook, and of the Provost Sergeant-Major whose tact was supreme. The lads came over for five days, had early morning tea in bed, breakfast, elevenses, lunch, tea, supper and late sandwiches for about five shillings a day. On their last evening there was always a dance and no lack of partners; these were great occasions. I used to go and help at the reception-desk and try and put in a hand where I could. We loved having the lads over and they loved being there (Appendix 6). There were no rules, to all intents and purposes; they could come in and go to bed when they felt inclined and so on; a considerable change from barracks; but we never really had any trouble from those who came. They behaved most decorously without failing to enjoy themselves.

Of course we had other visitors, hundreds of them and we tried to do our best for them. I remember well Colonel Ryde [Ride],[26] by normal avocation a professor of biology but then head of the army aid group I have mentioned, seated on the floor with a couple of other high-ranking officers playing dice on a low Chinese table. I remember an Easter when Good Friday saw forty, Saturday fifty and Sunday sixty officers of all ranks and forces in my house. I was, of course, completely defeated by the various forms of slang; it was also on this occasion that I swore I would no more make any attempt to remember names or make introductions. I remember a party of WRNS[27] the officers of which annoyed me; 3 officers and 3 ratings had to take four rooms because one officer could not sleep in a double room with a rating. That peeved me. But I was so very seldom peeved at anything and the way our people got on with the Portuguese was nobody's business. I don't think those who visited Macao will forget it.

We had also our repatriates to Macao; Fletch came back with Marjorie and re-assumed management of Melco; he had been controlling war-like stores and she had developed into a sculptress as well as having done war work. And there appeared the almost legendary Gellion,[28] of whom I was scared before I met him, and for whom I cared greatly when I met him. I have mentioned Melco as being one of my worst headaches; roughly, not to go into too much detail, the authorities said they must take the Company over or the Japanese would give no fuel and the city would be without light and water. I was a little sceptical; after all the Portuguese were in general keen to get into their own hands various foreign concessions. The joke was on me, and to some extent on the local authorities; the whole thing was fought and settled at a very much higher level than ours and after the war the Company came back to us as had been intended all along. The joke was on us in Macao, on me because of my furibund righteous indignation, on at least the second rank of local officials because they thought they had got the Company for good.

Anyhow Gellion came back, seemed grateful for my quite futile efforts on the Company's behalf and re-opened Skyline to take its pre-war place as the non-official (and even official from the point of view of lavishness) social highlight of the colony. Freddie liked poker and a game was sure to follow dinner at Skyline; but stakes were by arrangement amongst the players and no one was ever obliged to play for more than he felt he could afford; nor was the game too serious, nor, as was the Portuguese manner, was every other hand a variation on straight poker. Freddie was and no doubt is, the most genuinely hospitable person I know.

He was good enough to lend me Skyline with its wide terraces and lawns for the King's Birthday celebration in 1946. I am not sure that orders, wartime orders, were still not in force against official celebration; but in Macao it just <u>had</u> to be done. (And looking at that sentence, I feel it epitomizes much of our activities in Macao; they might be against orders but they just <u>had</u> to be done.) At the reception after champagne for the toast I served Pym's No. 1. This had surprising results amongst the high Portuguese officials and their wives, some of whom thought it was a soft drink.

All this time, of course, we were demobilizing, recording and generally clearing up. My staff fell as they were no longer necessary as they had mounted on becoming necessary. My orders finally came; I was to hand over a fortnight after the arrival of my relief and he was due on the 4th July. I asked Mr. Hall, our Consul-General in Canton, to come down and see our work which he most kindly did. I begged for more time; my graphs of expenditure, numbers under my care, comparative staff, disease incidence and so on could only be finished by September. There was inexorability, my complete statistical picture was unfinished; I had scored 99 and the captain had declared the innings closed.

One thing I like to feel is that I never hauled my flag down; by a strange coincidence on the day I handed over there was a typhoon which blew the flag from the masthead and I kept the tattered remains. They hang behind me now with our badge and that of the American Relief upon them. And before them hangs the gold and silver diplomatic sword subscribed for not only by the refugees but by many others inside and outside Macao who had never even entered my office.²⁹

Then of course the farewell parties concluding with one at the house from 10 a.m. till the moment I left for the ship. A crowd, including H.E. at the wharf, my flag at the masthead. "For he's a jolly good fellow"; a hard fight against tears. The ship draws away to cheering and *Auld Lang Syne*; as I pass the Consulate I dip my flag in last salute. Macao falls away in the distance, perhaps forever.

My tale is done. *Nunc dimittis*.

      H.M.S. *Ranee*   Rome
      August 1946.   January 1949

Appendix 1

SOUTH CHINA MORNING POST, THE HONG KONG TELEGRAPH, MONDAY, SEPTEMBER 3, 1945.

MACAO'S GREETINGS

British Consul Sends Congratulations

KEPT THE FLAG FLOATING

The British Consul-General, Mr. Reeves, has sent a letter to Lieut.-Governor H.E. Mr. F. C. Gimson, expressing his feelings at the relief of Hongkong.

He states: "After all this time my most sincere greetings and congratulations, both my own and all those under my charge, whether British subjects, Government servants or just ex-residents of Hongkong ......

"If such a thing be possible could you convey our rejoicing in their freedom to Hongkong? We have felt very deeply for you in the last years and, in fact, you have never been out of thoughts. If you feel that we have done little to help you, please believe that it was not our fault. Circumstances very much beyond our control have been responsible.

"It is, naturally, only by the mercy of Providence that we have been able to keep the British flag floating loyally here. I have felt very deeply the events in Hongkong of the last few days when your flag has gone up again. Our hearts are full as yours must be.

"May our re-united family never again be divided and nothing again separate the communities in these neighbouring colonies."

Appendix 2

Consul Cheered, Chaired

V-J DAY CELEBRATIONS AT MELCO CLUB

Melco Club on Sunday was the scene of gay festivity when the United Nations celebrated V-J Day and the spirit in which everyone joined in the activities of the day brought back memories of those "happy days" which, by God's grace, are once more to return to us soon.

Sunday's celebrations were as much an occasion for rejoicing as an opportunity to pay homage to the two men who have done so much for the refugees—His Excellency the Governor, Comd. Gabriel Mauricio Teixeira, and H.B.M. Consul, Mr. John Pownall Reeves.

The reception given them was spontaneous and sincere and these two will always be remembered by refugees—be they British, Portuguese, Indian or Chinese.

His Excellency the Governor, who was accompanied by Madame Teixeira, was received by Mr. Reeves and members of the Committee on his arrival. In the official party were also Capt. J. Silva e Costa and Mr. Pedro José Lobo. On the official party entering the hall of the club the Portuguese National Anthem was played by a band conducted by Eddie Guzman after which H.E. the Governor, accompanied by Mr. Reeves went up to the stage.

Opening Address

Addressing the gathering Mr. Reeves said:

"Your Excellency, our guests, ladies and gentlemen:

"On behalf of the Committee I thank you and all our guests for the honour they have done us by coming here this afternoon. By miraculous statesmanship, Sir, you have kept Macau neutral to the great benefit of us all. But we have sensed where your personal sympathies lay; you have felt for us in our black days and now you rejoice with us in our Victory.

"The flags of the United Nations have gone a long way since those black days but now are planted firmly in Berlin and in Tokyo where they will remain till the lesson is learnt that aggression simply does not pay.

"But Victory means more to most of us than that. It means return to our homes and to our lives. On behalf of my diminishing refugee family I thank the Government of Macau for all it has done for the citizens of the United Nations. And for myself I wish you each and every one—prosperity and peace."

Governor's Reply

In reply His Excellency the Governor expressed his thanks for all the kind references to him. He stated that from the beginning his heart was always with the Allies (Loud cheers), but his duty was to maintain the neutrality of the Colony at all costs.

In conclusion His Excellency wished all the refugees a speedy return to their homes and reunion with their families. He wished them all luck and expressed the hope that they will remember Macau where they will always find friends.

After the speeches Andy Hidalgo and his band played the dedicated song, "A Million Thanks to you, Your Excellency." The official party then went out to the lawn to watch some of the sports events which were by then in good progress.

Consul Chaired

During the tea dance the Starlettes rendered several of the latest song hits. The tea dance was well patronised and the floor was packed. An excellent exhibition of hula-hula was given by Baby Cespedes who presented, in true Hawaiian fashion, His Excellency and Mme. Teixeira and Mr. Reeves with Hawaiian "leis."

On the departure of Mr. Reeves, towards the end of the festivities, he was chaired by the gathering to the tune of "For He's a Jolly Good Fellow." He left amidst scenes of wild cheering.

Victory Punch

The whole programme of the day was carried out smoothly and provided fine entertainment for the spectators in the early part of the afternoon. The bar, which was set up outside on the lawn, proved a great attraction and was well patronized. The "Victory Punch" was by far the most popular drink.

The other bands in attendance during the day were Pabling Cespedes and his band which played on the lawn and the South Sea Serenaders which played during the billiards exhibition.

Appendix 3

MR REEVES EULOGISED BY HONGKONG PORTUGUESE COMMUNITY

The high esteem in which Mr. J.P. Reeves, H.B.M. Consul in Macau, is held was fully demonstrated on Wednesday at Melco Club where Hongkong Portuguese refugees gathered in large numbers to pay tribute to the man who has done and is still doing so much for the welfare of those who came to take refuge in this Colony.

In token of their appreciation, Mr Reeves was presented with a gold pocket watch which was inscribed by all the members of the Portuguese community here.

His Excellency the Governor, Comdr. Gabriel Mauricio Teixeira, accompanied by Lieut. Guedes de Andrade, and Mr José Pedro Lobo were present at the function.

On the respective arrivals of His Excellency the Governor and Mr Reeves the Portuguese and British national anthems were played.

Mr A.A. Lopes
Addressing the gathering Mr A.A. Lopes, President of the Commission Executiva de Refugiasdos said:

"Your Excellency, His Britannic Majesty's Consul, Ladies and Gentlemen:

"Having endured for over three and a half years the hardships of war, which, but for the providential and wise leadership of our beloved Governor, would have been unbearable, we rejoice with His Excellency, now that the blessing of Peace has been restored to the world; and although we have more than once assured His Excellency of our eternal gratitude, this assurance cannot be repeated often enough. It is deply [sic] rooted in our grateful hearts.

"Inspired by these same sentiments we are gathered here today to pay homage to His Britannic Majesty's Representative in Macau, Mr John

Pownall Reeves at a moment when our hearts are still glowing with joy over the glorious victory of the United Nations and when they are still turned to Almighty God in a fervent prayer of thanksgiving.

"Joy and Gratitude—these are the two predominant notes in our song of praise and thanks!

"We rejoice with Great Britain, the champion of liberty, justice and fair-play, under whose flag we lived, laboured, and fought. For one whole century our destiny has been bound up with that of the British Colony of Hongkong—our adopted home and the birthplace of our children, some of whom have even given up their lives in defence of their precious heritage.

"Ever since the day when the hazards of war made it necessary for our battered community to abandon and to seek refuge in Macau—the blessed land of our forefathers, where we were received with open arms—never for a moment have we wavered. We have remained firm in our faith in the Allied cause and loyal to the British Crown longing all the time for the happy day of liberation which came at last.

"But the melody of jubilation runs in perfect harmony with that of gratitude. We are grateful to all who have extended a helping hand to us in the hour of need; we are grateful to those who have given material and spiritual assistance; we are grateful to all who have rescued us from starvation, sickness and death."

Guest of Honour

"We have as our guest of honour today the man whom we owe an enormous debt of gratitude. We all know what Mr John Reeves has done for us, but I doubt if anyone could put in suitable words what that means, for it is something too deep—it is felt but cannot be verbally expressed. For Mr Reeves is one of those rare souls who give **with a heart**. I tell you that it is a brazen injustice to say that he has done these things of mere duty or courtesy … No! … He has been animated throughout by worthier motive for in each one of us he has seen a friend, a brother in distress.

"It is for this reason that he has endeared himself to us and that we have come to love and respect him. We see in Mr Reeves the perfect type of Englishman, whom no one can fail to admire.

"Mr Reeves: We know how inadequate is this demonstration of our respect and admiration for you. But I assure you that what I cannot interpret in words is deeply felt in each of our hearts; and I ask you to accept this souvenir, not for its intrinsic value, but as a token of sincere appreciation, esteem and gratitude of Hongkong Portuguese refugees in Macau."

As Mr Lopes presented the watch to Mr Reeves the band struck up "For He's a Jolly Good Fellow" in which the entire gathering joined in.

Appendix 3

H.E. the Governor

His Excellency the Governor associated himself with Mr Lopes' remarks that Mr Reeves, in carrying out his work of the past three years was not only fulfilling his duties but what he did was spontaneous and from his heart.

His Excellency said that he was very glad that the Portuguese refugees had taken this opportunity to pay homage to Mr Reeves for they would not be true Portuguese if they had failed to do so.

Mr J.P. Reeves

Mr Reeves, replying said that he was surprised by the occasion and that he felt embarrassed in accepting the gift. Recalling the arrival of the first refugees in Macau Mr Reeves said he had seen the refugees arrive and the poor condition they were in then. He had seen them organise themselves into sports teams, concerts and, in fact, all the activities that make up communal life.

He could not let the opportunity pass, said Mr Reeves, without a mention of the Volunteers. Although Macau had many rumours he had not heard of any bad rumour of the Volunteers.

In conclusion Mr Reeves said that if the Hongkong Portuguese showed the same determination and courage, co-operation and endurance as the Volunteers had done he felt sure that they would have in the future, as he heartily wished them, prosperity and happiness.

Volunteer Presentation

Capt. J.S. Rodrigues, on behalf of the members of the H.K.V.D.C., presented Mr Reeves with a beautifully painted scroll by C.S.M. Baptista in appreciation of what Mr Reeves has done "not only for the Volunteers but also for their families who are in Macau."

Dancing, which had started earlier in the afternoon was then resumed. Music was supplied by Art. Carneiro's Rivera Orchestra. During the interval the Starlettes, under direction of Art. Carneiro, rendered several popular songs.

Appendix 4

BRITISH EURASIANS PAY TRIBUTE TO CONSUL

Members of the community of British Eurasians met in large numbers at a reception at Grand Hotel yesterday afternoon when the opportunity was taken to present Mr. J.P. Reeves, British Consul with a fire screen in token of gratitude and esteem for all he has done for them.

Mr. C. G. Anderson, the chairman of the association presided and was supported by other members of the Committee.

The hall was specially decorated for the occasion and Ed. Guzman and his band supplied the music for dancing.

Mr. Anderson
"Mr. Reeves and Fellow Members:
 "With the war happily ended, one's thoughts are inclined to take a flight backwards to alight upon one's vicissitudes as well as those factors enabled one to survive. In counting their blessings the British Eurasian Community here finds that one of them lies in medical and financial aid provided by the Government, while another is found in the fact that throughout our war years with Japan, our Country has been represented in Macau by John Pownall Reeves, who honours us by accepting our invitation today. When adversity overtook us and necessity dictated fleeing from a home of which many of us knew no other, we arrived at this sanctuary, which is another of our blessings, to find our Consulate in a rather unhealthy neighbourhood with its insect as well as human pests and our Consul, a gentle son of Cambridge, almost entirely hemmed in by occupied territory, with an automatic at hip and bulldog determination to carry on with his arduous duties at all costs. And there was a sigh of relief over his personal safety when our little plot of England with its rose bushes and coy violets was, later, located along the Praia.

 "Ladies and gentlemen, in meeting our honoured guest, one's first

Appendix 4

impressions are his sincerity and friendliness. Shortly afterwards his strong and all-embracing humanitarianism began to manifest itself in his deep concern for all British subjects, and, a little later, when his contributions towards the wellbeing of everyone under his charge came fast and furious, he found a place in our hearts where he has remained ever since and where he will remain long afterwards. He has looked after our spiritual, educational as well as sporting needs. He has shared with us in our little joys and has felt with us in our hardships. He has even shown to us how to or how not to play hockey and, by this I mean, of course, that on the hockey field he has upheld a high standard of British sportsmanship. One early morning a few months ago when your chairman, much exercised in mind and with dark foreboding at heart, sought Mr. Lobo in his office on account of the acute rice situation, he found Mr. Reeves there on the same mission, which, unlike that of Sir Neville Henderson, did not fail. To our Association he has been a true and valued friend. In fact he has done all he could for us and, indeed, more than what one can reasonably expect of him, thereby winning both our admiration and our gratitude. If, today, I be permitted to express a slight tinge of regret it is that, when the good old country took it into its head to collect an empire, it did not give sufficient thought to the paramount importance of filling its Consular and Colonial Services with men of the caliber of Mr. J. P. Reeves and Dr. Selwyn Clarke, men of sympathetic understanding and of sterling character unknown to snobbery. Such men will provide the necessary stimulus, to the different sections of the British Community widely scattered within the four seas, to lead fuller lives, to realise themselves and to fulfill their destiny—a consummation deeply desired by His Majesty the King and by His Sire of Blessed Memory according to their speeches to the Empire and their Empire broadcasts—as small but staunch supports to the British Throne.

"Sir, the time has now arrived for us to part and, before we part, I beg of you to tender the gratitude of my community to our Government for its help, without which the lot of many of us would have been simply unthinkable. In the name of the Committee and members of the Association of British Eurasians of Macau and of our children, I have the honour to ask you to accept this souvenir as a token of our great respect for you as our Consul and our kind regards for you as a man. Our gift is both humble and inadequate; but if only a small part of our good wishes accompany it comes true, this screen, wherever it may be—in the home or in the Yamen in Macau or elsewhere—will serve as a sure shield against the slings and arrows of misfortune that may afflict one who, though young in years, has by his remarkable achievements as a war-time British Consul in a neutral Colony, endeared himself to thousands of different nationalities and who is justly entitled to be considered a credit to his family, to his University and to his Country."

Appendix 4

Reeves' Reply

In reply Mr. Reeves thanked the chairman for his kind words and for the help given him by the Eurasian Community. He added that a head depended on the community as much as the community depended on its head.

He mentioned the fact that one of the community's older members was among the first to return to Hongkong for important work and another younger member had been engaged in important work in his office for some years.

He expressed his thanks to all and wished everyone the best.

Appendix 5

A VOZ DE MACAU 22 de Outubro de 1945

Festa de homenagem

Com numerosa assistência onde predominaram os membros das Communidades filipina e sino-americana, realizou-se ontem, à tarde, no Clube Melco, a anunciada festa de homenagem e de gratidão das duas citadas comunidades ao Cônsul da Inglaterra sr. J. P. Reeves pelos serviçes e protecção prestados durante os criticos anos da guerra.

Foi uma festa extremamente simpática e mais uma a ajuntar às outras em homenagem ao simpático Cônsul que vê agora recompensados os seus esforços e os seus trabalhos particularmente árduos e dificeis com que teve de arcar durante quási quatro anos.

A festa iniciou-se às 15 horas. Meia hora depois chegou o sr. J. P. Reeves que, acompanhado pela Comissão Organizadora, ocupeu o lugar de homa na mesa que estava armada num dos lades da sala.

Depois dos acordes dos hinos inglês e americano executados pela orquestra sob a regência de Andy Hidalgo, fêz uso da palavra, em nome da comunidade sino-americana, o sr. Nathan Young.

Discursou, seguidamente o sr. R. J. Manalac, que representava a Comunidade Filpina.

Ambos os oradores salientaram os magnificos serviços prestados pelo homenageado a quem apresantaram os seus agradecimentos *utos* em nome das respectivas comunidades.

Em seguida, foi oferecido ao sr. Reeves um lindo e artistico escudo de prata que lhe foi entregue pelas meninas Corazon Manalac e Joyce Young.

Finda esta cerimónia, os convidados dançaram até às 19 horas acompanhados pela magnifica orquestra do sr. Andy Hidalgo, havendo entre os números de dança várias exibições de canto a dança pelas irmâs Tavares, Telma e Carmen, pela senhorinha Lorna Tavares e pela pequenita Baby Cespedes, quo nâo obstante os seus verdes anos, demonstrou grande habilidade.

A Voz de Macau, associando-se à simpatica homenagem cumprimenta o distinto homenageado e agradece o gentil convite quo lhe foi endereçade.

Tribute Party

Yesterday afternoon, in the presence of a large audience, predominantly from the Philippine and Sino-American communities, the previously announced gathering took place at the Melco Club so that the two communities could pay homage and express their gratitude to the British Consul, Mr. J. P. Reeves, for the services and protection he rendered during the critical years of the war.

It was a very pleasant gathering and yet another to add to others in honour of the popular Consul who now was being rewarded for his effort and particularly arduous and difficult work that he had carried out for nearly four years.

The reception started at 3 p.m., half an hour after Mr. Reeves arrived accompanied by the Organizing Committee, and had taken the place of honour at the table which was arranged at one side of the hall.

After the playing of the British and American national anthems by the orchestra under Andy Hidalgo, Mr. Nathan Young spoke in the name of the Sino-American community. He was followed by Mr. Manalac who represented the Filipino community.

Both speakers stressed the magnificent service rendered by the guest of honour and presented their thanks in the name of their respective communities.

Mr. Reeves was then presented with a beautiful and artistic silver shield which was handed to him by the young girls Corazon Manalac and Joyce Young.

After the ceremony, there was dancing until 19.00 accompanied by the magnificent orchestra of Andy Hidalgo. Between the dance numbers, there were performances of song and dance numbers from the Tavares sisters, Telma and Carmen, by Mrs. Lorna Tavares and by the little Baby Cespedes, who despite her youth demonstrated great ability.

The Voice of Macao is happy to associate itself with the friendly tribute to the distinguished guest of honour and also expresses its thanks for the kind invitation which was sent to the paper.

Appendix 6

MACAO LEAVE CENTRE VERY POPULAR

More than 300 servicemen from the Hong Kong area have already spent a leave at the new NAAFI/EFI leave centre in Macao. The centre is the former Bela Vista Hotel and is the only leave establishment in non-Allied or non-occupied territory.

The limited number of men fortunate enough to obtain the leave speak highly of the comfort and amenities of the centre and find the Portuguese colony interesting and pleasantly quiet.

The centre originated from a suggestion of Major General F. W. Festing, G.O.C., Hong Kong. The scheme was taken up by welfare workers with the assistance of the British Consul in Macao, Mr. J. P. Reeves, and the use of the Bela Vista was offered by the Governor of Macao, Commander Gabriel M. Teixeira.

"Beautiful View" is well situated on a hill at the southern and [sic] of the Colony and commands a full view of the harbour. When taken over by NAAFI/EFI it was entirely redecorated and refurnished and was officially opened in March.

Full hotel service is accorded the men on leave who pay only a nominal amount for the five days' stay. Each party at present consists of about 40 men from all Services but it is hoped to increase the figure to 60.

Well Organized

Management of the hotel—which has 30 rooms—is well organized and there is a minimum of restrictions, the lists of "Don'ts" familiar to Servicemen being noticeable by their absence. Men may wear civilian clothes if they wish and service extends to shoe-cleaning and the time-honoured morning cup of tea served in the bedrooms.

Four meals a day are served by a competent kitchen, a beer ration is available, and guests may be entertained. During each leave period, a football match is arranged with a Portuguese police team, a swimming party visits nearby Coloane island, and the centre holds a dance on the final evening of the stay. Such considerations make a Serviceman's leave very enjoyable and earns his full appreciation. The centre also caters for men on leave from H.M. ships calling at Macao.

Governor's Interest

With its quiet, old world atmosphere, wide avenidas lined with banyans, old forts and similar reminders of the past, Macao—oldest foreign Colony in the Far East—has plenty to interest the British Serviceman. He also learns of the Colony's precarious position during the war, when it was virtually surrounded by the Japanese, when it gave refuge to 10,000 British and American subjects.

The Governor of Macao, a Commander in the Portuguese Navy, takes a particular interest in the ships and men of the Royal Navy. He visited H.M.S. *Plym*, which called at Macao four hours after the surrender, and recently six B.Y.M.S. and three other mine-sweepers went to the Colony, the largest number of Royal Naval ships to visit at the same time. Both Admiral Lord Fraser, C.-in-C., British Pacific Fleet, and Vice Admiral Sir Cecil Harcourt, C.-in-C., Hong Kong have visited Macao.

The Governor has inspected the leave centre and wrote in the visitors' book " ... to all the boys ... we have been praying and well-wishing for them during the war ... we are thankful to them for what they have done."

Most Enjoyable

Bela Vista is under the management of Sergeant G. Wiley, of Sheffield, who had previously spent three years in Bermuda doing similar work. He is assisted by three members of the Women's Voluntary Service and has a local staff numbering 30. Mrs. D. Dalton, W.V.S., has flown several thousand miles on Service welfare work, and opened clubs and canteens in Malaya after re-occupation.

Her two colleagues at the centre, Miss Evelyn Shaw and Miss Haulwen Llewellyn, whose homes are in England, served at a jungle reinforcement camp in India and opened the Union Jack Club in Hong Kong.

The Bela Vista's visitors' book is already page after page of testimony to the success of the centre with such remarks as: "My most enjoyable leave."

Appendix 7

MACAU, SEPTEMBER 16, 1945   VOL. 1 NO. 19

HIGH TRADITION OF THE CONSULAR SERVICE MAINTAINED
BY MR. J. P. REEVES

*Unceasing Labour for the Welfare of Refugees
Will Not Be Forgotten*

Among the great services which millions of persons turn to in times of stress is that known as the British Consular Service. In an Empire covering a great part of the land mass of the world, with commercial and social relations in every other country, it is necessary that the representatives of His Britannic Majesty should be individuals possessing special qualifications in a very pronounced degree.

Of all the members of this Service during the War just ended, it is more than likely that few of his colleagues were called upon to face such problems as John Pownall Reeves, the genial British Consul in Macau. Few have tackled those problems with such enthusiasm and with so much interest in the welfare of those who looked to him for guidance and help.

Due to his efforts many women and children are alive today, and in the summing up of the success attending his efforts it will be seen that Mr. Reeves served his King and his fellow men far more than the mere letter of his instructions might have dictated. For this reason, the British have reason to be proud of their Consul who held this office in Macau during the difficult years that have just ended.

Hazardous Years

Looking back on those years, the most hazardous through which Macau has passed, it is indeed gratifying that the British should have, as Consul here, a man who rose to the occasion. It can indeed be stated that there was in

Macau a representative of Great Britain who knew how to maintain, with dignity and resource, the prestige of the British while he labored unceasingly under the most trying conditions for the welfare of those who came seeking his help.

Sympathy for his fellows, farsightedness in planning for dark and difficult days, dynamic in encouraging others to do their little bit for the community as well as for the common cause, resourceful in meeting ticklish situations, a good sportsman in every sense of the word, cut off from his fellow countrymen and standing alone as it were in the midst of a disintegrating world, he held the British flag to the mast in this little neutral Portuguese Colony, a symbol of courage and fortitude for all men to see.

Tower of Strength

Looking back on those dismal days when the whole world seemed crumbling, when the *Prince of Wales* and the *Renown* [sic] went down, when Hongkong fell on the sad Christmas day, when Singapore fell, when Allies were driven from the East Indies, and the Japanese were at the very door of Australia, he stood like a tower of strength inspiring his fellow countrymen as well as Portuguese and other friends who never wavered in their confidence as to the final outcome of the struggle.

Mr. Reeves has come to fill a place therefore in the history of Macau during the War, and all the activities which were created around the British refugees, who sought shelter in Macau and were generously admitted by Governor Teixeira, owe much to Mr. Reeves. Relief work was one of the principal contributions made by Mr. Reeves to the cause of the suffering human beings and its state that through the enormous remittances which he applied for and secured from the British Government a substantial contribution was made by him to the economic life of Macau.

The total number of those drawing British relief in Macau exceeded 9,000 persons. Connected with the work of relief there was the additional service of the medical office, with Hongkong doctors engaged to carry out their duties among their Hongkong fellows. For this Mr. Reeves expended large sums and spared himself not at all to achieve the best possible results with the material available.

Free School

A free school for the poorer children, a milk supply for needy children as long as it was possible to maintain this service, cheap rice when prices in the local market rose to exorbitant rates, were a few of the most obvious of the services which Mr. Reeves established in Macau.

All residents will recall the great efforts to secure funds for local charities. In this Mr. Reeves, enthusiastically seconded by Mrs. Reeves, contributed much to the good cause of charity in Macau.

Nor was Mr. Reeves' work limited to that of relief. There must have been, besides, much of a nature which is not divulged, for upon the cessation of hostilities Mr. Reeves was the recipient of a congratulatory telegram from his immediate superior H.B.M. Ambassador at Lisbon, expressing his gratitude to Mr. Reeves and his helpers for the work which he had so excellently performed throughout the difficult years of the war and the devotion [with] which he maintained the interests of his Government. The British Foreign Office has also shown its appreciation by a special message reading: "With the fighting in the Far East now at an end we take this opportunity of informing you that we have watched with great admiration the courage and devotion to duty which you have displayed and also your staff in such difficult circumstances. Your activities have been worthy of the Service."

Biography
John Pownall Reeves was born at Blackheath, London, on April 7, 1909, and as his name shows his father comes from old English stock.

His mother was Norman-French, being a native of the Channel Islands. He was educated at a preparatory school at St. Leonards-on-Sea whence he obtained a scholarship to Haileybury. This being the old training school for the East India Company, he feels he has a traditional association with Macau and has always shown interest in the history of the activities of the old John Company.

From Haileybury he went to Peterhouse, Cambridge, where he rowed and played hockey for the college. He had been destined for the Navy but not being able to pass the eyesight test he determined instead to serve the Government abroad and concentrated his studies on modern languages. The Consular Service gained, therefore, by this circumstance and he entered the China Consular Service and was posted to Peking. After studying Chinese for two years he was transferred to Hankow where he spent the next three years. While in Hankow he married Miss Rhoda Murray-Kidd, of a well-known family in Shanghai, and the following year a daughter was born.

"For a Rest"
He left Hankow by a special train for Canton under a somewhat doubtful safe conduct by the Japanese, the trip taking four days and not being destitute of excitement in the form of machine-gunning, bombing and acute food shortage. After home leave he returned to Mukden where for a while, he was Acting Consul General. From Mukden he received orders to come to Macau, being ordered there, as he grimly remarks, "for a rest."

In June 1941, Mr. Reeves arrived in Macau and he took office from Mr. H.D. Bryan on June 7. His staff then consisted of only one assistant—a steno-typist secretary—but this gradually increased and it now numbers 150. Six months after hostilities broke out in the Far East he lost contact with his superiors stationed in various parts of China.

On March 13, 1945, an acknowledgement of Mr. Reeves' invaluable

Appendix 7

service came from his Government. The British Foreign Office conferred upon him a double honour: they upgraded his post to full Consul, notwithstanding the rule that there should be no promotion in the Consular Service during the war. Telegrams of congratulations on this promotion came from H.B.M. Embassies at Lisbon and Chunking. Greetings both official and unofficial poured into H.B.M. Consulate, Macau, from all parts of the city.

Interest in Sport

Apart from his official duties, Mr. Reeves has played a prominent part in the sporting life of Macau during his years here. He was largely responsible for the reorganization of the Macau Hockey Club. He represented Hongkong in the Interport hockey matches and has turned out as often as his many duties allowed him to play. He took a close interest in all other organized sporting competitions in which Hongkong refugees participated.

Mr. Reeves' indefatigable efforts on behalf of the refugees under his charge will never be forgotten by the refugee community and all others who have known him. That he may long be spared to continue his splendid work and be blessed with many years of good health and happiness are the sincere wishes of all sections of the community.

Many Friends

Among the Portuguese, Chinese and other nationalities in Macau he has made many friends and admirers and it is certain that he will be long remembered by Macau for his charming personality, kindhearted generosity and for the part he played in Macau during a most difficult period. All those who know Mr. J. P. Reeves know that he will never forget Macau and the trying times which he contributed so greatly to alleviate—**J.M.B.**

Appendix 8

CHUNKING, Aug. 13: One of the most interesting stories [of] the Far East war will come from British Consul John Pownall Reeves who, since Pearl Harbour, has been isolated [on] the Portuguese island of Macao, 40 miles from Hongkong.

His Consulate is functioning next door to the Japanese Consulate.

An evacuee from Macau says that Reeves plays hockey with the Portuguese with a revolver strapped to his body and igno[res] Japanese spectators on the touchline.

Appendix 9

LOS ANGELES TIMES, SUNDAY, DEC. 30, 1945

CHINESE WANT BRITISH RULE FOR HONG KONG

HONG KONG, Dec. 29

Britain's century-old investment in Hong Kong is reaping dividends in native loyalty.

Almost alone among foreign held colonies, this Pacific outpost of empire trade so far has escaped the spreading fires of rebellion and revolt against the white man's rule in Southeastern Asia.

There have been no battles for independence here, no mass uprisings to throw out the "white master" on his ear. Order prevails, and Queens Road, the main thoroughfare, is as peaceful as Piccadilly, and as crowded as Times Square. There are plenty of exploding Chinese firecrackers as natives seek to blow the devil off their trail, but no grenade bursts to get the white man off their neck.

Want British Rule

As a matter of fact, while the rest of Southeastern Asia is rampaging to be rid of foreign political and economic dominations, most Chinese in Hong Kong don't want the British to pull out and permit this beautiful rock-crowned island to return to China's control. At least they don't want it to revert to China just now.

Of course the British certainly have no present intention of yielding this empire gem to other hands, but the quiet support they are receiving from the majority of Chinese here is tribute to their colonial administration of the sea gateway to all South China.

Bread and Butter

There are several reasons for this support. Chinese civil servants could be expected to back their present bread and butter. But support is equally

Appendix 9

strong among educated Chinese who, by virtue of birth here, are British subjects accustomed to British standards of justice, order and stability.

These qualities are appreciated by Hong Kong's large trading population, which fears that Chinese control might bring disruption of business and dissension and civil war to the island. They have had enough of war's chaos and now they want a return to peace and prosperity.

Earned Gratitude

Then, too, Britain earned considerable good will and gratitude by standing by the native population as best it could during the period of Japanese conquest. Several thousand Chinese who made their way to near-by Portuguese Macao during the war were given subsistence allowances by the British Consul on no other proof of British citizenship than sworn statements that they were born in Hong Kong.

"When China is completely unified under one government, matters would be different," one well-educated Chinese said. "But now we would like things to remain as they are."

In other words, they are content with Britain's bread until China can offer them cake.

Appendix 10

THE HONG KONG SUNDAY HERALD, SEPTEMBER 9, 1945

9000 Cared for in Macao

UNTIRING WORK BY BRITISH CONSUL

The story of activities of the British relief organisation in Macao, which apart from looking after the welfare of 9,000 people, aided many to escape. Both from Macao itself and Hongkong camps, is told in a very modest manner by Mr. A. Swemmeleer, who is now in the colony from Macao in order to find out about living accommodation in view of the many requests from Hongkong for the transfer of relatives and friends from Macao. He is also here to make arrangements for the despatch of food stuffs from Macao to Hongkong.

The organisation commenced on a small scale but it was not long before it found its resources severely taxed and requests had to made regularly for an increase in the monthly allowance from the British government—at first it was five hundred sterling and at the beginning of August this year it was approaching five thousand five hundred. As many as 1,000 people were suddenly placed under their care, so that they were always behind hand from a financial point of view, due to the length of time which elapsed between an appeal for increased funds and actual receipt of that increase.

British citizens and their dependents had the use of a medical clinic attended by five doctors—Eddie Gosano left for Hong Kong as soon after the surrender as he could, leaving four there—and six nurses, while there were free schools. The clinic was an expensive item as the average monthly cost for medicines and drugs was two thousand sterling. Occasionally they ran short of necessities and were forced to purchase in the Black Market at outrageous prices, and when this was not possible they fell back on prescriptions.

Appendix 10

The allowance received from Home allowed for a maximum of M.$150 per head (15 Macao dollars go to the pound sterling), though the majority received M.$80–85 per head.

Escapes Aided

Though it was not one of their official duties, the organisation always assisted where possible those who were attempting to escape either from Hong Kong and Macao and among those whom they smuggled over the border were Mr. and Mrs. Fletcher, Mrs. Geoffrey Wilson (wife of the A.S.P.). Mr Lessner (of Pan-[...................]) later harbor. There was no machine gunning of the city and damage of a minor nature and casualties very few.

Property Values

Mr. Swemmeleer went on to say that "Macao had prospered in a way." Many had made plenty of money and property values had soared—a house valued at M.$10,000 pre-war changed hands at M.$100,000, rich Chinese from Canton paying almost any price for suitable accommodation. The housing problem was the greatest one Macao had to face. The inhabitants lived in comparative comfort as labour was easy to find as there were few jobs to be had. An amah could be employed from M.$2–4 per month.

All who spent any time at all in Macao owe a big debt of gratitude to Mr. J. P. Reeves, the British Consul, who worked untiringly to improve conditions for all.

Mr. Swemmeleer, who is returning to Macao at dawn tomorrow by the "Fatshan", arrived in Hong Kong six months prior to the outbreak of hostilities, and was working for Messers. Warner Bros., the famous film company.

Appendix 11

This is a story about the Union Jack, symbol of Britain's greatness, which stirs the hearts of Britons in far places and of a man true to his British traditions.

He Kept the Flag Flying for Four Years

From David Divine
Daily Sketch Correspondent in Macao

The Union Jack has flown unchallenged in the Far East throughout the years of war beneath the balcony on which we sat yesterday when I heard the story of the British Consulate of Macao.

Cut off from the world in this tiny two-mile square fragment of Portuguese territory at the mouth of the great Pearl River from the moment of the capture of Hong Kong, the Consulate has maintained its tiny fragment of British territory intact.

More, it has performed a magnificent work for refugees of British, Portuguese, Chinese and other nationalities from Hong Kong.

When the refugees began to arrive Consul John P. Reeves had to set to work organizing the community within the community.

Rest Cure

Funds were provided by the Foreign Office and the Colonial Office at his request, and Mr. Reeves aided admirably by Mr. A. Zwemmeler a Dutchman in the colony, produced an orderly and workable method of life.

The whole story of the shifts, stratagems and contrivances cannot yet be told. Mr. Reeves had been sent down to Macao a few months before the outbreak of war for a "rest cure" from Mukden. He still has to have his rest.

His wife and daughter have been sent to Hong Kong for repatriation with Hong Kong internees, but peace has brought extra work to the consul.

Appendix 11

The work of the consulate has been from the very moment of the war in its complicated pattern of diplomacy and humanitarianism a notable page even in the long and honourable history of British consulates.

The Union Jack of Macao should be given an honored place among the treasures of the Foreign Office.

About *The Lone Flag* and John Pownall Reeves

By David Calthorpe

Time is a great healer, so it is said, but it is so often the case that healing, and the march of history, obliterates many memories of valiant works. So it has been for John Pownall Reeves, His Britannic Majesty's Consul in Macao, during the dark days of World War II. His lone flag had flown from the consular roof, only to be torn down by a typhoon on the day he handed authority over to his successor after the war, not neatly folded amid a glittering ceremony, but shredded and ripped into an untidy heap. 'Symbolic', John said of the once proud empire, after years of struggling against tyranny and the enemies of freedom. John had felt most passionately about the drama played out in this Portuguese enclave during the war years, putting pen to paper aboard HMS *Ranee* in 1946 and finishing these reminiscences in Rome in 1949. He called his memoir 'The Lone Flag'.

The Foreign Office refused permission for publication of Reeves' wartime memoir, in a letter dated 15 October 1949. The grounds for refusal were said to be government policy regarding the 'official experiences' of members of the Foreign Service. So, John became another gallant gentleman who bowed out with an OBE neatly pinned to his diplomatic uniform, straight into the shadows of history. While John and, indeed, Macao have been neglected in histories of World War II, one valuable source must be recognized—Alden's life of Charles Boxer.[1]

John was born in Blackheath, London, in 1909 and a birth notice in *The Times* announced the happy occasion. His parents were Herbert James Reeves and Katherine Margaret née Beaty-Pownall, whose family was from the Channel Islands. The Reeves were a middle-class couple, comfortably off with three servants. John was a first and relatively late child (both his parents were 40 when he was born). The family moved from the London suburbs to the country. John spent many years at the family home in the village of Hordle near the New Forest and went to the preparatory school in St Leonards-on-Sea, later obtaining a scholarship to Haileybury College, where he studied from 1923 to 1927. Danesford, the house at Hordle, was, by all accounts, a typical country retreat of one-and-a-quarter acres, sporting a tennis court, rose gardens and herbaceous borders. John's first photographic attempts with a Box Brownie give adequate evidence of an enquiring and active mind, as he captured all aspects of the house and garden in minute detail in the late 1920s. Lazy Sunday afternoons were often spent at a small summer house, built near a stream that meandered through the back garden, or with his uncle's naval friends at tennis parties.

Among his tiny amateur snapshots is a charming photograph, taken in 1929 on the tennis court at Danesford, of numerous admirals, in particular his highly decorated maternal uncle Vice Admiral Charles P. Beaty-Pownall and Admiral Seymour Erskine, who fought in the Boxer Rebellion in 1900 and later became aide-de-camp to King George V in 1911. With them is Admiral Lancelot Holland, who many years later was killed aboard HMS *Hood* when it was sunk by the *Bismarck* on 24 May 1941. In later years, John often spoke with great nostalgia about his family's maritime links and their informal gatherings.

The connection with the sea was to remain with him, albeit faintly, throughout his life, in quaint naval turns of phrase or in his passion for watching the junks manoeuvre about Macao harbour, as seen from the roof of the consulate. He told me that this was a favourite form of relaxation which he sorely missed. In his later years, John always claimed that one should wait until the sun was over the yard arm before engaging in cocktails or 'drinkies', as it was fondly called in the household. That ritual always took place after tea time, which was preceded by John's rigorous observance of the Portuguese custom of siesta—a wonderful remnant of his Macao years and an integral part of his retirement in Cape Town.

At that time, my mother was working with John's flamboyant companion and former secretary from Surabaya, Indonesia, Theresa (Tessa) Schukking. I was introduced at an early school-going age to their world of colourful nonconformity, at a time when a dour and repressive atmosphere prevailed in apartheid South Africa and all forms of eccentricity were frowned upon. This early introduction had a profound influence on my life.

John had been groomed for the navy but was refused entry because of extremely poor eyesight. He went instead up to Cambridge, where he studied languages. He flourished at Peterhouse, and rowed for the university in the famous race between Cambridge and Oxford. One of the victory oars, signed by all the team members from his early years, was recently returned to Cambridge. Hockey was his other love, as evidenced by his enthusiasm for the Macao Hockey Club. This English passion for sport, even in seemingly insignificant Macao, helped alleviate the enormous pressure on the beleaguered community of refugees, expatriates and colonial servants. It is indicative of that pressure that John always carried a pistol strapped to his shoulder in Macao, for fear of assassination, removing it only for ablutions or when he played hockey. He said that it took him many months to become accustomed to no longer wearing the holster, once hostilities had ended. I often remember his hand quickly moving into his jacket breast involuntarily when a car backfired in the street outside.

The Manchus' fall from grace in 1911 had given way to a long period of instability under warlords in the China of the early 1930s. It was in this tumultuous and fickle climate that John entered the British Foreign Service in 1933, as a student interpreter at the Legation in Peking (Beijing). This was a time of great excitement for foreigners living in the old capital. It was barely a decade after the deposed emperor, Pu Yi, had resided in the Forbidden City, acting out ancient ceremonies which were mere passing shadows of the old ways of the imperial court. Memories of the dowager empress, Tzu Hsi (Cixi), lingered on in the courtyards and gardens of the Summer Palace that she so loved, beyond the confines of the Forbidden City, with all its intrigues and jealousies. The markets were a haven for collectors of rare objects and antiques, sold by defunct court officials, Manchu nobles and eunuchs to support their extensive families. John used this period to indulge his passion for collecting. Among his first China purchases were beautifully carved blackwood cabinets, altar tables, chairs and thick-piled carpets. Yet it was the humbler, more exotic items that were so alluring, such as a silk-embroidered mandarin square from a court robe, depicting a stork, representing an official of the first rank, and bats, symbolizing good fortune/happiness. He had this set into a leather-bound portmanteau, which he used for all his personal documents throughout his China and Macao years and later in his retirement. It always remained close at hand on his favoured library table, as a reminder of his official days.

John had brought his Box Brownie with him from England and tested his photographic skills on all and sundry on his journey from Aden to Peking. These tiny photographs still grace the dusty pages of his Peking album. Pictures abound of his various explorations with friends. These are interspersed with images of the inter-port hockey matches at Tientsin (Tianjin) and the Peking race-course, along with glorious glimpses of the Ming tombs, the Temple of Heaven, Coal Hill and the Summer Palace. The album shows the dowager empress' lake barge, a favourite haunt of envoys posted to Peking, with its carved wooden-latticed windows and ancient attendant waiting for the imperial summons. A most amusing photograph remains of Adrian Holman, a consular friend, caught, according to the caption, in 'diplomatic contemplation' amid the carved blackwood furniture, with teacups, topees and straw boaters abounding. John's rather dry sense of humour remained with him all his life. 'Diplomatic contemplation' preferred to 'falling asleep'—an indication of John's flowery form of speech, which so characterized him.

Years later in Cape Town, John would often sit in his library of an evening and reminisce about his China years, with nostalgia and a hint of sadness in his voice. He knew that he would never again revisit those haunts of his early years. Most of the young men serving the empire had responsibility far beyond their years thrust on their shoulders. So it was with John Reeves, especially during his years in Macao. In the relatively carefree setting of the exciting and exotic Chinese capital, however, there was always time for play and enjoyment. The young men of the various legations would often hire a temple for weekend retreats in the Western Hills outside the ancient walls of Peking. It was common practice for European residents and Chinese pilgrim parties to hire such buildings from the Taoist or Buddhist priest-caretaker, for a few days in the rather wild, desolate area. Motorcars and donkeys were used for the exhausting trips through the hilly countryside, so evocatively conveyed in Anne Bridge's novel *Peking Picnic*, and as John also recounted to me. The old photographs taken by John testify to the unspoilt beauty of the rolling hills, dotted with temples and monasteries in various stages of dereliction. The days were filled with exploring the main temple compounds and their perhaps more enticing and mysterious architectural neighbours. A frequent guest of John was Molly Kaye, the well-known authoress whose works included the novel *The Far Pavilions*, together with her sister Betsy and mother, Lady Kaye. They visited the Temple of the White Pines, Fa Hai Ssu, so named for the white-barked trees which grew in the forecourt, flanking the large bronze incense-burner. John's Box Brownie captured during these memorable excursions the large, looming guardian figures which protected the main altar from malignant ghosts and evil-doers, as well as charming photographs of Molly Kaye. He would often talk of their languid days spent rambling in the hills, returning in the late afternoons to a well-spread tea prepared by their cook and bearers. He delighted in poring over the evocative photographs, lingering on a few in particular, which showed their party taking tea in the temple courtyard or grouped on the uneven stone stairs of mysterious pavilions, shuttered with ornate, peeling, lacquered doors in a landscape as yet unscathed. Molly was a dear and close friend of John, and many holidays were spent travelling with the Kayes. The last contact John had with the Kaye family was a visit from Lady Daisy Kaye, Molly's mother, in November 1974, when John was living in retirement in Malmesbury. She signed his visitor's book, *de rigueur* for all guests. John frequently told of the time when he and a few new consular arrivals in Peking had journeyed to the Western Hills to escape the excessive social formality, as well as the heat, that sometimes stifled one in the capital. Their temple retreat had been chosen for its remoteness. However, shortly after ensconcing themselves in their holiday domicile, a Chinese bearer arrived from a neighbouring temple with an invitation to dinner from its sole and august occupant. It was the British ambassador himself.[2] Their party could hardly refuse. They duly arrived at the temple's inner court in their finest holiday flannels to find His Britannic Majesty's representative attired in full evening dress, seated at a table laden with linen, crystal and the finest silver—all carried to that remote destination for the sole purpose of maintaining normal custom in the rhythm of life, no matter where one happened to be.

A favourite memory is of John seated in the library of his Malmesbury home, north of Cape Town. His mop of thick, wavy grey hair was invariably tied into a ponytail with a black velvet ribbon or let loose in Medusa fashion, and his carved ivory cigarette-holder was always held at an almost foppish angle, as he peered through bottle-bottom spectacles down the length of the library table laden with towers of books and exotic silver *bibelots*. In the glare of the late afternoon sun, a rich pattern of colour was always thrown onto the old faded Chinese carpet from a red amber statue of Kwanyin (Guanyin), the Goddess of Mercy, which stood on the window ledge. This, John said, had been an early favourite Macao purchase. Numerous dogs and a cat appeared scattered on the carpet, together with a large tortoise, aptly named Chronosky Aloysius Absalom. Aptly!

Why not? If you had seen so much and lived as dangerously as he did during those Macao years, you were entitled to name your tortoise as you saw fit. The tortoise always responded to its name. In winter, it was to be found between the dogs and the fire guard. Such was the man I first encountered. His had been a world peopled with saints and sinners, pimps, politicians, smugglers and assassins: a world on the edge of catastrophe. Yet the Union Jack of Reeves' Macao consulate was the only one flown, during those war years, down the whole length of the China coast. John was a relic of an age that was slowly dying. World War II destroyed it.

It became a haunting pastime to page through the old China album and pre-war scenic books on China, on wet Sunday afternoons before tea, surrounded by the faded trappings of a diplomat's life in the Far East. His rooms were filled with the books he so loved and with strangely carved Chinese blackwood cabinets, heavy with porcelain, ivories, rhinoceros-horn cups and richly decorated *cloisonné*. Silent Buddhas were forever seated in solemn contemplation of the shortness of time and of lingering memories. A stuffed baby crocodile peered down from a medieval French ecclesiastical cabinet used by the profane for drinks. 'Very sensible', we were told with a sideways glance. The crocodile had been a parting gift for John from his Indonesian manservant, when he had hastily left Surabaya during the tumultuous Sukarno years. He boyishly told how his open car sped through the dockside barriers, barely missing the booms, with the crocodile enthroned in the back seat amid the topsy-turvy leather suitcases, portmanteaux and hatboxes. This adventure always sounded to me as if it had come straight from the pages of a *Boys' Own Annual*.

My first visit to a restaurant as a child was with John. It was a rare treat for a South African child in the 1960s. He had decided that my horizons were to be expanded and the choice was obvious: Chinese! It was the only Chinese restaurant in Cape Town, John claimed, that served the genuine cuisine. He wore his long, black diplomat's cape, which he said had been made for him by his favourite tailor in Mukden. He would always ensconce himself against the wall furthest from the window, an old habit acquired from the years in Macao when he was constantly on guard against an assassin's bullet. (There is a beautifully carved blackwood cabinet that bears testimony to this, in the form of two neat bullet holes in the door, courtesy of a sniper, presumably Japanese or in Japanese pay, who had tried to shoot John from the garden outside the study window of the Macao consulate. The consulate building was situated below the Guia lighthouse, famously the first built on the South China coast.) With a flourish of the cape, he would sit down, placing his silver-topped Malacca cane on an empty seat. As he poured wine into goblets, one noticed for the umpteenth time the extremely long fingernails of his little fingers, grown in sympathy with a culture he so intimately assimilated into the daily flow of his life. He ate only with his own engraved ivory chopsticks, which he always carried with him, as any self-respecting Confucian scholar would. John entertained us—as always—with stories of Macao and China, a far distant land resplendent with dragons, curly-roofed temples, smiling, secretive Buddhas and forested mountains wreathed in coiling mist. These images were conjured up and supported by the many works to which he introduced me. They came from his extensive and seemingly endless library: Daniele Varé, Lin Yutang, Anne Bridge and Pearl Buck became everyday reading, alongside A. E. Grantham, Putnam Weale and Princess Derling, which I devoured in every detail.

Having studied modern languages at Cambridge and Mandarin in Peking, Reeves was clearly a gifted linguist. His Latin, German, French and Spanish were superb, as was, presumably, his Portuguese. He told us that he was able to speak only French until the age of six and burst into a flood of tears when his mother forced him to speak English! His knowledge of China was quietly displayed in most eloquent fashion, while other guests flaunted their knowledge after having spent only a few weeks doing the 'grand tour' of the East. The old visitor's book testifies to the many varied guests who called on him in his retirement here at the southern tip of Africa.

After his two years studying the language in Peking, John was transferred to Hankow (Hankou), moving after three years there to be acting consul-general in the walled city of Mukden in northeastern China. While stationed in Hankow, he married Rhoda Murray-Kidd, one of four siblings from a well-known Shanghai family. Lewis Murray-Kidd, her brother, was interned at Lunghua (Longhua) in Shanghai in May 1944, from where he subsequently escaped with four other prisoners.

John and Rhoda had only one child, a daughter born in Hankow in 1937, whom they named Letitia Mary. Very few snapshots remain from this period, other than one beautiful photograph of the proud parents with the sleeping child, taken at the nursing home. This he always cherished.

John rarely mentions his wife or child in the memoir—in fact, only five times. John told me that he and his wife had grown apart, but he never elaborated on that in later years. Indeed, he was terribly secretive about his married life. Rhoda and Letitia left Macao quietly on the HMAS *Fremantle* in September 1946. They transshipped in Manila to the USS *General A.W. Brewster*, bound for San Francisco, to return to England via America.

Rhoda had been interned after the fall of Hong Kong on Christmas Day 1941. Her daughter was in Macao at the time and they were reunited only 'after several months'. In testimony for the war-crimes tribunal, Ramon Muniz Lavalle, Argentine consul in Hong Kong at the time, refers to the case of Mrs. Reeves:

> Together with the Martin's case, I took up the one of Mrs Reeves, wife of the H.M. Vice-Consul at Macao. She was staying with them at the same place, also caught by the war in Hong Kong. She was not allowed to proceed to Macao, and her official position was not recognised. She was in an extremely bad state of nerves and general health, suffering from neurosis on account of a fracture of the base of her skull some time before. Her case was also serious and pitiful and I made all these particulars known to the Japanese authorities. As in the case of Mr & Mrs Martin, the reply was negative, and I could not obtain from the Japanese any alleviation of her situation.[3]

Press cuttings from Macao shortly after the Japanese surrender shed very little light on Rhoda, as she evidently never accompanied John to any of the official receptions given during the various victory celebrations. We can only speculate as to the reasons. Ill health could certainly have been a contributing factor. Despite her nervous disposition, she became involved with his work with the refugees when she eventually returned to Macao.

John and Rhoda were judicially separated after the war, but never divorced. I do remember John telling me that she was a Catholic and as such, out of respect for her, he never pursued the option of a civil divorce. Had John followed the latter option, he might well have continued to enjoy the successful diplomatic career which suited someone of his experience and obvious abilities. (The legal judicial papers could not be found after John's death. Although the executors of his estate made contact with Rhoda, by this time their daughter, Letitia, had died. Rhoda declined any benefits from his estate and Tessa was the sole heiress.)

Few photographs remain of Rhoda and John. One surviving photograph shows Rhoda with John's beloved canine friends at their bungalow, which was surrounded by large pine trees, somewhere on the China coast. (John's love for animals, particularly dogs, remained with him throughout his life. In later years, his favourite dogs Mira, a Doberman, and Scaramouche—a wild, black woolly animal, nicknamed the Yeti—would fall and clatter down the long wooden corridor like the baying hounds of Baskerville, whenever the doorbell rang at his Cape Town home.) From Mukden, John and family were sent to Macao for a 'rest cure' in 1939. While *en poste*, the Second World War was unleashed and John remained there until 1946, first as vice-consul and then consul—a most unusual honour, as promotions were seldom bestowed during wartime.

Macao always had a special place in John's heart. He would talk about it in a tone of a lover reminiscing over faded memories. Among his favourite haunts in the city was St. Dominic's Church, a splendid example of Portuguese colonial architecture gracing the cobbled central square. Another was the Protestant cemetery further up the hill, final resting place of Winston Churchill's uncle, Lord Henry John Spencer Churchill, and also graced with a splendid memorial to the great China coast artist, George Chinnery. John often mentioned this cemetery and its park-like atmosphere; he spent many hours there when wanting a break from his constant work among the refugees.

The refugee centre was evidently on the tree-lined Praia Grande, where John would watch the activity in the harbour over sundowners. He also loved to contemplate the city from the steps of the ruins of St. Paul's, a magnificent Portuguese Baroque stone edifice which was ravaged by fire in the nineteenth century. John lived in a house near the Guia lighthouse, next door, as it happened, to the Japanese consulate, the squeaky gate of which always alerted him to the nocturnal comings and goings of the 'enemy'. (His consular colleague, whom John described as 'a very fine man', was assassinated, some say, by the Kempeitai, because of his supposed neutral leanings regarding the war.) Macao was central to John's life and, indeed, the crowning point of a career that was curtailed by circumstances, both personal and otherwise. The fact remains that he was the right man, at the right time, to perform the humanitarian task which history entrusted to him. The course of his life up to that point seemed to have prepared him to fulfil his pivotal role in the lives of the British and Allied citizens. John was untiring in his efforts to assist the refugees who fled to Macao in the wake of the Japanese advance towards South China. His work speaks for itself in the memoir, yet to him it was more than just duty to king and country. It was a deep love for China and, in particular, the city of Macao and its people. His dealings with the Portuguese governor, Teixeira, and other officials in Macao often went beyond the call of duty and into the realms of friendship. On occasion, he was even called upon to act on behalf of His Excellency, the Governor—a most unusual occurrence in a neutral territory, where John represented a belligerent power.

There is, however, one rather unpleasant but telling tale which will always remain vividly etched in the mind. He told me once that, upon returning to his Macao residence one evening, he found the 'houseboy' had procured a most delicious-looking side of pork, prepared as a special treat in near-meatless wartime Macao. After a few mouthfuls of the repast, John set his knife and fork down to ask the silently waiting manservant where the pork had been obtained. The curt reply he received was 'the marketplace'. When John further pointed out that he had heard human flesh was on sale there, the inscrutable Macanese replied he too had heard this had been going on for some time, but that one could not tell the difference. John refused to eat any further.

He always strongly opposed any sort of unfair or, in his opinion, unwarranted behaviour from his peers. I remember a story concerning a small contretemps he had with the bishop of Macao at a diplomatic dinner, regarding his strong opinion that confirmees were far too young really to understand the relevance of confirmation. His Lord Bishop was much chagrinned at his apostolic authority being challenged, even in this minor way; they remained at a stalemate over this issue, to John's unending amusement. I think that he merely took delight in challenging the might of Rome, even if it be tilting at windmills. Strange to say, at a later stage he chose Don Quixote as the illustration for his bookplate. A night scene of the bishop's palace, painted by the Russian artist George Smirnoff, was one of his favourite paintings in his collection. Smirnoff, who lived in Macao during the war, was a prolific painter, primarily in watercolours; he had taught John's daughter, Letitia, among many other students. His magnificently executed views of Macao captured the ancient city in all its faded glory, much of which, alas, has been irretrievably lost.

In later years, John's active and erudite mind attracted men of the cloth to his table. It was not uncommon to find both Anglican and Catholic clergymen paying pastoral visits when John retired to the then small village of Malmesbury in 1972. Vatican Council II and its controversial amendments were diligently analysed amid the glow of candles at the library table, to copious amounts of red *vino* served with the demijohn slung over his shoulder—a habit acquired in Macao. 'The closer to Rome, the further from God', John often said, with wicked amusement in his eyes, set beneath the bushy eyebrows that made him look like a contender for the seat of Canterbury, straight from the pages of Giles.

After hostilities ceased with the surrender of Japan in September 1945, John stayed on in Macao until posted to Rome in 1946. In the same year, he received recognition for his wartime role by being created in the New Year Honours Officer of the Order of the British Empire in his capacity as consul in Macao. In Rome, he was responsible for consular matters pertaining to the Abruzzi, Molise, Sardinia and the Sardinian Islands, with effect from 15 September 1947. He was subsequently appointed in 1949 consul for the Province of East Java, to reside at Surabaya, where he met Tessa Schukking, who was to be his companion for the rest of his life. Her parents had been captured at the fall of Singapore, but Tessa had managed to escape on one of the last vessels to leave the city for Australia. She spent a few years there at a boarding school, St. Hilda's School in Cottesloe, and was reunited with her family after the war.

Leaving the Foreign Office after his Surabaya posting, they moved to a small farm outside Stellenbosch in the Western Cape. After his farming venture failed, he pursued a very successful career in broadcasting until his retirement in 1972. By his own definition, he considered himself, after the greater part of two decades, a veteran broadcaster.

His first entry to Cape Town was marked by a most unfortunate incident, which he still chafed at telling many years later. When the customs officials at Cape Town Harbour diligently searched this former consular official's personal baggage, they found his magnificent gold and silver diplomatic sword, which had been a gift from the community in Macao on his departure. John said that the gold content was so high that the sword bent under its own weight if held upright for too long. The customs officials declared it to be a 'dangerous weapon' and hastily prepared to confiscate it. No amount of pleading to the contrary was considered. John duly marched to the ship's side as it lay at anchor in Cape Town Harbour, saying that if he could not retain this ineffective 'weapon' then none would! With a flourish, he flung the golden sword far into the dark waters of Table Bay—there it lies to this day as a gift to Neptune, far from the greed of common man. Likewise, much of his magnificent collection of Chinese carved purple sandalwood furniture and valuable scrolls 'went astray' on leaving Surabaya. John believed that perhaps they were misplaced by another member of the *corps diplomatique* who had been entrusted with shipping the items. He could never be sure: his suspicions had no grounding other than a very fine gut feeling.

After Stellenbosch, John and Tessa moved to Cape Town, into a small house on the slopes of Signal Hill, overlooking the Atlantic. This cottage, said to be one of the oldest in Cape Town, was built around an inner courtyard in the midst of which an enormous lemon tree had taken root. The inevitable Cape winds constantly moved the heavy branches, laden with Chinese wind chimes, the sound of which he said 'called the temples of China to mind'. Their small drawing room reminded one of the sack of Peking with its disarray of 'chinoise objects', among which an ancient bronze temple drum on a carved wooden stand took pride of place, amid towers of books which they regarded as personal friends. This was the space where John was most at ease.

The kitchen, always a favourite haunt of John, was presided over by the 'kitchen god', whose roughly printed figure hung near the stove. His culinary exploits were legendary and the kitchen was a delight to behold, where new gadgets of every kind hung from peg-board on the walls. Pots, pans and bunches of onions hung from the ceiling, in true Iberian fashion, above a well-scrubbed Edwardian farm table, where a very large, fat, brown, glazed earthenware teapot held court after siesta. French onion soup vied with exotic Indonesian dishes as Sunday evening fare, which was rolled into the library on an old tea trolley laden with soup, breads, raw radishes and cheeses. It was a memorable tradition. Red *vino* flowed—as the evening drifted, we were always entertained with John's memories of Macao and Peking, amid the clatter of mahjong tiles.

One of his favourite souvenirs was a pair of Manchu shoes reputed to have come from the wardrobe of the dowager empress, and sold to him by a former court eunuch in Peking's Street of Antiques. True or not, John liked the story—the shoes remained as a faded reminder of Old Peking on the overloaded bookcase behind his library seat. The state of this bookcase was the result of years of avid collecting. But two books in particular were rather precious to him. One was a leather-bound Roman missal, given to him as a present and inscribed by Father Teixeira, the Macao historian; the other, a signed copy of *Sian: A coup d'état* had been given to him by Madame Soong Mei-ling, wife of General Chiang Kai-shek. They represented the two opposites in life, the sacred and profane.

When he moved to Malmesbury, he christened his home 'Guia', after the light that shone from the hill above his Macao residence, guiding the ships among the hundreds of islands that dotted the sea at the mouth of the Pearl River. His old Macao residence was demolished a week before I finally found it in 2005, with the help of Father Lancelot, a former Macao seminarian who had met John when having his passport renewed during the war.

One of my most precious memories of his gentlemanly behaviour was formed one wet winter afternoon in Malmesbury. John and Tessa had retired for afternoon siesta, ensconced with cats and dogs. I decided to do something useful that would perhaps please John. I stood on the lower half of the large bookcase and, with much stretching, removed a bronze standing figure of Gautama Buddha in the style of the Song dynasty. To my young and uninformed mind, it appeared far too dirty! So I proceeded to 'clean' away the offending dirt. Off came the patina from many years of gentle polish and burning incense. The cherished bronze now appeared cleaned and sparkling new! I awaited praise for a job well done. When they appeared in the library later that afternoon, I was met with absolute silence and no hint of offence on John's diplomatic visage, other than what I perceived to be a slight wince of pain from his knees. I was a little disappointed at the lack of enthusiasm for my afternoon's work, but promptly forgot about it. Years later, I was told that John had been absolutely appalled by my endeavours, yet his calm and assuring demeanour never wavered, even if I had noticed a slight wincing about his mouth. The patina has slowly returned to this benign deity, but it constantly reminds me that 'life is too short to stuff a mushroom', to quote a much-used phrase of his. John always was a gentleman and a diplomat.

His life slowly ebbed away, leaving him breathing with great difficulty, due to years of smoking, and barely able to walk, as a result of old knee injuries. He died in 1978 in the Swartland Hospital in Malmesbury, in a room overlooking the farmlands and mountains of the area. He never returned to his beloved Macao. He never saw China again.

I like to think that John Reeves 'ascended the dragon' knowing that he had done so much for so many, yet modesty and humility seldom allowed him to flaunt his deeds. It is to his memory that I dedicate these words and thank him *in absentia* for his guidance when I was young and its enduring enrichment.

John, your memoir is finally in print. *Requiescat in pace.*

Notes

Preface and Introduction

1. Wilhelm Snyman, 'The John Reeves Memoir, "The Lone Flag": Lifting the Veil on Wartime Macao', *Revista de Cultura* 23 (2007): 40–55.
2. Edwin Ride, *British Army Aid Group: Hong Kong Resistance 1942–1945* (Hong Kong: Oxford University Press, 1981).
3. Letter dated 5 June 1943 from Lieutenant Colonel Ride, head of the British Army Aid Group in China, to General Grimsdale, military attaché, British Embassy, Chungking (Chongqing), AWM (Australian War Memorial) PR82/068 2/34/10.
4. I am grateful to Jason Wordie for sharing with me their reminiscences on this subject.
5. Letter from Fukui to Telos de Vasconcelos, 15 September 1944. Macao Historical Archives MO/AH/A1/SA/01/25726.
6. AWM PR82/068 2/8/59.
7. Arnaldo Sales' comment, passed on to me by Stuart Braga.
8. See no. 74 on the main map. Another map in the Braga Collection at the National Library of Australia (1945 MAP G7947.M3 1945) marks the consulate here.
9. Stuart Braga's report of conversation with Geoffrey Wilson.
10. Adding to the puzzle, the diagram on page 34 lists, under the heading 'Skyline', eight guards who were operating from there. This forces one to ask what else was going on at Skyline.
11. This information, including the date of release, comes from a report by Mrs. Mary Erwin Martin of her time in Hong Kong before and after the surrender to the Japanese, http://groups.yahoo.com/group/stanley_camp/message /2842 (accessed 3 August 2013). Mr. Martin was consul general in Chungking; they too were trapped in Hong Kong by the Japanese attack.
12. Ken Cambon, *Guest of Hirohito* (Vancouver: PW Press, 1990), Appendix: Excerpts from War-Crime Trials, http://www.fourthmarinesband.com (accessed 5 July 2013).
13. AWM PR82/068 11/16/23.
14. Dauril Alden, *Charles Boxer: An Uncommon Life* (Macao and Lisbon: Fundação Oriente, 2001), footnote 11 on page 548.
15. I owe this observation to César Guillen Nuñez.

Macao during World War II

1. Reeves covers the subject of censorship and his own attempts to publish a newspaper. Another breach of strict neutrality was the transshipment of troops through Macao into China. The Japanese also ordered the Portuguese to remove their troops from Lapa, Dom João and Montanha islands.
2. Personal conversation with the author.
3. The game *fantan* involves scooping up a bowl of beads. These are counted out in groups of four: punters bet on the number remaining at the end—one, two, three or none.
4. Reeves uses the spelling *Saion* for this ship, but many references use *Sai On*.
5. See Chapter X of the memoir.

The Lone Flag
Chapter I   The Beginning

1. Correctly the SS *Sai On* although also referred to as the *Xi An*. She was a two-decked ferry, 225 feet long and 42 feet beam built at the Taikoo Dockyard in 1924.
2. It was the practice for Malayan Civil Service cadets to spend time in Macao to learn Cantonese.
3. R.G.K. Thompson escaped from Hong Kong and in early 1942 was in China. He did not stay long and joined Wingate in Burma. He went on to achieve fame after the Malayan Emergency as one of the world's leading experts on subversive warfare. His awards include KBE, CMG, DSO and MC.
4. While Mrs. Reeves was trapped in Hong Kong, their daughter Letitia, aged about five, must have been in Macao with her father.
5. By which Reeves means the Japanese consul, Fukui Yasamitsu.
6. Reeves is presumably referring to the three weeks between the start of the Japanese attack on Hong Kong and the fall of Hong Kong on Christmas Day 1941.
7. Mr. Fletcher was a manager of the Macao Electric Company (see Chapter III).
8. Donald Fletcher, 17, a student at the University of Hong Kong, served as a stretcher bearer during the fighting in Hong Kong but escaped to Macao in February 1942.
9. Lieutenant Colonel E.J.R. Mitchell took part in the defence of Hong Kong and replaced Colonel H.B. Rose as Commander of the Hong Kong Volunteer Defence Corp (HKVDC) on 20 December 1941. He spent the war as a prisoner of war (POW). His wife, Rose, and their two daughters had been evacuated to Canada in 1940 but returned in 1941 to a rented house in Macao.
10. See references in the Preface for further reading on the Battle for Hong Kong.
11. Margin note: 'Midnight mass cancellation'.
12. The Pearl River.
13. Macao was not joined to the mainland by a causeway but by a sand bar which in its early history could be submerged at high tide. Gradually it became a more permanent attachment and, by the time of the war, it had been considerably widened by reclamation and there was a road to the border crossing which was marked by the gateway known

Notes to pp. 13–19

as Portas do Cerco (Barrier Gate), preserved today as an historic structure. The two islands are Taipa and Coloane. Taipa was originally two islands but they were joined by reclamation. Coloane was first linked to Taipa by a causeway but is now inextricably linked by a broad band of reclamation—the Cotai strip, which houses many hotels and casinos.

14. Correctly: 'Não ha outra mais leal'.
15. This is one of Reeves' more puzzling statements as there seems neither records nor memories of universities coming to Macao, although certainly many moved within China to escape the Japanese. Some middle schools moved there from Guangzhou.
16. Commander Gabriel Maurício Teixeira was a naval officer. He became governor of Macao from 1940 to 1946. After leaving Macao he became governor-general of Mozambique (1948–58). He died in 1973.
17. Dr. Pedro José Lobo was born in Timor in 1892 and died in Hong Kong in 1965. He was appointed director of Economic Services in 1937 and went on to prosper after the war. At one time he was reported to have controlled all the gold imports.
18. Because of the International Date Line, V.J. Day was declared on 15 August in Japan and the Far East while it was on 14 August in the United States.

Chapter II   Getting Going

1. The SS *Perla* is mentioned in Tony Banham, *Not the Slightest Chance* (Hong Kong: Hong Kong University Press, 2003) as serving as an Auxiliary Patrol Vessel during the Battle for Hong Kong. She was a 326-tonne vessel with length of 185 feet. It is probable that she could have ferried 200 or more passengers across the sheltered waters to Macao.
2. Heenan report to the British ambassador in Chungking (dated 3 June 1942, NA [National Archives] FO371/41620). In this he states: 'as the Japanese have been pushing out Chinese and Portuguese from Hongkong and its new territories in a steady stream to Macao, as many as 1,000 per day having arrived at one period per junks and Japanese motor vessels such as the *Shirogano Maru*.'
3. Mrs. Wilson was the wife of Geoffrey Wilson who was an assistant superintendent of police in Hong Kong and was interned in Stanley. Until she escaped from Macao in 1943, she was the BAAG's contact agent in Macao. See Chapter X.
4. The Clube de Macau (Macao Club) still occupies part of the premises better known as the Teatro Dom Pedro V (Dom Pedro V Theatre). The building dates from 1860 and is the first Western theatre in China. The main façade was renovated in 1873 in a more neo-classical style, including pilasters and a triangular pediment. It is now preserved as one of The Historic Monuments of Macao (no. 72 on the map).
5. Correctly Dr. Elsa de Senna Fernandes.
6. The acting Portuguese consul in Hong Kong was Francisco Soares.
7. The work of the C.E.R. is described in Chapter VI.
8. Marginal note apparently reading 'Carrots'.

9. The battleship HMS *Prince of Wales* and battlecruiser HMS *Repulse* were sunk by Japanese aircraft on 10 December 1941; Singapore fell on 15 February 1942.

Chapter III "The Situation"

1. See below (page 23) for some brief comments on the story of the Consulate. See preface (page xii) for more on location of the consulate.
2. Here Reeves inserted a note: 'Burglar alarms'.
3. '[O]n 4 February 1945 ... Fukui Yasumitsu was assassinated ... An enquiry was conducted by the Portuguese authorities as to this incident. Consensus held that no political motive was impugned, merely an act of jealousy.' Geoffrey C. Gunn, *Encountering Macau: A Portuguese City-state on the Periphery of China, 1557–1999* (Boulder, CO: Westview, 1996), p. 127.
4. See Chapter VIII note 5 on the Netherlands Harbour Works Co.
5. John Company was the informal name of the British East India Company. Best known for their presence in India they were also granted a monopoly of trade with China. However, after the Indian Mutiny they were disbanded and trade became free. The English factor's house (more accurately the home of the president of the Select Committee for Macao of the East India Company) referred to still stands. It was and is commonly known as Casa Garden (no. 61 on the map) and is located next to the main Protestant cemetery (no. 60 on the map). It was still a museum in the 1970s, but later the museum was transferred to its current location within the Fortaleza do Monte (Monte Fort) (no. 66 on the map). Today the villa houses the Fundação Oriente (Oriental Foundation), an organization that promotes Portuguese culture worldwide, and an exhibition gallery, which houses exhibits of Chinese antiques, porcelain and contemporary art.
6. Much of this street, which runs behind the Ruinas de São Paulo (ruins of St. Paul's) (no. 65 on the map), has been renamed Rua de D. Belchior Carneiro, and only a short dead-end section is now called the Largo da Companhia (Square of the Company).
7. Haileybury had, after the demise of the East India Company, become a public school.
8. Although Moosa's store still exists on Rua Central opposite the Teatro Dom Pedro V (no. 72 on the map), it is now a shadow of its former self and one might pass it without a second glance.
9. The Indian Independence League was a political organization that operated from 1928 to the 1940s. It was set up to organize those living outside of India into seeking the removal of British colonial rule over India. Founded in 1928 by Indian nationalists, the organization was located in various parts of Southeast Asia and included Indian expatriates and, later, Indian nationalists in exile under Japanese occupation. The Japanese encouraged Indians to join the Indian Independence League so as to exert more pressure on the British.
10. Marginal note: 'Metropolitan'.
11. The Chinese Maritime Customs Service was run mainly by foreigners even though it operated as a part of the Chinese government. It was successful as it eliminated the

corruption that had prevented the government from receiving its proper duties. It became a powerful organization and effectively controlled commercial navigation in Chinese waters. Jean Fay, the commissioner of Chinese Maritime Customs in Macao, is mentioned later.

12. Ernest (Pat) Heenan was the representative of Royal Insurance based in Shanghai. He was in Macao 'pursuing a business connection' and was booked to sail back to Hong Kong on the *Sai On* on 8 December. Consequently trapped in Macao, he escaped to Chungking (Chongqing) in April 1942, where he wrote a full report on the Macao situation for the British ambassador in Chungking (dated 3 June 1942, NA [National Archives] FO371/41620).

13. In a report from Captain Olsen (NA HS/176): 'The Governor is pro-ally but cannot do much owing to the danger of antagonizing the Japs. The senior government members surrounding the Governor are very pro-Axis and do all in their power to embarrass the British Consul and community, even to the extent of falsifying reports before they reach the Governor. An official by the name of Silva da Costa seems to be the most vicious in the anti-British element.'

14. In 1889, Lewanika, chief of the Lozi, appealed for protection to the British, being threatened by the Ndebele. 'If the British did not intervene, clearly the Portuguese would expand into this unclaimed territory linking Mozambique and Angola. Rhodes was delighted ... to block the Portuguese.' Thomas Pakenham, *The Scramble for Africa* (London: Weidenfeld and Nicolson, 1991), p. 387.

15. The race track referred to was sited close to the border crossing with China. It was called the Hipódromo (Hippódrome) (no. 102 on the map). It had been built in the 1920s when Macao expanded into the areas that had previously been countryside. The area was redeveloped as an industrial and residential area after the war, the centre of which is now the Mercado Municipal do Bairro Iao Hon (Iao Hon Market). The roads bordering the area retain the word Hipódromo in memory of the track. A new race-course was built on Taipa Island and still holds regular meetings.

16. Heenan in his report describes George McCaskie as '27, British, Oxford, knowledge of Cantonese, Singapore Govt. Cadet'.

17. Heenan's description: 'Charles Michael Knaggs, 25, British, Varsity Cambridge; knowledge of Cantonese, Air certificate and Singapore Govt. Cadet.'

18. It seems that Reeves has the name wrong. Phyllis Harrop, working for the police in Hong Kong, escaped to Macao in January using fake German identity papers. She then went on to escape from Macao with the help of Nationalist agents. She endured a long trip overland to Chungking from where she returned to England. Her reports on the situation in Hong Kong were the first first-hand ones to reach London. In 1943 she published her memoirs as *Hong Kong Incident* (London: Eyre & Spottiswoode, 1943).

19. Kwangchowan (Zhanjiang) was a small enclave on the south coast of China near Hainan Island, ceded by Qing China to France as a leased territory and ruled by France as an outlier of French Indochina. The colony was invaded and taken over by Japan in February 1943, taken back by France in 1945, and finally returned to China in 1946.

20. Elsie Fairfax-Cholmondeley escaped with Israel Epstein, Ray O'Niell, Parker 'Dutch' Van Ness and Frank W. Wright. They found a small boat just outside the wire at Stanley,

and made it to Macao via Cheung Chau. The escape is described in I. Epstein, *My China Eye* (San Francisco: Long River Press, c. 2005).
21. Robert Stott escaped by sampan and then transferred onto a Macao fishing junk to reach Macao. He wrote a report (AWM PR82/068 9/7/13) to Lieutenant Colonel Ride of BAAG dated 6 October 1942 of his escape.
22. Heenan describes O'Neill as an American sailor and reports that when he last saw him, O'Neill was 'resting in Macao owing to a shrapnel wound in the back'. The fact that he had braved the escape from Stanley and many hours in a sampan making his way to Macao with this wound in his back gives a somewhat different sense of the man to that given by Reeves.
23. Pan American Airways' flying boat service was an American airline's first provision of a commercial flight service between the United States, Hong Kong and China. It operated between Hong Kong and Macao, then flew via Manila to San Francisco. It took about an hour for a flight between Hong Kong and Macao. Pan American operated two flights per week until Japan's invasion in 1941. Their 'property' was located on the east side of Macao roughly where the ferry terminal is today (a little northeast of no. 19 on the map). Pan American also had a radio station to which Reeves refers on the Colina de Barra (Barra Hill) (no. 83 on the map).
24. Heenan describes Redden as '30, American, Commercial Air Pilot of over 5000 flying hours experience; Radio operator's and Engineer's certificate P.A.A.; Pan American Airport Manager at Macao'.
25. The *Masbate* was built in Dundee in 1895 as the *Juno* and renamed in 1935, sold to Wallem & Co. Hong Kong but with the beneficial owner being South China Steam Ship Co. of Hong Kong. She sank in a collision off Fuzhou in 1949. Heenan reports her being 'in the Government Harbour, near to the *Joao de Lisboa*'.
26. Heenan mentions two other employees of the Chinese Imperial Maritime Customs, both ex Kongmoon: '?.T. Williams, 55, American who was Commissioner in Kongmoon' and 'A. S. Coppin, 50, British'.

Chapter IV   Organization

1. Amoy and Swatow are now Xiamen and Shantou.
2. V.R. would have indicated that the object dated from the time of Queen Victoria.
3. The origins of Cable and Wireless lie in a number of British telegraph companies founded in the 1860s. In 1928 the communications operations of the British Empire were merged into a single company, initially known as Imperial and International Communications Ltd., which became Cable and Wireless Ltd. in 1934.
4. It is interesting to note that Aycock was on a Japanese assassination list reported by BAAG to the British Embassy in Chungking. The others on the list were Reeves and the secretary of Fernando Rodriguez. This suggests there may have been more to Mr. Aycock than Reeves is telling us (FO371/46/99 24 July 1945).
5. See Chapter VII for more on the work of the clinic and the doctors.

6. Derek Anderson was a member of a distinguished Eurasian family. His sister, Joyce Symons, was later headmistress of Diocesan Girls' School in Hong Kong. Another sister, Phyllis Nolasco, was active in the BAAG. Their brother (Lieutenant Donald J. Anderson of the Hong Kong Volunteers) was killed in the Battle for Hong Kong. Hearing this, Reeves offered Derek, then sixteen, the position as archivist. See Vicky Lee, *Being Eurasian: Memories across Racial Divides* (Hong Kong: Hong Kong University Press, 2004), pp. 70–71.
7. See Chapter X for fuller discussion of secret activities.
8. José Maria (Jack) Braga (1897–1988) was an important historian of Macao. He accumulated a library on the activities of the Portuguese in the Far East. The war put a stop to his acquisition of books, but instead he began to record the life of the large English-speaking community in its efforts to maintain a vibrant cultural life in these extraordinary conditions. By mid-1945 it was obvious to local people that the war was finally coming to an end, as the growing number of air raids told of increasing American air supremacy. Braga began to collect newspapers, including the English edition of the Portuguese newspaper *Renascimento*, which by mid-1945 was able to give accurate information about the collapse of Nazi Germany. Now held in the National Library of Australia, these papers tell a dramatic story of rapidly growing excitement.
9. The Hong Kong Rehabilitation Committee 'of six men under Reeves which includes one Leo D'Almada … Other members are said to be Jack Braga (Portuguese), A El [grp undec] ulli (Indian), W.C. Hung (Eurasian) and C.Y. Kwan.' Message from Chungking to Foreign Office, 22 May 1945. The undecipherable name was clearly Abbas el Arculli. This initiative of Reeves outside his terms of reference caused considerable concern in Chungking and London to the degree that consideration was given to replacing him. See NA FO 371/46251.

Chapter V   Parochial

1. Miguel Senna Fernandes and Alan N. Baxter, *Maquista Chapado: Vocabulary and Expressions in Macao's Portuguese Creole* (Macao: Instituto Cultural, 2004) spell the name 'pacapiu' and describe it as a 'Chinese lottery'.
2. Government servants are still forbidden to enter the casinos in Macao.
3. The Porto Interior (inner harbour) is on the western side of peninsular Macao.
4. Ben de Senna Fernandes organized the Melco Orchestra, which apparently consisted of four players of the violin and cello.
5. 'Waits' are people who welcome in Christmas by playing or singing out of doors at night.
6. This further reference to the Chinese universities and schools suggests more research is needed to determine which institutions did move to Macao and where they were based within the colony.
7. See no. 13 on the map.
8. See no. 72 on the map.

9. The canidrome (see no. 49 on the map) was built only in 1940 and the sport had not yet matured so it is understandable that the racing was disrupted. Dog racing was resurrected after the war; the stadium is still in use today.
10. The tennis club still exists at the same location on the Avenida da República (no. 82 on the map) below what is now called the Palacete de Santa Sancha (no. 81 on the map).
11. No. 80 on the map.
12. Marginal note: '?Fat Siu Lao'. Despite its name, this is a well-known restaurant serving Portuguese food on Rua da Felicidade (no. 103 on the map).
13. The Central and Grand hotels are both on Avenida de Almeida Ribeiro. The Hotel Central is three blocks northwest from the Largo do Senado (Senate Square), while the Grand Hotel is at the western end next to the Inner Harbour.
14. The Portuguese Bank, or the Portuguese Overseas Bank, is correctly the Banco Nacional Ultramarino. The main branch is on Avenida de Almeida Ribeiro at the intersection with the Praia Grande (no. 8 on the map). Part of the original façade has been preserved.
15. This exceptional bank manager was Ade Santos Ferreira, who wrote Macanese songs.
16. No. 62 on the map.
17. Charles Boxer, among many other achievements, was an historian who specialized in the history of the Dutch and Portuguese in the Far East.
18. The grave is of Lord Henry John Spencer Churchill, who was in command of the HMS *Druid*, one of the fleet gathered in 1840 for operations with the expeditionary force in China. Lord Churchill died on 3 June 1840 of 'congestion of the brain complicated by an attack of dysentery'. See Lindsay Ride and May Ride, *An East India Company Cemetery* (Hong Kong: Hong Kong University Press, 1996), pp. 215–16. The cemetery is no. 60 on the map.
19. No. 68 on the map.
20. No. 18 on the map.
21. The poem is by Reeves, whose home and consulate, at least through most of 1942, was close to the Guia light, but see the discussion in the introduction of the location of the consulate.
22. No. 66 on the map. Marginal note: 'Mention murderers'.
23. Probably Hawker Ospreys, a navalized version of the Hawker Hind biplane, used as a fighter and for reconnaissance.
24. Lost over the years from the manuscript. It seems quite likely that the guide that Reeves refers to would have been *Macau, Oldest Foreign Colony in Far East, Founded in 1557* (Macau: Agência do Turismo, [1936]).

Chapter VI   Relief

1. Mr. Leo D'Almada e Castro was born in Hong Kong in 1904. He entered the University of Hong Kong at just fifteen years of age. He left the Faculty of Arts three years later before taking his degree examinations, and went up to Exeter College, Oxford, to read Jurisprudence. He left Oxford with a degree in 1926, was called to the Bar by the Middle

Temple in 1927, and returned to Hong Kong the same year to practise. His war years were spent in Macao serving as a liaison officer between the Portuguese and British governments in connection with refugees. Towards the end of the war, he and his wife made a difficult and hazardous journey through Japanese-occupied China to India, and thence to the United Kingdom, where he made a valuable contribution to the plans for post-war Hong Kong that were being drawn up in London. In 1945 he was appointed president of the General Military Court in Hong Kong, resuming his legal practice upon its dissolution the following year. In 1947 he took silk, and became recognized as the leading member of Hong Kong's Portuguese community.

2. Two D'Almada-Remedios brothers were in a list in KWIZ 51/4 dated 30 May 1944 (AWM PR82/068 10/13/13) as having 'been detained by the Japanese in Hong Kong. . . . The majority of those arrested had previously made trips to Macao and were probably suspected of contacting the British Consul there.' It is not clear whether either of these is the Mr. Remedios referred to by Reeves.

3. See Chapter III, n. 12.

4. This centre was in a house owned by the Remedios family on Rua do Barão (no. 100 on the map).

5. The dollars referred to in this passage are Hong Kong dollars, for which the exchange rate at this time was about HK$15 = £1. Macao's currency, the *pataca*, was before the war at par with the Hong Kong dollar. A catty is approximately one-and-one-third pounds, or 600 grammes.

6. *Compradore* is a Portuguese word meaning buyer. It was adopted in the China Trade as a term for the native manager who negotiated deals between Chinese suppliers and foreign buyers. Some such as Sir Robert Ho Tung, the compradore for Jardine Matheson & Co., became very rich and powerful.

7. Y. C. Liang was to be a very active agent of the BAAG in Macao, until eventually he was appointed the senior agent in mid-1943. Often referred to in the literature as 'Phoenix', his code name was in fact P.L. and Phoenix was Dr. Eddie Gosano. That mistake carries over into the following quotations. 'He [Liang] served as chief local agent for the BAAG. It was Phoenix who organized the escape routes on which Reeves dispatched Allied workers from Macao to Free China, and which served as the arteries for the BAAG's intelligence work.' With instructions from the Foreign Office, Liang reached Gimson in Hong Kong on 22 August 1945 'with Whitehall's official command to take power'. Both quotations from Snow, *The Fall of Hong Kong*, pp. 183 and 249 respectively. After the surrender, he was on the first Allied ship to arrive in Macao (see Chapter XII). Subsequently he was made Commander of the British Empire by the British government.

8. Marginal note: 'loyalty tests'. This probably referred to another of the fourteen tests that Reeves mentioned earlier.

9. Marginal note: 'Wong Ching Wei'. Given the context, this may be a mistake for Wang Jingwei and a reference to yet another form of currency which circulated in wartime Macao—that from the puppet Nanjing government.

Chapter VII   Medical

1. All the doctors returned to Hong Kong at the end of the war and nearly all later left for the United States. Dr. Eddie Gosano took over from Mrs. Wilson as BAAG agent in Macao. Dr. Ho Asgoe has not been identified.
2. Following the sighting of Our Lady of Fátima in 1917 by three shepherd children in Fátima, Portugal, she became a popular figure of devotion. Igreja São Domingos (St. Dominic's Church) in Macao was the first in the Far East to integrate the worship of Our Lady of Fátima into its religious services, and it is the starting point of the annual procession which carries her statue through the streets to Capela de Nossa Senhora da Penha (Penha Church) (no. 79 on the map). In the Catedral (Cathedral) (no. 9 on the map), there is a statue of Our Lady of Fátima and an inscription: 'Rainha do Mundo, Mãe de Portugal, Amparai Macau, 13.5.1943', which translates as 'Queen of the World, Mother of Portugal, Help Macao'. The dedication of this statue is probably the ceremony to which Reeves refers.
3. Porto Exterior (Exterior Port) at this time referred to the waters to the southeast of the town. Reclamation here had been carried out with the aim of stimulating trade but it never materialized—all the land has been built over.
4. The Kiang Wu Hospital still operates today on the original site (no. 58 on the map) but in a new building dating from 2000.
5. Hospital de São Rafael (St. Rafael Hospital) was founded in 1569 and operated up until 1974, when the organization decided to focus on the care of the elderly. The old building was taken over by the Portuguese government and, since the handover of sovereignty to China, has been used as the Portuguese consulate (no. 67 on the map).
6. Mr. Nolasco's pharmacy is the Pharmacia Popular, which still exists in the historic Senate Square (no. 69 on the map).
7. Sulfathiozole was a commonly used anti-microbial. 12/6 is a reference to pre-decimalization English currency and is equal to 62.5 new pence.

Chapter VIII   Other Countries' Interests

1. Bishop Adolph John Paschang (1895–1968) was an American Maryknoll priest. He was made bishop of Kongmoon (Jiangmen) in 1937. After the liberation of mainland China he chose to stay behind and was imprisoned and tortured by the Chinese Communist authorities. He was released to Macao in June 1952 and spent the rest of his life in Hong Kong.
2. Sergio Osmeña y Suico (1878–1961) was vice president under Manuel L. Quezon from 1935 and rose to the presidency upon Quezon's death in 1944.
3. The Riviera Hotel was on the Praia Grande near its junction with Avenida de Almeida Ribeiro (no. 7 on the map).
4. No. 86 on the map.
5. In the report written by Ernest Heenan to the British Embassy in Chungking, 27 May 1942, he says: 'The Netherlands Harbour Works, whose Manager in Macao is Mr. WoerKamp, have, in their sheds, to the North of the Macao Water Co.'s reservoir,

equipment, locomotives, rails and ironware to the value of some HK$3,000,000 and in the Government Harbour a dredger over which the Japanese have been casting an eye since before 8th December 1941. A party of Japanese boarded this dredger early in April. She is under the care only of Chinese watchman. Mr. WoerKamp has taken the matter up with the Hon. Consul for the Netherlands, Mr. Henrique Nolasco, Sr.' In *Macao: A Handbook* (Macao: Publicity Office, Harbour Works Dept., 1926), p. 19: 'the road passes Macao Siac where the "Netherlands Harbour Works Co" has established its workshops in connection with the Port Works of Macao.' This suggests that the company established workshops when working on the new port project of the 1920s and retained its property there to store equipment between projects. The area has now been reclaimed but a street on the reclamation named Rua da Doca dos Holandeses records the past Dutch presence.

6. The Japanese cut off the supply of rice to Macao and forced the Macao government to start negotiations for the transfer of the dredger to the Portuguese flag and for eventual re-sale to the Japanese. 'Negotiations took a couple of months before Gundesen, the man authorised to handle the case, who is at present in Shamshuipo Camp, gave power of attorney to Nolasco Sr., Honorary Dutch Consul, and instructions to sell if necessary.' SOE report, probably of May 1942 NA HS 1/176.

7. While the map has been lost, it is to be noted that in Chapter X, number 52 on the map is assigned to the Bairro Tamagnini Barbosa, which lies on the northwest of Macao near Green Island. This is no. 44 on the present map. The present map shows the firecracker factories at no. 43, just north of the Bairro Tamagnini Barbosa, with a dock just to their west. So it is likely that the floating Dutch equipment was moved near there before the 'accidental' scuttling of the lighter. Taking it right the way around the peninsula without intervention by the Japanese seems quite a feat.

8. Green Island or Ilha Verde was in the north of the Inner Harbour and was connected to the mainland of Macao by a causeway.

9. Russian Mountains is something of a misnomer. Montanha Russa is in fact quite a small municipal garden on the north side of Estrada de Ferreira do Amaral. Its modest hill features a spiral ramp (no. 38 on the map).

10. Consultation with native Norwegian speakers sheds no light on the meaning of this phrase.

11. 'To cut out' is to capture a ship from a harbour by getting between her and the shore.

12. Marginal note: 'Heard of since'.

13. Willy Reed was the youngest of seven brothers. Four were killed during the Battle for Hong Kong. Two were imprisoned in Sham Shui Po. Willy looked after his mother in Macao.

Chapter IX   Morale

1. The Sergeant's Club was on the corner of the Praia Grande and Rua do Padre Luís Fróis S.J. (near no. 7 on the map).

2. The library in the Leal Senado (Loyal Senate) is still there (no. 4 on the map), although most of the books are quite old and Macao has other, more modern public libraries.
3. Marginal note: 'lazy rice pickers'.
4. No. 78 on the map.
5. Chácara Leitão or Villa Leitão (no. 101 on the map) belonged to the Leitão family. It was located on the Estrada de Cacilhas on the seaward side of Monte de Guia (Guia Hill), very close to the water before the reclamation in front of it in the 1930s, 'of extraordinary charm and beauty, attractively laid out terraces and gardens, a private summer residence'. *Macau: A Handbook* (Macao: Publicity Office, Harbour Works Dept., 1926), p. 18.
6. With the Japanese occupation of Hong Kong, about 4,000 Portuguese families returned to Macao. To look after the youth, the Macao governor asked the Hong Kong Jesuits to set up a school with all expenses paid. The school, São Luís Gonzaga, began in January 1943 and closed its doors in December 1945.
7. No. 28 on the map.
8. Marginal note: 'First jack at opening'.
9. Deaconess Lee—actually Rev. Florence Li Tim-oi—was ordained by Bishop R. O. Hall in 1944 to serve the spiritual needs of Anglican refugees in Macao.
10. Marginal note: 'Defrock'.
11. Father Granelli was born in 1892 and arrived in Hong Kong in 1925. He was sent to Macao in 1942 to look after refugees and went back to Hong Kong on the first junk to leave Macao after Japanese surrender. He retired in 1969.
12. The church opposite the Clube de Macau is the Igreja de Santo Agostinho (Church of St. Augustine) (no. 71 on the map). Father Granelli was put in charge of this church.

Chapter X   Thrills, More or Less

1. Marginal note: 'chopsticks'.
2. Mr. Yamashita was the barber at the Hong Kong Hotel. He had been employed there since 1929 but when called upon he provided information to his fellow countrymen. Philip Snow, *The Fall of Hong Kong* (New Haven, CT: Yale University Press, 2003), p. 36.
3. Colonel Lindsay Ride of the BAAG.
4. Marginal note: '14 days'.
5. As previously mentioned, the coordinator was Mrs. Joy Wilson until she left for China; after that, her place was taken by Dr. Eddie Gosano.
6. 'Last month Chungking Embassy learnt that he had been communicating with the American O.S.S. in China. They at once instructed him … to stop this.' NA FO 371/46251.
7. Marginal note: 'Bunny'.
8. 'Savagely' is probably a mistype but it is thus in the original.

Notes to pp. 93–99   193

9. Despite Reeves' comment about his name, he is probably referring to Chan Tat-sun, who aided the BAAG in smuggling people out of Macao, including the four American pilots—see below.
10. Wolfram was mined in small quantities in Hong Kong.
11. The internment camp for civilians in Hong Kong.
12. Marginal note: 'Enlarge'.
13. That Reeves was right to be concerned is shown in Report from Chungking Embassy to Foreign Office (NA FO 371/46199 24 July 1945): 'Japanese assassination list includes the following names: Reeves . . . .'
14. It is likely that the concern of the Axis powers to ensure Portugal remained neutral also weighed heavily in the balance.
15. Marginal note: 'Frenchie'.
16. In Report from Chungking Embassy to Foreign Office (NA FO 371/46199 24 July 1945): 'Fernando Rodriguez head of Portuguese Red Cross Macao branch since 1942 was shot dead in Macao street on July 10th. Macao police arrested a man said to be body-guard of Wang Kung a reported enemy agent. Reason was non-cooperation and some financial issue.' It goes on to say: 'Dalmada [D'Almada] considers that might well have been result of some personal grudge.'
17. Muzzle-loading cannon were a common feature on junks even though they were considered obsolete by the military forces. Reports suggest that the gunpowder used was quite weak and the junk could not have been that close, so Reeves' concern was probably not fully justified.
18. BAAG did have plans to extricate Reeves if necessary, see AWM PR82/068 9/18/53. This description of the junk also tends to corroborate the argument that the consulate was on the Praia Grande at this time.
19. As Reeves noted in Chapter I, he had stopped the *Saion* (correctly the SS *Sai On*) sailing from Macao in December 1941 and thereafter the boat had been moored in Macao, most probably in the Inner Harbour. The incident described took place on 18 August 1943: 'one of the more provocative actions instigated by the Japanese during the war … the forced entry into Macau harbour of a large force of Japanese and Chinese auxiliaries who seized, by force of arms, a British ship, the *Sian* [sic], which the Portuguese had until now refused to surrender.' Geoffrey C. Gunn, *Encountering Macau: A Portuguese City-state on the Periphery of China, 1557–1999* (Boulder, CO: Westview, 1996), p. 122.
20. Marginal note: '14 days exactly'.
21. The Forte da Barra (Barra Fort) (no. 85 on the map) was built on the coast west of Penha Hill to guard the entrance to the Inner Harbour. The fort had a chapel dedicated to São Tiago, the patron saint of the army. Today, much of the fort has been transformed into a hotel, the Pousada São Tiago, and the chapel remains within the hotel grounds.
22. Despite this being a major disaster, there is curiously little information about it. The fire seems to have occurred on 4 February 1947. The ship was rebuilt after the fire and renamed the *Tak Shing*. She later became the *Tung Shan* and was always used on the Hong Kong–Macao run. She went to Japan to be broken up in 1974.
23. Photographs suggest this was on the reclamation below Guia Hill near the Pan-American base.

24. Stuart Braga, 'Rescued from Certain Death', *Casa Down Under* (the Newsletter of the Casa de Macao in Sydney) October 2011 gives their names as George W. Clarke, Don E. Mize and Charles Myers, and their date of arrival in Macao as 17 January 1945. He names the other airman as Basmajian and gives his arrival as two days later.
25. Skyline (no. 104 on the map) is very close to Penha Church, high up on the Estrada de D. João Paulino.
26. Father Patrick Joy, from 1927 to 1951, was one of the best known Jesuits in Hong Kong. Father Joy was appointed professor of moral theology of the Regional Seminary for South China in what is now the Holy Spirit Seminary, Aberdeen. He was appointed regional superior in the summer of 1941. As an Irishman he escaped internment, but he was arrested individually in 1945. The end of the war found him in prison. For two years after the war he supervised the restarting of the Jesuits' activities that had been interrupted by hostilities and the occupation.
27. Marginal note: 'Burglars'.
28. The numbers refer to the original map. The Bairro Tamagnini Barbosa is no. 44 on the present map and the 28th May houses are no. 50. The account implies the *Tungwei* was at the very eastern end of the North Patane Basin and the *Masbate* was a little to the west of the *Tungwei*.
29. The Portuguese government lodged a protest with the United States and compensation was eventually paid in 1950. This amounted to US$20,255,952 for 'damage caused when American planes bombed Macao's harbour during World War II on 16th January, 25th February and 11th June 1945, mistaking it for Japanese occupied territory'. Specific compensation was also paid for the damage to the *Masbate* and injury to Captain Jorgensen on 25 February 1945.
30. Chungking was by this time the capital of Free China. The Chinese were very much dependent on the support of the Allies and hence they did not want to see any harm come to the British consul.
31. The anti-piracy team was led by Lieutenant Commander Gick. Their anti-piracy work is well described in Gick's obituary: http://www.telegraph.co.uk/news/obituaries/1381964/Rear-Admiral-Philip-Gick.html.
32. Marginal note: '"Macao" film'.

Chapter XI Odds and Ends

1. Argentina Gonsalves was the nanny or governess of Reeves' daughter, Letitia.
2. Marginal note: 'Incident over band at Riviera'.
3. The Hong Kong Planning Unit was set up in London in 1943. Staffed mainly by ex-Hong Kong civil servants, it was headed by David MacDougall who had escaped from Hong Kong on a motor torpedo boat. See Tim Luard, *Escape from Hong Kong* (Hong Kong: Hong Kong University Press, 2012). The aim of the unit was to prepare for when the Japanese were defeated and ensure that Hong Kong had a smooth return to British rule. See Steve Tsang, *A Modern History of Hong Kong* (Hong Kong: Hong Kong University Press, 2004), p. 130 et seq.

4. Reeves identifies this in a marginal note as okra.
5. Marginal note: 'all whites'.
6. Marginal note: 'belle level?'.
7. Marginal note: 'secret radios'.
8. See Migual Senna Fernandes and Alan Baxter, *Maquista Chapado: Vocabulary and Expression in Macao's Portuguese Creole* (Macao: Instituto Cultural de Macau, 2004).
9. Correctly, the Mocidade Portuguese—a nationalist boy-scout kind of organization.
10. The Duke of Kent was killed in a puzzling air crash in Scotland on 25 August 1942.
11. Marginal note: 'Pimms No. 1'.
12. M.L. stands for motor launch. They were larger than a motor torpedo boat but still quite small.
13. Marginal note: 'Red Rice'.
14. Marginal note: 'Del...'?
15. Bernardo de Senna Fernandes.
16. This last sentence is an addition which Reeves marked for insertion after 'Fleet Air Arm'. It was felt this would disrupt the flow and so it was moved to the end of the paragraph.
17. Reeves' account is a little over-compressed. As the Japanese grew closer to Australia and had already bombed Darwin, Australian and Dutch commandos were landed on Portuguese Timor as a defensive move. However, within a week of insertion of this force, on 20 February 1942, the Japanese invaded and succeeded in forcing and pushing back the Australians into the interior of the island. However, resistance continued until 10 February 1943, when the final remaining Australians were evacuated, making them the last Allied land forces to leave Southeast Asia.

    In obvious violation of Portugal's neutrality, the Japanese then interned the whole Portuguese administration (in appalling conditions). It was the report of the invasion of Timor that must be presumed to have led Reeves to destroy papers in the expectation that the Japanese would treat Macao similarly.

    Although Salazar protested the Australian-Dutch invasion, his real anger was with the Japanese. So he required that access be provided and that Captain da Silva e Costa visit Timor, threatening to break off diplomatic relations if this was not done. The Japanese flew Captain da Silva e Costa to Timor and back on military planes. This was in March and April 1944, not after the war as Reeves states.
18. The bishop of Macao from 1942 to 1954 was João de Deus Ramalho.
19. See Chapter IV page 34 for organization diagram.
20. The New Cemetery is now a section of the Cemitério de Nossa Senhora da Piedade (Our Lady of Mercy Cemetery) (no. 39 on the map), which is located on Av. do Coronel Mesquita. The Protestant area is in the northwest part close to the Montanha Russa Garden and is a peaceful oasis well worth a visit.

Chapter XII   Post-War

1. BAAG successfully delivered a Union Jack to Reeves and this was reported in a letter to Lieutenant Colonel Ride dated 23 June 1943.

2. Quite what Reeves meant by 'four hours later' is not clear. The BBC announcement was on 14 August. Admiral Harcourt reached Hong Kong on 30 August and the first British ship, presumably that 'grey shape', arrived off Macao on 2 September (War Diary, C-in-C, British Pacific Fleet [NA FO 371/46258]). However, as Reeves and the governor were clearly waiting for the ship's arrival, perhaps the four hours refers to the time from their being notified of its coming and its arrival.
3. The Miramar radio station is no. 22 on the present map.
4. HMS *Plym* was a River class frigate. Interestingly, she was used as the detonation platform for the nuclear bomb test on 3 October 1952 in the Montebello Islands, Western Australia. Despite some reports that HMAS *Fremantle* was the first Allied ship to reach Macao, it is clear that the *Plym* preceded the *Fremantle*: from War Diary, C-in-C, British Pacific Fleet [NA FO 371/46258] (Admiral Harcourt): '2nd September. HMS *Plym* sailed for Macao on 2nd September as escort for a small vessel which went to collect rice and returned on the 3rd September, having had an enthusiastic welcome in that Portuguese port which has harboured so many Hongkong residents during the war.' 'The HMS *Plym* was assigned the task of escorting a Chinese delegation to Macao to negotiate with the Portuguese settlement for food and supplies . . . Since Portugal had not declared war on Japan it was assumed that Macao was not occupied and would have surplus stores to feed the people that were literally starving in Hong Kong. As a Telegraphist with the official landing party I took the first step on the jetty to make way for the Chinese delegation. The Portuguese Governor, dressed in all of his medals and finery, clearly mistook me for a member of the delegation and promptly greeted me with a hug and kiss on each cheek.' D. T. Tudor, *Blue Waters—The Memoirs of a Canadian Submariner* (Victoria, BC: Island Blue Print Co., 2006).
5. The ship was an Australian minesweeper, HMAS *Fremantle*, which took them to Manila where they transferred to the USS *General A.W. Brewster* bound for San Francisco to return to England via America.
6. Marginal note: 'Mention the HK dinner'.
7. Marginal note: 'Mention officers first arrival'.
8. The artist was CSM Marciano F. Baptista. Dr. Solomon Bard, who was in the camp with CSM Baptista, comments: 'Baptista, who was a local Portuguese, undoubtedly had contacts with the outside, either family or friends. It would have been easy for them to send him paints in a parcel, which were allowed in (except during punishment periods).' The scroll has sadly been lost. It was numbered Appendix 3.
9. The journalist was David Divine and the name of the company is a typo for Kemsley Press—a major newspaper publishing group in the United Kingdom at the time.
10. The *Nieman Reports* come from the Nieman Foundation for Journalism at Harvard. The Reports publish articles about the rights and responsibilities of news organizations.
11. Marginal note: 'film'.
12. The plane was the Supermarine Sea Otter—the last biplane in service with the RAF.
13. Insertion above the text: 'there'.
14. Marginal note: 'Nip Consul's remarks to H.E.'

Notes to pp. 128–174

15. As Consul Fukui had been assassinated, there was a new Japanese consul, Maseki Yodogawa. Iwai (given name unknown) may have served between Fukui and Yodogawa. See US War Dept Magic Reel XII 1078 March 8, 1945.
16. Marginal note: 'Time when Hughie did it to Commodore'.
17. Marginal note: '. . . my rank'.
18. Marginal note: 'Carnival'.
19. Major General Francis Festing was appointed Commander of British Forces in Hong Kong from August 1945.
20. No. 15 on the map.
21. No one of this name can be found in the French naval records. The most likely person was Vice Admiral Philippe-Marie-Joseph-Raymond Auboyneau. The French were using Hong Kong as a re-supply base around this time, so a side trip to Macao would not be surprising.
22. Admiral Sir Bruce Austin Fraser GCB, KBE, took command of the British Pacific Fleet in December 1944. He signed the Instrument of Surrender of Japan on behalf of the United Kingdom on the USS *Missouri*.
23. The Navy, Army and Air Force Institutes (NAAFI) is an organization created by the British government in 1921 to run recreational establishments needed by the British Armed Forces.
24. Here was inserted a reference to no. 31 on the original, missing map.
25. The Women's Voluntary Service was primarily established to help civilians in the United Kingdom, but foreign offshoots were set up during WWII.
26. Lindsay Ride was professor of physiology at the University of Hong Kong and after the war was appointed vice chancellor. A lieutenant colonel in the Hong Kong Volunteers, he became a prisoner in Sham Shui Po Camp after Hong Kong fell. On 9 January 1942, with the help of Hong Kong guerrilla forces, he managed to escape to Chungking (Chongqing), a feat for which he was appointed O.B.E. Ride formed and commanded the British Army Aid Group, headquartered in Kweilin (Guilin), Kwangsi (Guangxi).
27. The Women's Royal Naval Service (Wrens).
28. Frederick Johnson Gellion was managing director of the Macao Electric Company (Melco) but was away in San Franciso during the war years. He was referred to by some as 'the uncrowned king of Macao'.
29. See the biographical essay for the rest of the story of this sword.

About *The Lone Flag* and John Pownall Reeves

1. Dauril Alden, *Charles Boxer: An Uncommon Life* (Macao: Fundação Oriente, 2001), Appendix 1.
2. Presumably, Sir Archibald Clark-Kerr or Sir Miles Wedderburn-Lampson.
3. Ken Cambon, *Guest of Hirohito* (Vancouver: PW Press, 1990), Appendix: Excerpts from War-Crime Trials, http://www.fourthmarinesband.com (accessed 5 July 2013). The Martins were the British consul general at Chungking (Chongqing) and his wife, who were caught by the war in Hong Kong.

Index

28th May Houses 103, 194n28

Admiralty 131
Admiralty Instructions 5
Africa, territory stolen from Portuguese 25, 185n14
air raids xxiv, 74, 99–100, 103
Air Sea Rescue Launches 129, 131
Alden, Dauril, *Charles Boxer: An Uncommon Life* 167, 181n13, 197n1
Allied nations, other 77
American (U.S.)
  air raids xxiv, 187n8
    compensation paid for xxiv, 104, 194n29
  airmen 101–102, 194n24
  amphibian 127
  citizens xxi, 27, 71
  Embassy in Chungking 71
  Government 71
    money owed for relief 71, 73
  intelligence service and O.S.S. 93, 192n6
  interests 37, 72, 74
  Red Cross 71
  relief 73
American Republics, Central and South 77
Amoy 31, 186n1
Anderson, Derek 37, 77, 187n6
Anderson, Lieutenant Donald J. 187n6
"Angel's Roost" 28
Anglo-Portuguese relations 117

Archivist 37, 187n6
Arculli, Abbas el 35–36, 57, 187n9
Argentinian Consul in Hong Kong, Ramon Muniz Lavalle xiv, 174
Argonauta Club 44
Armacao refugee centre 51, 80, 82
Asiatic Petroleum Company 23
assassination xxiii, 22, 94, 169, 172, 175, 184n3, 186n4, 193n13
Auboyneau, Vice Admiral Philippe-Marie-Joseph-Raymond 197n21; *see also* d'Aubignan, Admiral
Australia xix, xxii, 21, 156, 177, 181n8, 196n5
Australia, National Library of xi, xv, 181n8, 187n8
Australian troops in Timor 118, 195n17
Avenida da República 188n10
Avenida de Almeida Ribeiro 77, 188n13, 188n14, 190n3
Avenida de Horta e Costa xxiii
Avenida do Coronel Mesquita 195n20
avitaminosis 66
Axis powers xxi
Aycock, Wilfred 32, 35, 36, 37, 57, 60, 119, 186n4

baccalao (dried codfish) 116
Bairro Tamagnini Barbosa 103, 191n7, 194n28

Banco Nacional Ultramarino xxiii, 46, 188n14
bandits 102
Banham, Tony, *Not the Slightest Chance* xv, 183n1
Baptista, CSM Marciano F. 145, 196n8
Barcos, Lieutenant Correia 117
Bard, Dr. Solomon 196n8
Barnes, Dr. 61
Barra Fort 98, 193n21
Barrier Gate *see* Portas do Cerco
Barros, Frederico 44
Barrow, Graham 126
Barry (of Hong Kong Government Rice Control) 126
basketball 88
Basmajian *see* American (U.S.) airmen
Bastille Day 76
BBC xi, 121, 196n2
Bela Vista Hotel xx, 83, 134, 153, 154
bicycle 26, 68
Bishop of Hong Kong (Bishop R.O. Hall) 89, 192n9
Bishop of Macao 114, 118, 176, 195n18
Blackheath 157, 167
Blair, Jimmy 127
bodyguards xxiii, 95, 97, 104, 105, 111, 119, 126
bombing xxi, xxiv, 11, 55, 75, 99, 100, 103, 157, 194n29, 195n17
bombs, assassination and terrorism 43, 96, 112, 115
Bond, Miss 71
books xiv, xvii, 80, 81, 171, 172, 173, 178, 187, 192n2
Borras, Mr. 24
Botelho, Mr. 50
bowls (lawn bowls) 88
Boxer Rebellion 168
Boxer, Major Charles 46, 188n17
Braga Collection at the National Library of Australia xi, xv, 181n8, 187n8
Braga, Jack 38, 187n8
Braga, Mr. J.P. 38

Branco, Fernando Augusto, Portuguese foreign minister xix
Brazil xxii
bridge (card game) 44, 81, 86
British
 ambassador (in Peking), dinner in Western Hills 171
 ambassador in Chungking 183n2, 185n12
 community 12, 18, 148
 Consul for Abruzzi, Molise, Sardinia and the Sardinian Islands 177
 Consul for East Java 177
 Consulate-General in Canton 23, 136
 Embassy in Chungking 71, 95, 123, 181n3, 186n4, 187n9, 190n5, 192n6, 193n13, 193n16, 197n3
 Embassy in Lisbon 53, 157
 firms 54
 flag *see* Union Jack
 government 18, 52, 56, 156, 157, 158, 163
 intelligence service xi, 93, 94, 189n7
 nationality xxi, 17, 24, 53
 nationals/subjects 3, 4, 6, 17, 18, 24, 52, 53, 65, 71, 73, 94, 102, 139, 148, 162, 175
 Pacific Fleet 154, 197n22
 passports 53
 subjects, relief for 49–60, 156, 163, 175
 unengaged during Dutch attack 13
British American Tobacco Company 104
British Army Aid Group (BAAG) x, xiv, xv, xxiv, 181n2, 183n3, 186n21, 186n4, 187n6, 189n7, 192n3, 193n9, 193n18, 195n1, 197n26
 agent/coordinator in Macao 92, 183n3, 190n1, 192n5
British Consulate in Macao xvi, xix, 3, 12, 34, 43, 97, 123, 125, 137, 158, 165, 166, 167, 168, 173
 accountants 32, 36
 administration cost 60
 coat of arms 35

Easter 135
expenditures 33, 60
farm cooperative 111
   chickens and ducks 111, 112
   rabbits 112
   turkeys 112
filing system 33
financial record 33, 59
funds (from London) 53, 156, 163
   distribution of 54
   statistics, of refugee funding 60
furniture 31
intelligence services, coordination 94
isolation xix, xxii, 172
junk outside Reeves' window xiii, 97
location of xii–xiii, xvi, xix, 3, 12, 21, 23, 43, 147, 159, 181n8, 184n1, 188n21, 193n18
proximity to Japanese Consulate 21
school see M.S. School
secret 38
secretary, Reeves' 37
staff
   administrative 60
   Ah Chiu 99
   Ah Wong 111
   Ah Yu 105, 111
   growth of 32
   James 111
   Joseph 111
   medical 69
   youth of 32
Britto, Freddie 65
Bryan, Mr. H.D. 23, 157
Bunny 38, 107
Burma xxi
B.Y.M.S. (British Yard Mine-Sweeper) 129, 154

Cable and Wireless (Ltd.) 32, 186n3
cable, international xxiv
Cabral, Commander Amerigo 116
Calçada da Vitória xii, xiii
Calçada do Gaio xii, xiii

Calthorpe, David ix–xii
Cambon, Ken, *Guest of Hirohito* 181n11, 197n3
Cambridge 157, 168, 169, 173
Camoens Grotto and Garden see Jardim Luís de Camões
canidrome 188n9
cannibalism 14, 176
Canton 23, 44, 129, 136, 157, 164
Canton Police vs. Macao Police (football game) 86
Cape Town xvi, 168, 170, 171, 172, 175, 177, 178
Capela de Nossa Senhora da Penha (Penha Church) 190n2, 194n25
Casa Garden (English factor's house) 22, 184n5
Cathedral (Sé Catedral) 190n2
Catholic Cemetery see Cemitério de Nossa Senhora da Piedade and Cemitério de S. Miguel Arcanjo
Catholics 37, 118, 174
catty 51, 189n5
Cemitério de Nossa Senhora da Piedade 119, 195n20
Cemitério de S. Miguel Arcanjo (St. Michael's Cemetery) xx
censorship 119, 182n1
Central Hotel 42, 46, 73, 188n13
C.E.R. (Refugee Commission), Commission Executiva de Refugiados 18, 49, 50, 61–62, 68, 83, 84, 143, 183n7
   Executive Committee 50
Cespedes, Pablino 72
Chácara Leitão (Villa Leitão) 83, 192n5
Chan, Tat-sun 38, 93, 101, 193n9
Chang, Mr., owner of *Masbate* 28
charity dance, altercation at 105
charity drives 109
Chiang Kai-shek 179
Chief of Cabinet (Chefe de Gabinete) 50
China coast xxiv, 76, 172, 173, 175
China Sea 131

China Travel Service 104
Chinese
  antiques 169, 171, 172, 178
  beneficiary owner 28, 76, 104
  Central Government 44, 76
  Communists 106
  community 13, 38, 85, 124
  Embassy in Washington 77
  gangsters 85, 95, 105
  intelligence services 93
  nationalists xxiv
  restaurant in Cape Town 172
  New Year 42
  universities and schools, moved to Macao 44, 183n15
Chinese Maritime Customs Service 24, 29, 76, 184n11
Chinnery, George 175
Choa, Rudy xiv
cholera 62, 123
Cholmondeley, Miss (Elsie Fairfax-Cholmondeley) 27, 185n20
Christians, money for Christmas 58
Christmas Day 1941 xxi, 11, 13, 90, 156, 174, 182n6
Chungking xiv, 21, 185n12, 185n18, 194n30, 197n26
  auxiliaries 105
  gunmen 96, 97, 104, 105
Church of England 89, 192n9
Church of St. Augustine *see* Igreja de Santo Agostinho
Church processions 114
Churchill, Lord Henry John Spencer 175, 188n18
Churchill, Winston 24, 46, 175
claims for property destroyed 120
  tortoise 120
Clarke, George W. *see* American (U.S.) airmen
Clark-Kerr, Sir Archibald 197n2
Clube de Macau (Macao Club) 16, 19, 44, 81, 89, 183n4, 192n12
coal 104

cocktail parties 5, 12, 128
coding of messages 22
Colina da Penha (Penha Hill) xiii, 193n21
Colonial Secretariat of Macao 17, 50
Colonial Secretary of Hong Kong *see* Gimson, Franklin C.
Commercial Diplomatic Service 3
Commissioner of Police, Macao 109
Commodore Hong Kong 11, 132
comprador (buyer) 52, 189n6
Confucius 124–125, 173
Consul for Holland, Mr. H. Nolasco Sr. 22, 75, 191n6
Consul for Thailand, Mr. Fernandes 22
Consular Corps, dean of 113
Consular Instructions 5, 32
Consular Officers 4, 6, 24, 53, 113
  as Jacks of all trades 4
  as members of local community 5
  duties of 6, 7, 24, 77
Consular Service 3, 157
Consul's flag (blue ensign) 132
Consul's launch 132
Corregidor 73
corvettes 129
Cotai strip 182–183n13
cyphers 6, 92

da Silva, Antonio Maria 81, 123
da Silva, Carlos 88
da Silva e Costa, Captain 50, 118, 141, 185n13, 195n17
Daily Sketch 126, 165
d'Almada e Castro, Leo xii, 49, 50, 81, 109, 110, 187n9, 188n1, 193n16
d'Almada-Remedios brothers 189n2
Darwin, Australia 195n17
d'Aubignan, Admiral 133, 197n21
Davies, Mr., missionary 71, 72, 102
D-Day 25
Deaconess Lee (Rev. Florence Li Tim-oi) 89, 192n9
Diocesan Girls' School 187n6

Index

Diplomatic and Consular Services, amalgamation of 4
Diplomatic Officers 53, 113
Diplomatic Service 3
Divine, David 126, 165, 196n9
doctors 36, 56, 57, 61, 64, 65, 66, 67, 74, 82
  import from Hong Kong 61, 156
  number of 17
  youth of 32
dollars, Chinese National 59
Dom Pedro Theatre 183n4, 184n8
Dona Maria II Fort xxiv
Dredger, Dutch 22, 75, 190–191n5
Duke of Kent, memorial service for 115, 195n10
Dutch
  attack, in 1622 13
  commandos 195n17
  interests 75
Dutch East India Company 22
dysentery, amoebic or bacillary 66

East India Company (John Company) 22, 23, 157, 184n5, 184n7
embarkation of officials to return to Portugal 116–117
Epstein, I. 185–186n20
escapes 38
  expenditures on 33
  from Hong Kong xxiv, 26, 27, 164, 182, 185n18, 185n20, 197n26
  from Macao 26, 27, 101–102, 185n12, 185n18
espionage 91, 94–95
Esquire 28, 126
Estado Novo 50
Estrada de Cacilhas 192n5
Estrada de Ferreira do Amaral 191n9
Estrada de João Paulino 194n25
Eurasian community 38, 88, 147, 149
evacuation of Portuguese from Hong Kong 15, 16
exchange problems 59
executors of Reeves' estate 174

Exterior Port *see* Porto Exterior

fantan 41, 42, 182n3
  played with bodies xxii
Far East xix, 13, 41, 44, 47, 76, 119
Farrell, FBI 106
Fat Siu Lao 188n12
Fátima, Our Lady of 62, 114, 190n2
Fay, Jean 29, 76, 77, 184–185n11
F.B.I. 106
fencing 129
Fernandes family 44
Fernandes, Ben de Senna 187n4
Fernandes, Bernardo de Senna 117, 195n15
Fernandes, Dr. Elsa xviii, 16, 183n5
Fernandes, Mr. 43
Ferreira, Commander 116
Festing, Major General Francis 131, 134, 153, 197n19
Figueiredo, Mr., Accountancy School 38
Firecracker Factory 75
firecrackers 43, 97, 124
firewood 51
first Allied ship to Macao 196n2, 196n4
Fletcher, Donald 182n8
Fletchers, Mr. and Mrs. 12, 16, 18, 23, 24, 79, 102, 117, 135, 182n7, Plates 9–10
Fong, Mr., killed by bomb 43
food
  coupons to buy grain xxi
  stocks shared with Hong Kong 126, 163, 196n4
  supplies and prices xxi, xxiii, 14, 16, 51, 52, 196n4
Football Club 45
football, miniature 86
foreign currency xxiii, 96
Foreign Office, in London x, 6, 53, 58, 65, 107, 113, 157, 158, 165, 167, 169, 187n9, 193n16
France, Indochina and other possessions 185n19

Fraser, Admiral Sir Bruce Austin 134, 154, 197n22
Free China 26, 27, 33, 71, 73, 74, 93, 97, 102, 103, 111, 194n30
Free French 29, 76
freemasonry 118
French Naval Forces 133, 197n21
French territories, in the Far East xxi
fuel
 for generators 117–118, 135
 for refugee centres 51, 82
 target of bombing xxiv, 100
Fukui, Japanese Consul in Macao xii, 21, 22, 91, 113, 114, 175, 181n5, 182n5, 197n15
 assassination of 12, 22, 175, 184n3
Fundação Oriente 184n5

Galloway, Mr. and Mrs. 24
Gambling Inspectors 36
Garrett, Richard, *The Defences of Macau* x, xiv
Gellion, Mr. F.J. xiii, 23, 101, 117, 135, 136, 197n28
Germany xx, 24, 119, 187n8
Gick, Lieutenant Commander 106, 194n31
Gimson, Franklin C. 122, 139, 189n7
gold xxiii, 183n17
golf 45, 88
Golf Section of Civilian Tennis Club 25
Gomez dos Santos, Madame 43
Gonsalves, Argentina 109, 194n1
Gonsalves, Johnny 65
Gonsalves, Micao 37
Gosano, Dr. Eddie xii, 36, 113, 163, 189n7, 190n1, 192n5
Government Harbour 186n25
Government Medical Service 16, 61, 62
Government of Macao 15, 17, 24, 84, 100
 pharmacy 65
 servants, forbidden to gamble 42, 187n2
Governor Gabriel Maurício Teixeira
 and the Royal Navy 115, 122, 130, 132

 at opening of NAAFI Centre 153, 154, 156
 attendance at celebrations at war's end 113, 114, 124, 137, 141, 142, 143, 145, 153, 154
 attendance at refugee events 80, 83, 85
 efforts to avoid conflict with Japanese xxii, 90, 121
 permits medical practitioners from Hong Kong 61
 pro-Allied 24, 185n13
 requires only money from BNU used xxiii
 residence *see* Palacete de Santa Sancha
 suppresses *Macau Tribune* 100
 suppresses mutiny of troops 115
Governor's Palace xiii
Graça, Jorge xxii
Grand Hotel 46, 73, 147, 188n13
Granelli, Father 89, 192n11
Gray, FBI 106
Green Island (Ilha Verde) xxi, 75, 112, 191n8
Gremio Militar (Military Club) 44
Grimsdale, General 181n3
Guangdong Province xx, xxi
Guangzhou xx, 183n15
Guia Hill xii, 192n5, 193n23
Guia Lighthouse 47, 173, 175, 179, 188n21
guidebooks xi, 48, 188n24
guidebook to Macao xi
Gundesen, Mr. 191n6
Gunn, Geoffrey, *Encountering Macau* xiv, 184n3, 193n19
guns xiii, xxiii, 39, 96–99, 104–107, 119–120, 122, 126–128, 159, 169
Guterres, Dr. 61

H.D.M.L. *see* Motor Launch
Hague Convention xix
Haileybury 23, 157, 168, 184n7
Hall, Mr., Consul-General in Canton 136
Hankow (Hankou) xiv, 157, 173
Harbour Office 112

Index 205

Harcourt, Admiral 123, 131, 154, 196n2, 196n4
Harrop, Phyllis (Reeves named her Pam) 26, 185n18
Heenan, Ernest (Pat) 24, 26, 28
  report 183n2, 185n12, 185n16–17, 186n22, 186n25, 190n5
Henry the Navigator 116
Hipódromo 25, 26, 185n15
  bicycle gymkhana 26
  race-meeting, cancelled 26
  used for farming 26
Ho Tung, Sir Robert 189n6
Ho, Dr. Asgoe 61, 190n1
Ho, Vincent xi
hockey 87, 115, 126, 159, 169, 170
  club 44, 45
  Consulate team (Valentes) 87, 100
  ground 63
  interports 87, 158
Holman, Adrian 170
Hong Kong
  Battle for xv, 182n9, 183n1, 187n6, 191n13
  bombing of 55
  dollar 53, 59, 71, 189n5
  fall of xxi, 11, 13, 90, 156, 165, 174, 181n10, 182n6, 187n6, 192n6, 197n3
  Government 37, 126
  liberation of 122, 123, 139, 163, 189n7, 196n2
  Pan-American service to 186n23
  police 16, 183n3, 185n18
  refugees from ix, xxi, 15, 16, 21, 52, 66, 87
Hong Kong Hotel 192n2
Hong Kong Legislative Council 49
Hong Kong Planning Unit 110, 194n3
Hong Kong Portuguese Community 143
Hong Kong Rehabilitation Committee 110, 187n9
Hong Kong Volunteers 12, 125, 145, 187n6, 197n26

Hongkong and Shanghai Banking Corporation 23
Honolulu 116
Hordle village, near New Forest 168
Horne, "Trader" 129
Hospital de São Rafael (San Rafael Hospital) 63, 117, 190n5
Hung, W.C. 187n9

Iao Hon Market 185n15
Igreja de Santo Agostinho 192n12
Igreja São Domingos (St. Dominic's Church) xviii, 47, 175, 190n2
Igreja São Lourenço (St. Lawrence's Church) xiii
Ilha Verde see Green Island
Immigration Office xiii, 12
  permit 12, 26
Imperial and International Communications Ltd. 186n3
India xix, xxii, 76, 102
Indian and Malay community 85
Indian community 24, 35, 38
Indian Independence League 23, 184n9
Indo-China 104, 185n19
Inner Harbour (Porto Interior) xxiii, 187n3
inoculations 61
Inter-Allied Celebration 125
Irish Jesuit Fathers 84, 102, 118
Isamu, Sergeant Major Honda xiv
islands 13, 43; see also Lapa, Dom João and Montanha islands
  Coloane xxi, 182–183n13
  Taipa xx, xxii, 182–183n13, 185n15
Iwai (given name unknown), Japanese Consul 197n15

Japan
  attack 11
  authority to carry out house-to-house searches in Macao xxiii
  decision not to annex Macao 96, 193n14

Japanese
  advisers xxiii
  aggression in China xix
  assassination list 95, 96, 186n4, 193n13
  Consul 21, 105, 106, 128
  Consulate xii, xiii, 21, 27, 91, 128, 129, 159, 175
  cruelty 50
  Departments, Naval, Military, Gendarmerie and Financial 14
  district bureaux for register of births, deaths, etc. 110
  espionage 21
  Gendarmerie 22, 94
  interference in Macao's internal administration xxii, 110
  invasion of Timor 195n17
  occupation of Hong Kong 192n6
  occupied territory 73
  prisoners of war 128
  property in Macao 128–129
  sea blockade xxi
  secret police xxiii, 175
  surrender xi, xxiv, 104, 121, 127, 177, 189n7, 197n22
  troops xxii
Jardim Luís de Camões 46
Jardine Matheson & Co. 189n6
jeep 14
Jesuits 84, 192n6, 194n26
Jiangmen see Kongmoon
Jick, Commander see Gick, Lieutenant Commander
João de Lisboa 116, 186n25
Joeselyn, Mr. 133
joint ventures, Japanese with Hong Kong and Macao businessmen xxiii
Jorgensen, Trygve (Trigger) 28, 75, 104, 194n29
José Conde Fernandez house xiii
Joy, Father Patrick 102, 194n26
junks xiii, 31, 73, 97, 99, 101, 102, 123, 193n17–18, 197n22

Kaitak Aerodrome 127
Kaye, Molly, Betsy and Lady Kaye 170–171
Kempeitai see Japanese, secret police
Kemsley Press 126, 196n9
Kiang-Wo Hospital (Kiang Wu) 63, 190n4
King's Birthday 115, 136
King's Regulations 5
Knaggs, Charles 26, 27, 185n17
Kongmoon (Jiangmen) 186n26, 190n1
Kowloon 127
Kwan, C.Y. 187n9
Kwangchowan (Zhanjiang) 27, 103, 185n19
Kweilin (Guilin) 102, 111, 197n26

Lam, Dr. P.K. 68
Lammert, Mr. and Mrs. 24
landing craft loaded with butter and kerosene 133
Lapa, Dom João and Montanha islands xx, xxiii, 182n1
Largo do Senado (Senate Square) 188n13, 190n6
Leal Senado 13, 114
Leal Senado Biblioteca 81, 192n2
Lee, Vicky, *Being Eurasian* 187n6
Letitia see Reeves, daughter
Li Tim-Oi, Deaconess Florence see Deaconess Lee
Liang, Y.C. 52, 189n7
Lima, José and Janet 129
Lisbon xxi, xxiv, 53, 117
Little Flowers of Mary 84
Lobo, Dr. Pedro José 14, 18, 25, 50, 83, 105, 114, 141, 143, 183n17
London xxiv, 53, 110, 117, 123, 167, 187n9
  communications with 53
Lopes, A.A. 50, 51, 52, 143
Lourdes 62
Lowry, Miss 71
Loyal Senate see Leal Senado
Loyal Senate Library see Leal Senado Biblioteca

Luard, Tim, *Escape from Hong Kong* 194n3
Lusiads *see* Os Lusíadas
Lyceum 100
Lyttleton Road, Hong Kong xiv

M.S. School 85
Macanese (language) 113, 187n1
Macao
  brothels xxiii
  building styles 13
  business xx, xxiii, 46
  carnivals 42, 129
  casinos xx, xxiii
  cinemas 43, 82
  clubs xxi, 44, 45, 84, 154
  concerts 43, 80, 145
  dance halls 82
  death rate, of population xxii, xxiii
    deaths from starvation 14
  Director of Medical Services 43, 61
  dog-racing 45
  dried fish (industry) 43
  economy xxiv, 14
  gambling xxiv, 36, 41, 42, 54, 74, 81, 110
    bidding for the monopoly 41, 42
    taxes xxii
  garrison xxi
  hospitals 17, 54, 74, 106
    access to 63
  hotels xx, 46, 182–183n13
  map xi
  navy xxi
  neutrality xix, xx, xxi, xxiv
  opium dens xxiii, 41
  population expansion xxi, 13–14
  post-war visits 129–134, 153, 154,
  prostitution 41, 43
  restaurants xx, xxiii, 45
  stood alone xxi
  theatres 43
Macao Club *see* Clube de Macau
Macao Electric Company (Melco) 23, 117, 118, 130, 135, 182n7, 197n28

Macao Electricity Company, Portuguese take-over 117, 118
Macao Naval Aviation Centre xxiv
Macao Tribune 38, 100–101, 118–119
Macao Water Company 23
Macau Siac 190–191n5
Macau, gunboat xxii
MacDougall, David 194n3
Mae West 127
mah-jonng (mah-jong) 81, 178
mail, lack of 14
malaria 83
Malay, origin of Macanese vocabulary 113
Malaya xxi, 154
Malayan Civil Service 11, 23, 26, 182n3
Malmesbury 171, 176, 179
Manalac, Mr. 72, 151
Manchus 169
Mandarin 173
Manila 73
Marjorie, Duchess of Macao 28
Martin, Mrs. Mary xiv, 174, 197n3
Maryknoll Fathers 27, 190n1
McCaskie, George 26, 27, 185n16
medical service, of British Consulate in Macao 61–69
  clinic 33, 36, 57, 60, 61, 63, 64, 67, 68, 163
    administration 65
    consultations 64, 68
  house visits 68
  identity card 57, 67
  Medical Board 66, 68
  medicines 33, 54, 62, 63, 82, 163
    atropin 62
    carotene (carrotin), Vitamin A 66
    cod-liver oil 64, 66
    cost of 64, 65
    share stocks with Hong Kong 126
    sulfa guanadin 66
    sulfathiazol 65, 190n7
    sulphanilamide 42
    supplied to Portuguese 65
  prescriptions 62, 63

Melco *see* Macao Electric Company
Melco Club (Watco and Melco Staff
    Club) 25, 44, 45, 88, 105, 117, 125,
    141, 143
Melco Orchestra 43, 187n4
Micky (security guard) 104
midnight Mass 90
midshipmen 134
Military Club *see* Gremio Militar
milk 16, 156
Milk Board 109
mines 99
Miramar 121, 196n3
Mitchell, Lieutenant Colonel E.J.R. 182n9
Mitchell, Mrs. 12, 24, 182n9
Mize, Don E. *see* American (U.S.) airmen
Mocidade Portuguesa xiii, 114, 195n9
Mohammedans 24, 37, 58
money
    to support refugees xxii
    Chinese xxiii
    coming from bank 58–59
Montanha Russa (Russian
    Mountain) 191n9, 195n20
Monte Fort 48, 184n5
Mooney, Alfred 109
Moosa, Mr. Cassim 23, 184n8
Morrison, Robert 46
Motor Launch (M.L.) 115, 129, 130, 131,
    132, 195n12
motor torpedo boat 194n3
Mozambique 183n16, 185n14
Mukden 157, 165, 173, 175
Mukden Incident xix
Murray-Kidd, Lewis 173
Murray-Kidd, Rhoda *see* Reeves, Mrs.
    Rhoda
Myers, Charles *see* American (U.S.) airmen

NAAFI Leave Centre 134, 153, 197n23
Não ha outra mais leal (There is none more
    loyal) 13, 183n14
national anthem
    American 124
    British 80, 124, 143
    Portuguese 143
nationality
    dual and master 17, 32, 53
    questions of 53
Navy, Army, Air Forces Institute *see* NAAFI
navy vessel
    on breakwater 129–130
    on rocks 130
netball *see* basketball
Netherlands Harbour Works Co. 22, 75,
    130, 184n4, 190–191n5
New Forest 168
newspapers xxiii, 14, 100, 126, 182n1; *see
    also* Macao Tribune
Nieman Reports 126, 196n10
Nolasco, Frederico 44, 87
Nolasco, Phyllis 187n6
Norwegian interests 75
nurses 69, 163

OBE (Order of the British Empire) 167,
    177, Plate 12
oil *see* fuel
oil-lighter aground 130–131
Olsen, Captain 185n13
O'Niell, Ray 26, 102, 185n20, 186n22
opium 41, 42
optician 68
Oriental Foundation *see* Fundação Oriente
Os Lusíadas 46
Osmena y Suico, Sergio, Vice President of
    the Philippines 71, 190n2
Osprey airplanes 48, 188n23
Otter *see* Sea Otter
Oxford and Cambridge boat race 169
Ozorio, Dr. 61

pacapiu (*pakapiu*) 41, 42, 187n1
Pacific War 114
Palacete de Santa Sancha (Palace of Santa
    Sancha) 45, 188n10
Pan American Airways 27, 28, 74, 99, 100,
    104, 186n23, 193n23

Index 209

motorboat 74
stew 28
Panamanian interest 76
Paschang, Bishop 27, 71, 190n1
patacas (Macao currency) 52, 59, 96, 189n5
Peak, the 123
Pearl Harbour xix, xxi, 11, 116, 159
Pearl River 13, 165, 179, 182n12
Peking (Beijing) 157, 169, 170, 171, 173, 178
Penha Church *see* Capela de Nossa Senhora da Penha
Penha Hill *see* Colina da Penha
Perry, Mrs. 85
Peterhouse 157, 169
Pharmacia Popular 64, 190n6
pharmacy, Mr. Nolasco's *see* Pharmacia Popular
Philippine
 community 151
 dance band players 73
 seamen 71, 102
 subjects 71
'Phoenix' 189n7
pirates 106, 107, 126, 134
P.L. (code name) 189n7
platinum xxiii
poet (Chris) 131
police 45, 110
 football team 86
Portas do Cerco (Barrier Gate) 182–183n13
Porter, Jonathan, *Macau: The Imaginary City* xv
Porto Exterior xxiii, 43, 62, 74, 187n3, 188n13, 190n3, 191n8, 193n19, 193n21
Portugal, Spanish occupation of 13
Portuguese 17, 38, 80, 100, 113
 armed forces 50
 attitudes to war 24
 community in Hong Kong 113
 Consul in Hong Kong, Acting 17, 183n6

Consulate in Hong Kong 53
Consulate in Macao 190n5
doctors 61, 63
flag 124
garrison 48
government 52, 75, 80, 194n29
 in professions 46
Law 18, 61
nationality 53
naval air service 48, 99, 117
neutrality xix, xxii, 99, 195n17
occupation of Macao, in 1557 13
overseas xx
papers 53
police 56, 105
Portuguese Naval Yard 74, 132
pro-Allies 24
pro-Germany 24
Red Cross 96, 193n16
volunteers 102
Portuguese Bank *see* Banco Nacional Ultramarino
Portuguese Residents Association of Hong Kong (P.R.A.) 49
Pousada São Tiago 193n21
Praia Grande xiii, 12, 175, 188n14, 191n1, 193n18
Praia Grande No. 3, refugee centre 83
Protestant
 cemetery 46, 115, 118, 175, 184n5, 188n18
 churches 88, 115
 schools and colleges 44
Provost Sergeant-Major 134
Public Enemy No. 1 85
Pym's No. 1 (Pimm's) 136

Q-junks 106

race course *see* Hipódromo
radio xxiii, xxiv, 14, 95, 100, 121, 129, 186n23–24, 196n3; *see also* wireless
RAF 196n12
Ramadan 58

Ramalho, João de Deus *see* Bishop of Macao
Ramon Muniz Lavalle *see* Argentinian Consul in Hong Kong
Red Cross 31
Redden, Earl 28, 186n24
Reed, Willie 77, 191n13
Reeves (British Consul in Macao)
　assassination attempts 96
　broadcaster, later career as 177
　cats and dogs 171, 174, 175, 179
　daughter, Letitia xiv, 112, 120, 157, 165, 173, 174, 176, 182n4, 194n1
　exploring region around Peking 170
　family, maritime links 168
　farming, venture in South Africa 177
　kitchen, culinary exploits 178
　leaving Macao 137
　marriage xiv, 173
　modern languages, learning of 173
　Mrs. Rhoda xiv, 12, 22, 101, 109, 123, 156, 157, 165, 173, 174, 182n4
　navy, intended career 168
　next posting (Rome) ix
　parents 167
　photography 168, 169–170, 171
　President and Member of Merit, Hockey Club 44, 158
　promotion to Consul 158
　resignation from Melco Club 25
　reward for assassination 95
　sword, gold and silver diplomatic 136, 177
　tortoise 171, 172
　visitor's book 171, 173
　Western Hills, weekends in 170, 171
refugee centres 16, 19, 84, 175
　chiefs 83
　conditions in 19, 65
　cooking in 82
　dances and music 19, 20, 79, 80, 82
　sanitation 19
refugees
　accommodation for 16
　and gambling 36, 54
　charity drives for 109
　clothing allowances 58, 74
　death rate 64
　dental treatment 58, 68
　difficulty in washing clothes 19, 65
　duties 81, 83
　education for 37
　end of war celebrations 125, 137, 141–145
　family scam 56–57
　funds for relief 33, 58, 67
　girls acting as dance hostesses 82
　good behaviour to Japanese 90
　identity cards 33, 57
　illegitimate children 82
　medical history 33
　medical issues *see* medical service, of British Consulate in Macao
　moral standard of 82, 90
　morale-raising activities 49
　numbers of 17, 55
　qualifications for obtaining relief 35
　ration cards 33
　rations for 51
　religious provision 89, 90, 192n9, 192n11
　skin diseases 19, 65
　subsidy to 33, 51–58
Rehabilitation Committee (post-war of Hong Kong) 38, 110
relief
　cases 33, 35
　for American citizens, Committee for 72, 74
　problems 102
　criteria for deciding level 54–56
　mechanics of giving 56, 58
religious
　festivals 58
　teaching 85
Remedios family 189n4
Remedios, Mr. 49, 50, 189n2
remittances, for Chinese from USA 77–78

Index   211

reports of Battle for Hong Kong 15
reservoir 28, 130
Reuters 126
Revista de Cultura (*Review of Culture*), Macao ix, 181n1
Ribeiro, Dr. 61
rice
　control 126
　price of 33
　supply of 51, 191n6
rickshaws 114
　coolies 104
　for transport of doctors 68
Ride, Colonel Lindsay x, 92, 135, 181n3, 186n21, 192n3, 195n1, 197n26
Ride, Edwin, *British Army Aid Group* 181n2
Ride, Lindsay and May Ride, *An East India Company Cemetery* 188n18
'Rigor Mortis' 131
Riviera Hotel 16, 73, 102, 190n3
Rocha, Mr. 17
Rodrigues, Mr. (Portuguese Red Cross) 96; *see also* Rodriguez, Fernando
Rodriguez, Father Lancelot xii, 179
Rodriguez, Fernando 186n4, 193n16
Roman Catholic Church xxi, 84, 88, 89
Roman Catholic priests 71
Rome 31, 51, 84, 177
Roskill, Hughie 130
Royal Insurance Company 24, 185n12
Rozario, A.P. 112
Rua Central 184n8
Rua da Doca dos Holandeses 190–191n5
Rua da Felicidade 188n12
Rua de D. Belchior Carneiro 184n6
Rua de Henrique de Macedo xii, xiii
Rua do Barão 189n4
Rua do Padre António xiii
Rua do Padre Luís Frois S.J. 191n1
Rua Horta e Compania (Largo da Companhia) 22, 184n6
Ruinas de São Paulo (ruins of St. Paul's) 175, 184n6
rumours 15
Russian Mountain *see* Montanha Russa

safe-conducts, Allied and Japanese 104, 157
safe combinations 6
Salazar, Dr. 50, 118, 195n17
Sales, Arnaldo 181n7
Salesian Fathers 16
Salesian orphanage brass band 124
Salvation Society of Macao xx
sampan 26, 38, 74, 101, 102, 123, 131, 132
San Francisco 78, 117, 174, 186n23, 196n5, 197n28
São Januário Hospital 133
San Luiz Gonzaga School (São Luís Gonzaga) 81, 84, 192n6
San Rafael Hospital *see* Hospital de São Rafael
sanitation xxii, 110
Santos-Ferreira, Ade 44, 188n15
São Tiago (St. James) 193n21
saudade 48
Schukking, Theresa (Tessa) xvi, 168, 177, 178
scroll from POWs xi
Sea Otter, Supermarine 126–127, 128, 196n12
Secretary for Chinese Affairs 24
security risk x–xi, 189n2
Senate Square *see* Largo do Senado
Sergeants' Club 80, 191n1
Sham Shui Po xi, xv, 191n6, 197n26
Shanghai xx, 44, 157, 173, 185n12
Shaplen, Bob 126
Shekki pigeon 45
ships
　HMAS *Fremantle* 123, 174, 196n4–5
　HMS *Druid* 188n18
　HMS *Duke of York* 134
　HMS *Plym* 122, 154, 196n4
　HMS *Prince of Wales* 20, 156, 184n9

ships (*cont.*)
    HMS *Ranee* 137, 167
    HMS *Repulse* 20, 156, 184n9
    SS *Lourenço Marques* 116
    SS *Masbate* 28, 75, 103, 104, 186n25, 194n29
    SS *Perla* 15, 183n1
    SS *Sai On* xxiii, 11, 23, 97–99, 182n1, 185n12, 193n19
    USS *General A.W. Brewster* 174, 196n5
    USS *Missouri* 197n22
Shirogano Maru, Japanese motor vessel 183n2
shoes, Manchu from dowager empress 178
siesta 168, 178, 179
Sikhs 24
Silva, Jerry 36, 60
silver xxiii, 171
Singapore xxi, 20, 44, 76, 156, 177
Sino-American Community 151, 152
Sino-Portuguese intelligence group 92, 95, 101
Skyline xiii, 101, 123, 129, 136, 194n25
sloops 116, 129
Smirnoff, George 176
Snow, Philip, *The Fall of Hong Kong* xiv, 189n7, 192n2
Snyman, Wilhelm 181n1
Soares, Francisco 183n6
softball 87
Soong, Madame Mei-ling 179
Sousa, Eddie 50, 51
Sousa, Mickey 37
South Africa ix, 168
South China Morning Post xiii, 139
speculation in currencies 59
sports 45, 85–88
St. Dominic's Church *see* Igreja São Domingos
St. John's Day 13
St. Lawrence's Church *see* Igreja São Lourenço
St. Leonards-on-Sea 157, 168

St. Michael's Cemetery *see* Cemitério de S. Miguel Arcanjo
St. Paul's, ruins of *see* Ruinas de São Paulo
St. Stephen's College, Lyttleton Road, Hong Kong xiv
Stanley internment camp 26, 27, 95, 123, 128, 183n3, 185n20, 193n11
State Department (USA) 27, 71, 72
statistical record 136
steamers, for repatriation 123
Stellenbosch, Western Cape 177, 178
sterilizers 63
Sterling 59
Stott, Robert 27
Supreme Court 47
Surabaya, Indonesia 168, 172, 177, 178
Swatow 31, 186n1
Swemmelaar, 'Swemm' or 'Sandy' 35, 36, 54, 57, 60, 62, 64, 67, 99, 100, 163, 164, 165
Symons, Joyce 187n6

T.B. 64, 66
Tak Shing 193n22; *see also* SS *Sai On*
Teixeira, Father 178
Teixeira, Governor Gabriel Maurício *see* Governor Gabriel Maurício Teixeira
Teixeira, Madam 134, 141
telegraphic transfers 53
Telos de Vasconcelos 181n5
Temple of the White Pines (Fa Hai Ssu) 170
Tennis Club, Civil 45, 188n10
Tennis Club, Military 45
Thompson, R.G.K. 12, 182n3
three-dice game 41, 42
Tighe, Dixie 126
Timor xxii, 118, 183n17, 195n17; *see also* Australian troops in Timor
torture 92, 99, 103
Travessa do Padre Narciso xiii
Tsang, Steve, *A Modern History of Hong Kong* 194n3
Tudor, D.T., *Blue Waters* 196n4

Index   213

Tung Shan 193n22; *see also* SS *Sai On*
Tungwei 103, 194n28
typhoon xi, 136, 167

União Nacional 81, 118
Union Jack xi, xxii, 21, 121, 123, 136, 139,
    165, 167, 172, 195n1
United States (USA) 72, 123
universities, moved to Macao from
    China 13, 183n15
The University of Hong Kong 182n8,
    188n1, 197n26

vaccines 62
van Ness, Parker 'Dutch' 185n20
van Woerkom (WoerKamp), Mr. 75,
    190n5
VE-Day 24, 122
venereal disease 82
Victoria, Queen 186n2
Vieira, Sam, acting Governor 116
Villa Lille Norge 76
visitors' book 28, 154, 171, 173
VJ-Day 14, 25, 106, 116, 41, 183n18

waits, spirit of the 44, 187n5
Wang Jingwei (Wong Ching Wei) 189n9
Wedderburn-Lampson, Sir Miles 197n2
White Ensign 121, 122
Wilson, Geoffrey 181n9, 183n3
Wilson, Joy 16, 18, 24, 79, 102, 183n3,
    190n1, 192n5

wine 27, 116, 173
wireless 11, 12, 74, 112, 116; *see also* radio
Wolfram 95, 96, 193n10
Wong Koon-Kit 106
Wong, Warren 72
Wong Tai Co 52
Woodham, Peter 127
Wordie, Jason xv, 181n4
World War I (First World War) xx
Wright, Frank W. 185n20
writings on China 173
WRNS (Women's Royal Naval Service,
    Wrens) 135, 197n27
WVS (Women's Voluntary Service) 134,
    154, 197n25

Xavier, Freddie, Liaison Officer Portuguese
    Affairs 36
Xavier, Mrs. 16, 80
Xavier, Toni and Freddie 112

Yamashita, Mr. (barber) 192n2
yen, Japanese military 59, 96
Yeung Yuk-Kwan 105
Yodogawa, Maseki, Japanese
    Consul 197n15
Young, Nathan 72, 151, 152

Zhanjiang *see* Kwangchowan
Zhongshan County xxii

www.ingramcontent.com/pod-product-compliance
Ingram Content Group UK Ltd.
Pitfield, Milton Keynes, MK11 3LW, UK
UKHW021834210426
5322IPUK00012B/202/J